PRAISE FOR CHERR

"Can I just say that I adore Cherríe Moraga's work and that she is absolutely essential?"
—JUNOT DÍAZ, author of *The Brief Wondrous Life of Oscar Wao*

"Cherríe Moraga is an iconic figure—one of the pioneers of fierce Chicana, feminist, queer activist contemporary North American literature! What more can I say?"
—JESSICA HAGEDORN, author of *Dogeaters*

"I've long been a great admirer of Cherríe Moraga's work; I think she's a terrific, beautiful, daring, electrifying writer!"
—TONY KUSHNER, author of *Angels in America*

"When future generations look back at the first generation of Latino/a literature, Cherríe Moraga's formative work will be one of the cornerstones of what by then will be American Literature. Without her work, many of us would not have felt the solidarity and power or had the critical vocabulary or understanding to give voice to our own stories."
—JULIA ALVAREZ, author of *Saving the World* and *Once Upon a Quinceañera*

"Without a bit of hyperbole, I can say that I hold Cherríe Moraga in the same kind of reverence that a whole generation of young African American poets held Gwendolyn Brooks—that is, with gratitude and awe for the role a writer can play in shaping a literature and empowering its younger writers toward distant, more creative boundaries."
—MANUEL MUÑOZ, author of *What You See in the Dark*

BOOKS BY CHERRÍE L. MORAGA

ANTHOLOGIES

This Bridge Called My Back: Writings by Radical Women of Color
   (co-edited with Gloria Anzaldúa)
Cuentos: Stories by Latinas
   (co-edited with Alma Gómez and Mariana Romo-Carmona)

ESSAYS AND POETRY

The Last Generation
Loving in the War Years: Lo Que Nunca Pasó por Sus Labios
Waiting in the Wings: Portrait of a Queer Motherhood

PLAYS

Heroes and Saints and Other Plays
The Hungry Woman
Heart of the Earth
Watsonville: Some Place Not Here
Circle in the Dirt: El Pueblo de East Palo Alto

A Xicana Codex of Changing Consciousness

A Xicana Codex of Changing Consciousness

WRITINGS, 2000–2010

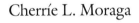

Cherríe L. Moraga

Drawings by Celia Herrera Rodríguez

DUKE UNIVERSITY PRESS
Durham & London 2011

Printed in the United States of America
on acid-free paper ∞
Designed by Jennifer Hill
Typeset in C & C Galliard by
Tseng Information Systems, Inc.

Library of Congress Cataloging-in-Publication
Data appear on the last printed page of this book.

To Celia, in gratitude
for the daily lesson
de su conciencia Xicana Indígena.

THE COLOR OF A NATION

They thought of the desert as colorless,
blinded by its high noon bright.
They saw no hue,
its original habitants equally invisible,
their footprints camouflaged by the dusty imprint
of wagon wheels and hoof tracks.
Her name, too, was written there in the dust.
Did you see her? She who wrote without letters
the picture of a disappearing planet?
She knew in advance what it would mean, their arrival.
She saw us, her pueblo, a cactus tuna
bleeding in the heat.

Contents

Drawings by Celia Herrera Rodríguez

La Jornada

Prólogo: A Living Codex

This collection not only appears at the close of the first decade of the twenty-first century, but according to the Maya calendar, its publication occurs while the final epoch of the world, as our Mesoamerican ancestors understood it, comes to an end. I have no intention of discussing New Age or Hollywood predictions for December 22, 2012. Suffice it to say, much commercial profit has already been made from sensationalized misinterpretations of the ancient Maya predictions, especially when they are said to forecast a doomsday, in which the world ends in one great tidal wave of destruction and despair. Countering such apocalyptic scenarios is, on the one hand, the less dramatic but more politically useful position that Mesoamerican calendric predictions are being realized daily in the ongoing violence resultant of more than five hundred years of continued colonization and its legacy of slavery, misogyny, and environmental indifference. On the other hand, the emergence of a new "Sun" (epoch) as predicted by the Maya also foretells a much more benevolent final outcome, if we can fulfill its mandate. It is a whimsical promise, a cosmic contract for a fundamental change in human consciousness.

Like the Mesoamerican codices of our original American ancestor scribes, I use these pages to reflect on the imminence of this period of profound global transformation, measured by my own stumbling steps of evolving political and spiritual awareness and activism. I describe these writings as *codices* because the Nahuatl word evokes the oral impulse that first birthed this record of essays, poems, and meditations. As Xicanas and Xicanos, one of our oldest written traditions resides on the indigenous ground of the spoken word, interpreted from the painted black marks of resin wept from trees onto a piece of amatl paper. MeXicanas and MeXicanos have always told stories aloud: as weapons against traíciones, as historical accounts and prophetic warnings, as preachers and teachers against wrongdoing, as songs of celebration, as exhalations of laughter, as prayer in the presence of the divine. And through this storytelling one's awareness of the world and its meanings grows and changes. There is no other common way, really, to explain an old way of using words; maybe even to justify it in the context of an unjust Western literary canon that extols the privately read, soundless word and abstract thought over the canto of cuento. As with the Mexica concha, the reader/singer of this work provides the breath that runs through the aural shell of these pages, giving it voice, body, propósito.

The pre-Columbian manuscripts offered images of flora and fauna, myth and history, genealogy, war, and ritual—from the mundane practices of daily life to ceremonies of great sacrifice. The function of those original manuscripts was to create a cartography of time and place and of the divine energies that animated through them. Painting serpentine paths of journeying, the tlacuilos[1] inscribed the progressive footprints of our collective ancestors. Most codices that survive today were painted after the arrival of the Spanish, the smoke from the smoldering graveyards of the original texts still lingering in the olfactory memory of their creators. That is to say that they were works created within the context of colonization.

This book follows in that tradition, reflecting a map of my own journeying in the first decade of this new century—as writer, teacher, teatrista, mother, daughter, and lesbian lover. Each step is marked by written glyphs depicting the daily advance of *neo*colonialism: the mosque in flames surrounded by U.S. troops; the family in Middle America sitting on the curb before their foreclosed home; plants and animals, villages and people-of-color communities disappearing into an ocean of melting glacier and broken levees; the dollar bill that makes it all possible.

This decade-encompassing collection of writings is framed by major historical events that impacted us in the first ten years of the twenty-first century—from the 9/11 attacks to the election of the first Black president; from national tragedy to great political optimism; from the predictable and brutal economic betrayal of working people by Corporate America to finally, the *un*predictable outcome of movement in the earth's alignment and of a disillusioned nation in the heart of change. The book is also shaped by private events made public here in the effort to make peace with, and politic through, them.

While the general structure of the collection follows the chronology of public addresses I presented throughout the decade, its arrangement most closely reflects the Mesoamerican cyclical sense of time, space, and movement, in which to advance forward is to return again and again to the site of origin.[2] Here patterns of Xicana feminist thought, which first surfaced for me more than a quarter of century ago, return to the present point in time, circling backward in memory as they progress forward in imagination and in living practice.

Life is not a progressive plot line. As Xicanas and Xicanos, we reside in the contradictory metaphor of an "America sin accento."[3] We are told we are citizens of a country which crafted its nationhood by thieving our own original nations. We are told to forget those origins, even as we witness our migrant Native American relations suffer a state-sanctioned racism and an abuse of civil rights unparalleled in this country since Jim Crow and Japanese internment during the Second World War.[4]

As much as Hollywood would like to (literally) bank on it, we are not headed for an apocalypse; the apocalypse has already occurred for those of us standing in the line of cruelty's fire, and ultimately, for the cruel and the fire-armed. All the while, the infinite possibility of recuperative social movement exists in that great empty site of nascent change. "Ground *zero*," they call it, the hole that remembers rupture. It is an apt enumeration, according to Maya mathematics. We count backward from there, placing our carbonless footprint across the face of this planet, the face of the female, divined. Our scribes record the journey, as our ancestors walk with us. Staff and gourd in hand, we enter that mouth in the mountain, the rebirth of collective consciencia.

Xerí L. Moraga
Oakaztlán, Califas

Agradecimientos

Already embedded in each of these writings is an implicit thank you to every person mentioned in these pages, living on this side of time or in the timelessness of the ancestors. Each one's corporeal and spirit life inspired this collection in some small or grand way. Beyond this, what makes this book fundamentally possible is my familia—de sangre y corazón, especially those I have lived with on a daily basis—my partner, Celia; my son, Rafael; my daughter of heart, Camerina; and nuestra nietita, Cetanzi. I thank you all for your part in creating both the obstacles and apertures in my writing process over this decade (and more), for without the context of this (extra)ordinary Xicana lesbian life, these pages could never be. I thank my sisters, JoAnn Moraga Lawrence and Cynthia Moraga García, because of their infinite faith in my work. I thank my father for his kindness and the example of his unprejudiced mind.

I also thank my students of color at Stanford University—those Native and mixed-blood, in diaspora and in lucha, queer and querying young folks—whose open and hungry minds proffered me the opportunity to think aloud many of the ideas presented in this collection, and whose heartfelt intellectual engagement supported me along the way. Gracias to Jennie Luna for the use of her home in the final days of completing this manuscript and to La Red Xicana Indígena for providing a critical community base in which I could ground in practice my imaginings and political inquiries.

Thanks to the Duke University Press editorial team, including: the assistant managing editor, Neal McTighe; the editorial assistant, Danielle Szulczewski; the copy editor, Molly Balikov; the designer, Jennifer Hill; the editorial associate, Leigh Barnwell, and the editorial director, Ken Wissoker. Their engaged professionalism made for a productive and relatively stress-free process. Also, thanks to Ricardo Bracho for his precise eye and vast cache of political-cultural language as indexer.

And, finally, I thank Stuart Bernstein, my friend and agent, for his tenacity and uncompromising loyalty to my vision, even when it doesn't please the "market." As he is a rare find, I thank Helena Viramontes for finding him for me.

A Xicana Lexicon

Throughout this text, I spell *Xicana* and *Xicano* (Chicana and Chicano) with an *X* (the Nahuatl spelling of the "ch" sound) to indicate a re-emerging política, especially among young people, grounded in Indigenous American belief systems and identities. I find especially resonant Roberto Rodríguez's observation in his treatise *The X in La Raza* that *X* in many ways reflects the Indian identity that has been robbed from us through colonization, akin to Malcolm X's use of the letter in place of his "slave" name (86). As many Raza may not know their specific indigenous nation of origin, the *X* links us as Native people in diaspora. When Chicano and Chicano appears with "Ch," it indicates the word's usage by the person(s) to whom I refer or, at the time period, referenced.

I use *Latino* when referencing, as a group, people whose ancestors originated in Central and South America, also including Mexicans, Chicanos, and caribeños.

I use *MeXicano* to mean Mexicans and Chicanos.

Although many academic texts do otherwise, I continue to capitalize and do not hyphenate people-of-color identities—for example, Black, Native, Asian American, and Third World—in keeping with the tradition of activist writers who emerged from the people-of-color movements in the 1960s. The writing style was an act of racial and cultural identity-affirmation, intended to distinguish us from the assimilationist agenda of mainstream America. I have maintained this style throughout my tenure as a published writer.

For the most part, I refrain from using *America* and *American* to refer exclusively to the United States, since the peoples of all the Americas are, in fact, Americans or americanos. When I do use *America* to mean the United States, it is always qualified by the word preceding or following it; for example, "middle-class America." *América* with an accent refers to the entire American continent, North, Central, and South. "America" in quotes indicates that the term's conventional meaning is contested.

Spanish words are neither translated nor italicized (unless for emphasis) in order to reflect a bilingual Xicana sensibility. No glossary is provided, since most readers, if they do not have some basic knowledge of Spanish, will easily be able to find a Spanish dictionary.

Last, a note on naming. With a few exceptions, I refer to people by their actual names. In the case of my compañera/companion/comadre that I have lived with and loved for over thirteen years, I use two names. *Celia Herrera Rodríguez* is a visual and performance artist, public intellectual, and educator. When referencing her professionally, I use her full formal name. When speaking of her more intimately, as my mate, I use her familial name, *Linda*, as it is pronounced in Spanish: "leen'-dah." The two names are an attempt to distinguish the public person from the private in my own writing and for my readers.

one   **Existo Yo**

La Consciencia Xicana

A XicanaDyke Codex of Changing Consciousness / 2000

In 1996, I wrote a memoir titled *Waiting in the Wings: Portrait of a Queer Motherhood*. The book, initially prompted by my seven-year-old son's premature and threatened birth in 1993, was completed three years later, marked by the deaths of my son's paternal grandfather and a beloved uncle. And in this manner passes the generations, and our lives.

Waiting in the Wings is an extended narrative describing my growing relationship with my child through conception, his birth in Los Angeles, his many months in the hospital, the first three years of his life, and his final emergence into a thriving boyhood. I began to learn to write "fiction" in composing that narrative, drawing from whatever skills about dramatic tension and character development I had garnered as a playwright. Through the act of writing that so-called autobiography,

I learned that a story well told is a story embellished and re-visioned just like the stories that poured from my mother's mouth in our family kitchen some forty years earlier. The fiction of our lives—how we conceive our histories by heart—can sometimes provide a truth far greater than any telling of a tale frozen to the facts.

Through writing *Waiting in the Wings*, I learned to reconfigure and rearrange dates, names, and chronologies to create a true narrative of my experience, generated by a relentless faith in dreams, memory, and desire. Since the completion of that memoir, my journal entries have moved away from an "I" fixed on the exact record of my experience to, I hope, something much deeper: I have encountered the "I" of "character" who is and who is not me, one which allows me the freedom of incorrect politics and a bravery not realized in my own life. So in that sense, this writing is as much an autobiographical narrative as it is a dream waiting to happen, based on some irrefutable facts.

THE FICTION OF OUR LIVES

Fact. I am a middle-aged lesbian living in Oakland with my beloved and her sometimes-grown son, Mateo, and her growing preteen granddaughter, Camerina, and my blood-son, Rafael Angel.

Fact. I've got it all. A ridiculously high mortgage, compensated by a sunset I can witness every clear night la creadora provides right from my front porch. Above it all. I sit above it all, above the bay's horizon and the airport Hyatt and Alameda's military base, turned-back Indian territory, and the Fruitvale barrio. I live with the barrio in my horizon, just south of my Berkeley whitedyke days and eight miles east of my early woman(of-color)hood in San Francisco. I got history in this territory and a woman my age who's as old as the hills, which is why I took her on new, cuz she remembered the hills of her own girlhood in Sacramento and southward all the way to Sandias, Tepehuanes. And that matters to both of us.

She taught me how to smoke rolled tobacco like you're praying to some god; although I knew it before. Somehow. When she taught me I remembered, like with most things she taught me, that it was a matter of remembering. She taught me how to build and burn a fire, even in the city. She taught me the importance of fire on a daily basis. Something you have to keep watch over, tend, nurture, coax along and control . . . just like the boy you're raising. Who'da thought we'd live this long, raising babies and our babies' babies into our middle age? Like I said, I got it all.

Fact. My literary and theater career has been "marred" as much by my politicized cultural essentialism as by my sexualized undomesticated lesbianism, to say nothing of my habitual disregard for the requirements of genre and other literary conventions. I don't know that I am a good writer. I believe I have, at times, well-articulated moments of insight, but I am not always convinced, no matter how many letters I get from those lonely queer and colored ones telling me that my words save lives that, in fact, words can.

Fact. We are a colonized people, we Chicanos; my woman reminds me when I find my stomach tied in knots each time I sit down to write. I experience myself writing beneath the suffocation of a blanket of isolation and censorship. The most virulent is self-imposed and lacks the high drama of senator-sanctioned obscenity charges. The censorship I have experienced has come in the not-so-idle threats of gun-toting, mad-dog envidiosa coloreddykes and in just plain ole commercial disregard, where the money you need to do the work you do ain't there for the kind of work you do. This has especially been the case with my work in theater. I don't know, really, who my friends are as a writer, those with whom I share common cause. I wonder why so many of us, Chicana and Chicano writers, remain so enamored with white people, their privileges, and their goodies: the seduction of success. Why do we remain confused about who we are? Not Black. Not Indian. Not white. Then what? I believe that our confusion causes our writing to fall miserably short of the truly revolutionary literature it could be. I tend to read American Indian writers these days because they aren't afraid to betray "America" and always Toni Morrison because she's stayed Black looking back.

Fact. I have always lusted for women and am grateful that there was a lesbian feminist movement in 1974, which when I was twenty-one allowed me to recognize and act on this loving without shame, justified it without apology, and propelled me into oppositional consciousness with patriarchy. Mostly, I am grateful to that movement for saving me from many years of heartbreaking repression, I'm sure.

I'm also grateful—plain and simple—for her, my beloved, that there was a Chicano movement that invited her entrance, politicized and betrayed her, right around the same time that the white entitlement of lesbian feminism betrayed me. I am grateful for those first moments of consciousness, always born from a living experience of injustice turned to righteous rage, that first experience of genuine collectivism, that blessed epiphany of art-inspired action. And I am equally grateful for those early betrayals that forced both of us to keep looking elsewhere for a radical re-visioning of our lives. Those betrayals have shaped my political consciousness more profoundly than any easy solidarity. There is no home, I learned, except what we build with a handful of others through a tenacious resistance to compromise.

A RESISTANT COMBATANT

In the small world that is my queer familia we live as if our values shaped the world at large or more accurately as if our values might chisel away at some monolithic monoculture we attempt to subvert with our art, our blood, our daily prayer. This may be the truest fiction we inhabit, but it sustains us. For now.

Another maker of fiction, Sherman Alexie (Spokane/Coeur d'Alene), writes: "I made a very conscious decision to marry an Indian woman, who made a very conscious decision to marry me. Our hope: to give birth to and raise Indian children who love themselves. That is the most revolutionary act."[1] When I stumbled upon these lines in Alexie's *One Stick Song*, my heart opened at the pure courage and simplicity of the statement. I felt him to be my relative in the naming of what I, as a Xicana lesbian, have kept secret for so long. For as taboo as it is to admit within the context of the firmly inscribed multiracial social democracy progressives paint of their imagined "America," I had a child to make nation, one regenerated from the blood-nations Mexicans born in (or coming to) this country are forced to abandon at the border. I had an Indian child to counter the loss of my family's working-class Mexican Indianism with each succeeding generation. I had a Xicano child cuz Raza's turning white all over the States.

Sometimes I think it is the "social advantage" of looking white enough to travel unnoticed among mainstream America that has put me in the position to recognize on a visceral level how spiritually unrewarding Gringolandia is. *It may feed your belly but not your soul*, I tell my Xicano students. And beneath this writing, I hear my son ask about his beloved Anglo grandpa, my father: "What about Papa Joe?" How do you teach a seven-year-old the difference between institutionalized ignorance, racism, bigotry, class arrogance, and the individual white people, breeds, and mixed-bloods that make up his family? How do you teach a child the word *genocide* and still give him reason to love beyond his front door?

The evolution of my own changing lesbian Xicana consciousness led me to make the same basic decision Alexie made: "to marry an Indian woman" and "to give birth to and raise Indian children who love themselves," not necessarily in that order, but, I believe, prompted by the same moral imperative. I can't write those lines, however, without acknowledging that from the perspective of some less informed North American Indian activists, Xicanos hold no rights to their indigenous identity by virtue of their Mexicanism. This perception is aggravated by the fact that the majority of Mexicans in the United States and México have historically denied (and been denied) their Native identities. I also can't write those lines without conceding that when most heterosexuals of color discuss breeding as a revolutionary act, they aren't necessarily thinking of their lesbian sisters and gay brothers as comrades in those reproductive acts of sexual and cultural resistance (especially given the white-washing queer identity has suffered in the public imagination). Historically, we may have been invited to bed by those cultural nationalists, but not to the tribal councils.

But for Indian children to love themselves, they must love their sex organs and their sexual desire. They must love the full range of their community, including their lesbian mothers and aunties and queer fathers and cousins. They must develop a living critical consciousness about their land-based history (outside of the White Man's fiction), a history that remains undocumented by mainstream culture and is ignored by the queer, feminist, and "Hispanic" communities. They must remember they were here first and are always Xicano, Diné, Apache, Yaqui, or Choctaw; for that memory can alter consciousness, and consciousness can alter institutionalized self-loathing that serves cultural genocide. Our children must become rigorous abolitionists of the slavery of the mind. They must think the taboo thought and cultivate in their own lives a profound knowledge about who they are, outside the framework of the U.S. nation-state. I don't know exactly how to teach a counter-culture of courage to my children, but I am working on it. And in this I am not alone.

For these reasons I believe my conversation about strategies for revolution as a Xicanadyke mother resides more solidly within the cultural-political framework of American Indigenism than in any U.S. gay and lesbian or feminist movements. At their cultural core these movements remain Euro-American, in spite of a twenty-five-year history of people-of-color activism. I have for the most part removed myself from conversation with the gay and lesbian feminist movement because most of its activists do not share my fears and as such do not share my hopes or strategies for political change.

Genocide is what I am afraid of, as well as the complete cultural obliteration of those I call my pueblo and the planet that sustains us. Gay men and lesbians (regardless of race) have, in the last two decades, become intimately connected to the question of survival because of the AIDS pandemic. But, as AIDS activists have already learned—sometimes the hard way—AIDS and its threat of death impacts people-of-color communities differently, be they gay or heterosexual. The pandemic is just one more murderous face in the long history of the systematic annihilation of poor and colored folk across the globe.

So, I fear AIDS as I fear gang violence as I fear the prison industrial complex as I fear breast cancer. I also fear the loss of Nuevo México to New York artists; the loss of Mexican Indian curanderismo to new age "healers"; the loss of Día de los Muertos to a San Francisco–style celebration of Halloween; the loss of indigenous tribal and familial social structures to the nuclear family (gay and straight); the cultural loss for children of color through adoption by white parents (gay and straight); the loss of art to commerce.

I think of Adrienne Rich's words from a generation ago: adapting John Donne, she wrote, "Any woman's death diminishes me."[2] Twenty years later, I would amend Rich's statement and assert with equal lesbian feminist passion, "Every barrio boy's death diminishes me." I never knew I would experience it this way; this intimate sense of a pueblo in the body of a boy. Maybe motherhood has changed me. And then I think not, except for a growing compassion for those I have loved the most intimately in my life: Mexican mothers, unspoken and never spoken for. This love is what fundamentally propelled me to be a lesbian in the first place and it continues to do so. And so, I suffer their sons, their fathers, our men, while remaining a resistant combatant.

LOST TRIBE

The police delivered Linda's son to our door just before dawn this morning. He returned home a broken boy, crying as his mother, my woman, patched him up from a yanked hospital IV. Twenty-six years old, but in our bathroom, he is a boy of sixteen, wondering what had gone wrong. Everything was going all right—the job, the car, the room, the "stuff." "I was doing so good," he cries. I watch the back of his neck as his head falls onto his chest, wet with tequila tears, the sun-darkened brown of his skin against the white shirt collar, still crisp with Saturday night's starch. I see in him my own son's elegantly sculpted neck, the same silk of brown-boy color. I want to look away from this meeting of generations, this juxtaposition of contradictions. My son of seven sleeping safely between the sheets, my woman of forty-seven, hours later, on the street with her grown son in search of the car he had abandoned that night after a tequila- and testosterone-driven fistfight; after macho bravado and police threats; after father failure and mother abandonment. Or so he sees it.

A week later, the white Mexican therapist asks Linda, "What are you afraid of?" "That he'll be killed," she answers. I watch the therapist's face. She is exaggerating, this is hyperbole, he thinks. My woman, a veterana of a war the therapist does not witness. How is it we feel that our children's ability to flourish, to achieve some kind of real ánimo in their lives, is on our backs to carry, that their failure is our failure? How do we separate mother-guilt from an active resistance to the genocide of men of color by requiring them to grow up? How?

I am reminded of my comadre Marsha Gómez. How she acknowledged in her mid-forties that she would never be free of the burden of her boy, that her son's "condition," as she called it, meant he would never be a fully functioning adult. I felt an unbearable sadness for her. Although her son was diagnosed schizophrenic, I sometimes wondered if his condition was anything more than colored and queer in the United States: mixed-blood, mad, and male? A year later, he would murder her. Marsha, like me, like my woman: a Xicanadykemamá.

He was one of the lost tribe. No romance about it. One of the lost ones who are so many of our sons now. I gotta boy following him. Somehow I think if I do good by Linda's boy, twenty-six going on sixteen, my little boy gotta chance. But it's hard to live up to. Big boy ain't my blood. I tell his mother, "I didn't break it." But I know in that resides the lie. "We all 'broke it,' him, them." And I'm only as good as the chance I give him, even if we fail. His blood is on my hands. I write these words like the beginning of a fiction about the end of a fact, but the question of his survival remains for both his mother and me. Somehow, this notion of us as a people, un pueblo, makes us mutually and collectively responsible for one another's survival. The privatization of the Anglo-American household makes no sense to us. He is family because he is Raza, although he holds my and his mother's lesbianism in contempt. A living contradiction: the mutuality of our responsibility to one another in an individualistic culture that divides and most surely continues to conquer us through those divisions. This son of ours: my antagonist and this country's volatile victim at once. This threatened and threatening machito, who is my gente, child, and brother. I want to write "brethren," for it is biblical, this grand story of nations and dislocations, exile and homecomings.

HOMECOMING

On Día de los Muertos, Linda gathers all the orphans together— Mexican Indians and a few dispossessed white folk—and we pray. It is a vigil of sorts. By 9:00 PM my son is already a bundle of bones and cobija on the hardwood floor. Linda's granddaughter, Camerina, on the threshold of her moon, stays up. Is it the pending menstruation, the hormonal eruption of her body, which keeps her up? She has something to strive for.

Some days, I strive only for my son. Some days the pure joy I experience watching him jump off the play structure in the school playground at the sight of my car pulling up to the curb, his running toward it at full speed, backpack falling off one shoulder, an earnestness in his face, is enough. This pure recognition of a moment in *his* world: *those monkey bars, that asphalt playground with painted-on kickball fields and tetherball circles, this mama arriving to pick me up as promised, knowing the afternoon snack will be waiting, the two hours of homework sitting at the kitchen table with sorta sister across from me, we both working word problems onto a sheet of photocopied preguntas. Momma working all the time with her hands, as we are with our minds, cleaning the kitchen, banging around pots and pans, chop chop chopping ajo, cebolla, celery into our evening dinner. My momma is not a housewife. She is queer and writes books, and wants something more for herself and us.* Something more than careers and portfolios and mortgages. And what I want is enough for all of us for now.

I am wondering what is happening in my middle age. I have changed. I have less hope, it seems, a deepening sadness accompanied by a growing wakefulness. I refer to my son as I do because I know this is a fleeting moment of well-being, extended in his blessed childhood, where he is awake and full of hope, which propels him forward into his life like the gestating hormones of his sister. My lover's hormones and mine are not gestating so much any more. They are, I imagine, taking leave of their previous missions, four babies in total between us. Is this why I am sad? This death of the illusion that we are not dying.

Days later, I am on a plane returning from Los Angeles and my mother's eighty-sixth-birthday celebration. I measure the ages of the passengers around me. There are those striving upward, ignorant of death. They are making money, careers, plans. There are those whose careers are a done deal. "Success" achieved or not, their bodies now worry them so. They try not to think about it, their bulky weight (the daily discomfort of those extra thirty pounds), the aching left hip, frozen knee, the sudden palpitations of the heart.

My mother is eighty-six years old today and continues to change into a woman I have never met, but must quickly learn to know. She repeats descriptions of events from yesterday and last week over and over again because they still interest her, as she remembers them as brand new with each telling. She asks the same question two and three times within a ten-minute span of a conversation. She brings out the same cup of coffee to serve someone, forgetting in the trip from kitchen to dining room who the someone was. She has already asked and been told twice. The coffee she offered to serve me goes cold.

My mother is eighty-six years old today. My mother and Linda's son teach me daily not to expect anything. She is a deep bruise in my heart; he, the constant ache of uncertainty. As I return home to Oakland, the sun sets pink and purple outside my window. I read the Xicano poet Alfred Arteaga's new collection of verse, *Frozen Accident*. He writes:

> tlahcuiloco of floricanto, as well
> as Gato and Xeritzín and all other
> souls alive, live only in the inks,
>
> in the red and the black, for only in
> codices do bodies truly animate[3]

Then, I think, can't we just make art? I am reminded there is a prayer in the act of writing. How is it I stray so far away from that home site? How is it I do not daily drag my woman, a painter, into this prayer of art that sustains in the face of grave disappointment, all the small dyings of heart?

SOME OF MY BEST FRIENDS . . .

Nearly thirty years out of the closet and I really don't know what I have left to say to the white gay and lesbian community,[4] except that I continue to be one, a lesbian; that just last night, on the eve of my woman's forty-eighth birthday, I made love to her like I remember wanting it as an adolescent. Thirty years ago, desire was a sad dream, and I remember thinking how *queer* (in the pre-eighties sense of the word) it was to want as I did.

Lesbian. Dyke. Queer. "I'll go to the grave queer," I announce, fully knowing that no one can shake me from that rock-bottom place of conviction about my desire. My racial identity has always been more ambiguous. The ground it stands on is built upon a knowing for which I can make no clear accounting. I never met one of my Yaqui ancestors; never a relative who named us anything but Mexican so Mexican it is, but since my earliest childhood I knew Mexican meant Indian. And it was the naming of "Chicano" in the seventies that reminded me of that fact and that sent most of my relatives into political hiding. So, I knew "Indian" was dangerous, like lesbianism. Knew it could not be domesticated, tamed, colonized. Like "dyke." People (white, black, and brown alike) have tried to dislocate me from Xicanismo, half-breed that I am; but it is getting harder and harder to do so. I'm getting older. I've been standing on this ground for too long now to be moved. In hubris and deception reside enemies from within and without. I've slept under the same roof and in the same bed with women for whom I remain unknown and unknowable. The bitter irony is that they never knew that they didn't know me. And that's a fact.

Several years ago, Ricardo Bracho, a playwright and my compadre, asked me how I identified myself politically, as a "Chicana lesbian" or a "lesbian Chicana?" As wordsmiths, of course, these distinctions matter to us. I remember there was some discussion about how the Spanish language forces one to choose, since *lesbiana* (the noun) and *lésbica* (the adjective) occupy distinct locations as parts of speech. English, in contrast, allows for a bit more ambivalence, since *lesbian* is used for both the noun and the adjective and its signification relies exclusively on syntax. At the time, nearly a decade ago, we both agreed that I was surely a Chicana lesbian, in that order, where Chicana is the cultural modifier of the indisputable fact of my lesbianism. In a call for just such cultural specificity and in critique of white middle-class women's cultural hegemony of lesbian sexuality throughout the 1970s, I wrote in 1982: "What I need to explore will not be found in the lesbian feminist bedroom, but more likely in the mostly heterosexual bedrooms of South Texas, (the Eastside of) L.A., or even Sonora, México."[5]
    What I didn't know was how a thorough exploration of that sexuality on the sheets of my bed and the sheets of my writing would eventually separate me from the lesbian and gay movement. In contrast to what Ricardo and I had concluded in that kitchen conversation in the early nineties, today I feel that my lesbianism modifies a growing Xicanismo, where the revolutionary consequence of my cultural identification generates my activism, my art, and my sexuality.

I've still got white friends (most at a distance now), queer girls who sleep with each other and some who sleep with men, and who remain my friends because they are not safe women. They do not go to sleep at night with false confidence. They do not believe middle-class security will secure them. They are not fooled by professions and insurance policies and retirement funds. They are not tricked into believing that postmodern theory is the same as radical action or that tenure is a tent against the harsh elements of oppression. Therefore, they remain my allies, these white women. Still, I don't see them that much anymore.

There was a time, living in New York City in the early eighties, when I ran with a buncha white and Black literary girls and we had a shared purpose. Cuz I was still thinking kind of in black and white back then, never naming, except with great pains in my own private writings, what really tormented my soul at night: a desire for return more primordial than any simple cross-country relocation to Califas could fulfill. A longing for that Mexican Indian "Madre" waiting for me at home in the body of my relatives here and gone, in the body of a woman my age and wanting.

For me, New York in the early 1980s was *Conditions* magazine, Kitchen Table: Women of Color Press, and the women-of-color caucus of New York Women Against Rape. It was a burgeoning feminism of color that grew in its autonomous conversation just among us culludgirls. And as that conversation evolved, so grew an activism that separated many of us from white women, drawing us closer and closer not only to one another, but also to our specific cultural experience as Chicanas, cubanas, and Lakota; English- and Spanish-speaking Afro-Caribbean women; and Chinese Americans and immigrant Southeast Asians.

In that specificity, I learned that, for the most part, when white women spoke of women of color and racism, they were usually thinking of Black and white relations and, too often and to my disappointment, many African Americans were equally politically engaged in the same bipolar version of the history of U.S. race relations. In spite of my theoretical faith in the cross-cultural feminism of color proposed by *This Bridge Called My Back*, four years after its publication I found that my feminism was taking on a decidedly Chicana formation in practice.

In the meantime, at night me and the Puerto Rican girls and the Black girls that could dance salsa went out and made out in bathrooms and on dance floors, drunk with desire, and somehow in that juncture there was a place to be me. Me, a light-skinned mixed-blood Chicana with lousy Spanish in a Nueva York that still sold tortillas in cans.[6] And I thank Sandra Camacho and Alma Gómez and Vienna Carroll y las dos Myrthas (Quintanales and Chabrán) for that. I thank Leota Lonedog for an underground urban Indianism I couldn't quite put a name to back then but knew my heart was working to live out in another decade. I even thank all "the women who hate me," to quote the title of Dorothy Allison's collection of poems.[7] Maybe cuz inspiring hatred gotta mean something was given and got up and gone when you left and that's somehow a tribute to what once was.

Reading Amber Hollibaugh's *My Dangerous Desires*, the history of a poorwhitegypsytrashfemcommiedyke is rendered in the manner of a beautiful adventure book. It is my friend Amber's history and fantasy at once, the facts that make up her fiction. Closing the book, I think, "A damn worthy life and she ain't even dead yet." Through the particular history of this complex and compelling woman and activist, the history of a movement is documented. I must confess I was a bit jealous of Amber's story; that for all its class betrayals, the gay and lesbian movement—that one movement—is where Amber finally found her home. I was jealous because no movement has ever sustained me like that. My history, a solo journey it seems, traverses many movements of diverse, seemingly contradictory identities.

A few weeks ago, Linda returned home with the news of Dolores Huerta's critical condition.[8] Dolores is mostly recovered now, but earlier that day I had a premonition of sorts about her vulnerable health. I remembered César Chávez's funeral, how I was unable to attend. How the "circumstances" of my life had prevented it. Today those circumstances have changed. Thinking of Dolores, I vowed that upon her passing one day, I would be present con mi familia, that *this* time I had a familia with which to *be* present. Selfish thoughts about the markers of meaning in our own lives. These leaders are both persons (our friends) and at the same time symbols. Audre Lorde was a symbol and a person and a friend. The artist-activist Marsha Gomez's intimate death at the hand of her son continues to symbolize something great and powerfully humbling in my life. Maybe I, too, am a symbol to others, to young ones, as I age. I don't write this to aggrandize myself, only knowing that we are all just moments, creative at best, in a small and troubled history of a planet and its people.

I watch my mother age daily and I move inside her body; watch the markings of my own body like the prediction of the future she already lives. I can't wait until after she dies to write of that history. I can't wait to be a centenarian to remember. I remember now a future I fear I will witness and I quiet my justified paranoia by writing counter-tales of courage I may never fulfill in life. It is autobiography in the truest sense: a record of my imaginings, as much as that of my experience. So that when I write in the voice of some one-hundred-year-old Xicana-dyke, armed and barricaded in her desert adobe, her lover for sixty years by her side, it is as much "me" as I can conjure in the best and worst of scenarios.

The centenarian tells us: *We are in a war against the United States government. We knew (hoped) it would finally come to pass, this meaningful way to end our lives here. Too horrible to think of dying without a fight, without reason for fighting. When I turned fifty, I began to mourn my ancestors, the recent ones known in my lifetime, who left with little resistance, except an entrenched bitterness. My woman and I share this, this commitment to not die as one of them, to leave for our ungrateful children a legacy of self-defense, por lo menos.*[9]

The old women of this story, as much as the personal and political portraits painted in an essay, are my Xicanadyke codices of changing consciousness. As a child in the early 1960s clandestinely dreaming of women, I could never have imagined how "legitimate" in some select circles queerness would become. I also never knew how the color of that queerness (and its political consequences) would once again render my desire not only unlawful but thoroughly revolutionary in its political promise.

A codex is a history told and foretold. I know a little bit about where

I've been in the almost fifty years that is my life. I don't know where we're going. I can only conj(ect)ure, which is why I write, to allude to a future for which we must prepare. And so, to that end, may we strive always for illegitimacy and unlawfulness in this criminal culture. May our thoughts and actions remain illicit. May we continue to make art that incites censorship and threatens to bring the army beating down our desert door.

From Inside the First World / 2001

ON 9/11 AND WOMEN-OF-COLOR FEMINISM

> and when we speak we are afraid
> our words will not be heard
> nor welcomed
>
> Audre Lorde,
> "Litany for Survival"

Beginning this writing on the afternoon of the tragedy of September 11, 2001, I had misgivings about foregrounding a new edition of *This Bridge Called My Back*, clouded by my own doomsday, albeit justified, reflections.[1] My hesitance was fleeting, for one fact remained unalterably true: the conditions of invasion, war, and terrorism have existed for people of color in this hemisphere since the mistaken arrival of Columbus to our shores.

What has changed after five hundred years of colonialism is the degree to which economic globalization, and the concurrent cultural and military domination by the United States, has engendered for Third World peoples (both within and outside of this country) a necessary expanded citizenship as members of a global community. Geopolitical borders mean little when the technological capacity of destructive weaponry available to countries (as well as the "terrorist" discontent) ensures our shared status as a world population of potential victims. In a very brutal way, all that has changed with the attacks of September 11 is the illusion that U.S. borders protect those who reside within them, an illusion seldom shared by this country's residents of color.

LOVE IT OR LEAVE IT

I remember from my days as a somewhat naive anti-war protester in the late sixties that the John Birch Society had put out millions of bumper stickers addressed to us "peaceniks." "Love it or leave it," they read. And I see how even today I fall so easily into the trap of believing that somehow the U.S. government gets to determine what "America" is. In the same manner, a generation ago, men of color tried to determine what *revolutionary* meant, censoring women from voicing their opposition within the people-of-color movements of the late sixties and early seventies. In the name of a different "nation" they protested, "Love it or leave it," and many of us did in fact leave, but not forever.

We returned. We returned twenty years ago on the pages of *This Bridge Called My Back* and the streets of this country, veteranas of the Chicano, Black Power, Asian American, and American Indian movements. We returned, veteranas of the anti-war and anti-imperialist movement against the United States' involvement in Vietnam. We were among the hundreds of thousands that forced a U.S. president out of office (Richard M. Nixon) and we went on to declare our rights as feminists, lesbians, and renegades from some of the most radical social change movements of the period. We were driven by the conviction that the established race-based política was not radical enough, for it did not address a fundamental root of injustice, the gender-defined divisions of labor and loving. Then in the mid-seventies, feminism too betrayed women of color in its institutionalized Eurocentrism, its class prejudice, and its failure to integrate a theory and practice that proffered whole freedom for the body politic of women of color. My disillusionment with the movements of the period marked my own coming of age politically, for it required of me, as it did for so many women of color, the development of a critical consciousness that had not yet been reflected in any mass social movement in the United States. To be sure, I was not alone in 1978, but there were hardly thousands sustaining those beliefs.

A generation ago, our definition of a U.S. feminism of color was shaped by a late 1970s understanding of the history of colonialism and neo-colonialism in the United States, as well as our intracultural critique of the sexism and heterosexism in race-based liberation movements. We recognized and acknowledged our internally colonized status as the children of Native and African peoples ("the first and forced Americans," as the poet Gloria Yamato once put it to me, quoting Amanda White[2]), and we found political alliance with the great-granddaughters of the disenfranchised Chinese railroad workers of the late 1800s and the daughter-survivors of the internment of Japanese Americans during World War II. Today's women of color have increasingly diverse demographics, with an ever-expanding range of political concerns: from Dominican women combating AIDS in New York City to Puerto Rican independentistas forging a campaign to remove the U.S. Navy from Vieques Island; from Native Hawaiian women activists struggling for the sovereignty of their homeland to South Asian women organizing in opposition to domestic and sexual violence against immigrant women. And, as we fear a full-scale (un)holy war against Islam, Arab American women emerge full-scale in opposition to this terrorist war against "terrorism" and its impact on the lives of women and children in the war zone.

The continually changing demographics of people of color in the United States are the product of its cultural, military, and economic invasions around the globe. As "refugees of a world on fire,"[3] women of color seek a liberation that is not confined to our state-imposed identity as residents of the United States. Instead our origins oblige us to assume a transnational activism, while at the same time honing a politic which addresses our concerns as Native and Asia- and Africa-originated women living within the nation-state.[4]

What then is the radical woman-of-color response to these times of armored embattlement? U.S. Representative Barbara Lee (D-Calif.) took a decidedly radical woman-of-color position when she stood alone among the members of Congress to state her opposition to war in western Asia. She was one individual Black American woman refusing to fall prey to U.S. patriotic propaganda. If we take the idea of democracy at its word, it obligates my congressional representative and myself, as women of color, to protest not only this war but also the conditions that helped create it: namely, U.S. foreign policy.

On the morning of September 11, I turn on the news to watch the twin towers of the World Trade Center fall to the ground. I am deeply shaken, as is everyone, by the immensity of the assault. My children, leaving their morning oatmeal, run to the TV set. I watch their mesmerized eyes. The scene is right out of an action thriller. "This is really happening," I say. I am, I believe, afraid—but of what? In the futuristic action film that is now our lives, the "bad (foreign-looking) guys" blow up the World Trade Center and "good (Anglo-looking) guys" bring out the big guns to defend the United States against the assault. But this scenario can produce nothing but pure hopelessness because terrorism will never be defeated by big guns, only by a collective reckoning with the United States' own history of global economic terrorism, and "the fundamentalism of free enterprise."[5]

As the Pentagon represents the armored core of the military industry in this country, the World Trade Center represented the pinnacle of Corporate America and globalization, housing some of the most powerful financial, technological, legal, and manufacturing firms in the world, all doing business with the United States. World Trade Center workers were killed en masse on September 11—the majority not six-figured shareholders and bank investors and corporate lawyers (although they too were sacrificed), but office clerks and service workers and janitors and waiters and secretaries. Knowing this, how can Corporate America elude at least *shared* responsibility for these deaths?

President George W. Bush may not have been flying the plane that crashed into the World Trade Center, but he is the most recent pilot of this turn-of-the-century disaster. Individuals govern the United States at the highest level, a ruling corporate-government elite who personally wield political power for profit. These individuals, at an unprecedented rate in the last generation, have destroyed the lives, livelihoods, environment, and political autonomy of Third World peoples around the globe from whom the greatest profits can be made with the least amount of resistance.[6] Shielded by corporate affiliations, protected by government legislation, and in cahoots with the military industry, the same individuals will learn only one lesson from this disaster: they must devise ever more aggressive means of preserving their freedom to make a profit at the expense of a majority non-Western population and the working classes. Tragically, their strategies will only serve to further endanger the lives and threaten the well-being of the peoples of the United States.

As hard as it is for this nation to admit, the so-called terrorists were not "cowards," as Bush referred to them, but people who believed so fundamentally in their cause that they were willing to kill and die for it. In the same way, many of our sons and daughters will be willing to kill and die in this impending world war in order to protect the freedom of enterprise, erroneously understood in the United States as "democracy." Suffice it to say, I denounce the murderous acts of September 11 with the same outrage with which I, along with so many others, had condemned the murder of tens of thousands of Iraqis civilians in the United States' "defense" of its oil interests in Kuwait. President George H. W. Bush executed that war in 1991. Ten years later, it's junior's turn. But as a global citizen, Xicana, and passport-carrying "American," I am interested in the root causes of violence, especially those perpetrated in my nation-state's name.

The position of greatest power—like that of those twin towers which once stood sentinel, shadowing "the gate to the New World," as the news anchor Peter Jennings described the Statue of Liberty[7]—also occupies the location of the greatest vulnerability. As members of a global citizenry, we are forced to acknowledge that the United States has appropriated well beyond its share of world's resources, and as such becomes, rightfully, the most visible target for the world's discontent. The bigger you are, the harder you fall. I speak in clichés, or are such phrases, which now rise to the surface of our daily discussions, simply tried and true axioms that this country has forgotten?

By four o'clock on 9/11, my idea of the necessary politics of our times—what I envision for a future of radical activism—has shifted as dramatically as the collapsing spine of the World Trade Center. I am shocked and horrified by the disaster, but, I confess, I am not surprised. The assault reverberates with a profound sense of the inevitability of the United States' demise as monolithic power. Upon the news of the attack, major network television ran images of Palestinians dancing in the streets. Although there was no credible evidence to confirm that the filming in fact occurred after the World Trade Center and Pentagon attacks (which raised serious questions regarding the U.S. media's role in manipulating U.S. anti-Arab sentiment), the images struck me with a profound sense of awe, as they forced the general public to recognize how thoroughly the United States is hated by the victims of its policies. For more than fifty years, the Palestinian people have watched their sons and daughters and elders die opposing the Israeli occupation of much of their land. Bombs dropped on Palestinian civilians bear a U.S. insignia. Is not $4 billion a year to support the Israeli state a form of terrorism against the Palestinian people? Are Palestinian children, mothers, fathers, and elders any less deserving a viable life than any citizen of the United States?

When my son asks me why the people as brown as him are celebrating in the streets of Palestine, I respond, "We are not the good guys." Why is this so difficult for the United States to acknowledge? Do we really believe the Hollywood version of our story? We are always the good guys. They, those "others," are always the bad. The speeches for the National Day of Remembrance on September 17 reflected exactly this kind of national solipsism, in which speakers for the most part espoused a chest-pounding, self-aggrandizing moral superiority over the "uncivilized" Islamic world. If the truth be told, all the token gestures made toward U.S. Muslim and Arab communities since September 11 are just that—token—and belie a profound xenophobic distrust and disdain of cultures that elude the West's ethnocentrism.

The United States may be the only country in the world that feels entitled not to suffer the consequences of its actions. This country constructed through acts of thievery and invasion imagines it will never be robbed or invaded. Even western Europe endured the bombing of its cities and countryside during both world wars. The attack on Pearl Harbor was only a tiny taste of assault against the United States, but one that instigated a revenge unparalleled in world history: the atomic bombing of Hiroshima and Nagasaki. To be sure, the United States "won" that war and, by its perverse militaristic definition, it will surely "win" the war it currently wages against the Islamic world, but at what cost? It is incalcuable.

In my recurring dream of a different América, just as in the replays on the network news, the World Trade Center along with the Pentagon surely fall to the ground in defeat; but, in my dream, there are not nearly twenty thousand workers inside. In my dream, we, the workers, are not fodder for U.S. crimes of greed. In my dream, the profiteers pay, not us. As I told a friend, "If Indigenous América had blown up the Pentagon, I'd be dancing in the streets too." Is it heresy to state this? But that is just a dream. In real life, I sit at the kitchen table and shake my head in despair, in full knowledge of the deaths to come. And they will surely come to our communities: barrio boy–turned-soldier as dead and as brown as any Afghan.

Eyes glued to the TV screen, my child of eight is frightened. "Will they bomb here?" he asks, and I realize that in all honesty, I cannot answer, "No, not here," as I would have before September 11. Because we live on the edge of the ocean, on the borderline of this nation-state; we live in a major metropolitan city, in the shadow of the Golden Gate Bridge and the Transamerica Pyramid; we are the symbol on the West Coast of the greed and arrogance that is the United States. "I don't know," I answer. How do you teach a child a politic where there is no facile "us and them," where the "us" who are his ostensive protectors against the bombing of his home city are at the same time the "them" who brought the bombs down onto this soil?

OUR CIVIL WAR

It is an hour before the dawn of my forty-ninth birthday. The house sleeps. Linda stirs as I leave our bed to find my journal and scratch out these words. I pass by darkened open-door'd rooms on my way to the kitchen and my morning café. I discern my son curled into the bottom bunk of his blue-painted room, under quilt and cotton sheets. There is a full basket of action figures and other plastic toys by his bedside. Across the hall our girl, Camerina, lies with one adolescent leg tossed out of the covers, spanning the full length of her bed diagonally, the same position her "Nana" assumes once I leave our bed for these early aurora-instigated writings. In a few hours, la familia will all rise and ready themselves for school and work. I'll pack lunches. Linda will make avena con fruta and our day will begin. It is the most peace I have ever known.

Last night an awesome storm broke over the Bay Area: bold strikes of lightning crisscross one another in the early evening skyline, followed by a quaking thunder. My young son calls me to the bathroom, where he finishes his bath.

"I'm afraid," he tells me.

"Of what?" I ask. The lightning cracks behind our voices.

"That a new world is emerging and I will lose you."

The day before, we had joined with friends and familia in a fire ceremony against the impending war. The kids were in and out of the circle, left to play around the yard and house as their relatives sat and prayed and analyzed until the sun had set and the half-moon had risen over the bay waters. I realize my son had heard the tenor and tone if not the substance of our remarks and rezos, and carried with him his own concerns about the war. *Emerge* is the word my eight-year-old used and I thought much of this afterward. Is this in fact what we are bearing witness to: the end of one epoch and the painful birthing of another?

At the ceremony, Linda remembered and acknowledged the pre-Columbian prophets. She spoke of the message they had given to our ancestors as they suffered the near-conquest and its five-hundred-year consequence: "When we no longer have to grow our own food and build our own houses," she recalled, "when every moment of our lives is not exhausted in sheer effort to survive, we, their descendants, would rebel." Did the prophets mean we would "emerge" a wronged and righteously resistant people? Is this the time?

Stupidly, with the ethnocentrism of a North American, I had imagined that real radical movement would arise from us, the U.S. citizenry. I had not dreamed that the world would rise against the United States and that we would have to take a side. But this is exactly what is required of us now: to suffer the slings and arrows delivered by our own compatriots as they name us traitors to "American principles." But what exactly are those principles beyond the freedom to buy? With the collapse of the World Trade Center, our "selected"[8] president assures his citizenry in speech after identical speech, that he, his lawmakers, and the military will continue to preserve "our way of life." I imagine this means the level of comfort and convenience and anesthetization from world events that the U.S. middle-class enjoys and has come to equate with democracy. And, indeed they have preserved our way of life at the expense of the majority people-of-color and non-Christian populations of the world. They have made us, as dutiful consumer citizens, speechless accomplices in an indefensible globalization, which continues to threaten the cultural integrity and economic stability of most of the Third World. And so we must die too, finally. In this sense then, those workers murdered at the World Trade Center become our first public martyrs for the war of resistance we, as U.S. citizens, have refused to fully wage against our nation-state. We are not yet witnessing the same mass graves as El Salvador in the 1980s, but this is our twenty-first-century civil war, in which our compatriots are being buried under corporate skyscrapers.

This morning I dreamed the bodies of the fallers, those who jumped off the top floors of the blazing World Trade Center—not to save their lives, but their skins, to escape that deadly burning of flesh. They drop head over heels, their arms stretched out against the sky in their wish for wings. Upon awakening, I remember my poem from twenty years ago: "I'm falling . . ." the murdered child cries, dropping off the cliff. "Can't you see . . . I'm falling?" And I hear the echoing voice of America's children, all of us abandoned by our country.

We are witnessing an incredible opportunity for the collective character of this country to distinguish itself from that of its bandit-leaders and make reparations for injustices done. As citizens, we must require the United States to assume a politic of mutually interdependent economic and ecological responsibility with the nations of the world, in which the natural resources of nondominant countries are no longer mined for corporate profit and their cultures ultimately disappeared in the process. Unfortunately, we citizens are being schooled daily in passive acceptance of the standard, uncritical story of Western world entitlement, where Capitalist Patriarchy, in concert with Judeo-Christian fundamentalism, becomes the rule of law and is propagated every night on the network news hour and each morning in the daily paper.

One evening, a few days after the 9/11 attacks, I step outside our home and watch the city lights. Something is changed, something beyond the sudden flash of red-white-and-blue draped from every third house. There is a pervading quiet lying over the city, the obvious result of an aircraft-empty sky. Everything has slowed down, stillness settles over the city. Express mail means trucks, not jets, and Linda reminds me how I always ask for this, for everything to slow down. If a plane never flew again, I would not miss it. But the quiet also betrays a profound somberness. I do not believe it is only the nearly three thousand dead that the country mourns, but the death of our illusion of invulnerability, of plain old safety as demarcated by U.S. borders. As the Egyptian writer Nawal El Saadawi tells us, "Scared people are easy to control."[9] And so a very frightened citizenry agrees to relinquish its power to corporate-funded leaders, surrender "a few civil liberties," postpone critical thought, and cloak its national anxiety under a red-white-and-blue security blanket called "patriotism." It is also patriotism that protects us from the deeper, harder acknowledgment of our complicity with those three thousand deaths and the thousands more to come. I look out over the Oakland skyline and I am stunned by the realization that what has ironically resulted from 9/11 is the dramatic intensification of the national deception. I dream of a full-scale assault to expose the lies. I look behind me for sister-warriors.

REMEMBERING TRAUMA

In 1981, *This Bridge Called My Back* called for a radical restructuring of this country, a country built on the shaky ground of a duplicitous and strategic amnesia, resultant of a five-hundred-year history of invasion, beginning with the first European colonizer-settlers and their wholesale theft of Native lands. The historical trauma of invasion is carried by both victim and perpetrator, while further acts of invasion are daily perpetrated to throw more displaced bodies between remembering and ourselves. If we must wear ribbons,[10] then let us tie them around our finger to remind us of the daily practice of countering U.S. collective amnesia.

The writer and activist Toni Cade Bambara, who first introduced *This Bridge Called My Back* twenty years ago,[11] countered institutionalized amnesia in her own dangerous writings before her untimely death from cancer in 1995. She wrote in her novel *Those Bones Are Not My Child*: "Maybe you *are* a crazy woman, but you'd rather embrace madness than amnesia."[12] In this statement resides our shared resistance mission as women-of-color writers and activists living inside the numbing forgetfulness of an "occupied América." Our task is to remember.

As the Palestinians remember daily the illegal and brutal occupation of their rightful territories since 1947, a situation supported by the United States for decades with weaponry and funds to the tune of $1.5 trillion; as the Maya-turned-Zapatistas remember through armed struggle their original land-right to the territory of Chiapas; as the women of Afghanistan do not forget who trained those terrorists whom the United States now calls enemy.

I remember.

In my lifetime. . . . Should I start the list? In my lifetime, Victoria Mercado, a unrelenting union organizer, a communist, and a lesbian was gunned down under "suspicious circumstances" by a virtual stranger (she was thirty-one years old); Ingrid Washinawatok (Menominee), a sovereignty educator and activist, was kidnapped and executed in the U.S.–aggravated civil war in Colombia. In my lifetime, AIDS wiped out a full generation (mine) of gay men-of-color activists, writers, and artists. In my lifetime, I witnessed the CIA's overthrow of Chile's democratically elected president Salvador Allende and ten years later, their usurpation of the Sandinista revolution in Nicaragua. In my lifetime, the United States has force-fed to Native, Asian, African, and Spanish-speaking América a poisoned economic alphabet soup (WTO, IMF, NAFTA, FTAA) in which "development" has meant little more than la finca being replaced by la maquiladora.

Sanctions against a dissident América are imposed to such a degree that it is taboo to even say aloud that we do not stand "united" as every billboard, new car dealership, dry cleaners, and auto repair shop attest. But we do not stand united. María Elena sits among two dozen or so of us around the circle of the fire. With full conviction, she states: "I am an Indian. This is not my country, but it is my land." Myrtha, puertorri-queña, cries full-bodied tears: "I hate this country. I want to burn down every American flag I see." When the Cuban missile crisis occurred in 1962, she packed it up and left for Puerto Rico. She did not want to die on U.S. soil, she told us. Nearly forty years later and Puerto Rico is still not a free and sovereign nation. Millicent's got ancestors calling to her in her dreams. They urge her to come on home with them; this slavery has been a long enough, deadly enterprise.

Oh yes, I *am* a traitor, a traitor to the geopolitical borders that divide nations of people, which separate me from identifying with the loss and death of human relatives across the globe. Who are truly my allies? Cer-tainly not those U.S. leaders who exercise genocide in my name. The tragic events of 9/11 effectively erased me of any residue of unthinking loyalty to the nation-state. I have seen the hate the anesthetized mind can foster. I awaken with renewed commitment to the work of a re-constituted América.

SISTERS OF THE CORN

As women of color re-member trauma, re-collecting the pieces of our fractured histories, we look to origins erased from the official record and to contemporary progressive movements that attempt to remedy the cultural ruptures and economic injustices our pueblos have suf-fered. To date, however, few politically progressive movements in this country have fully incorporated the specificity of the woman-of-color experience into their analyses of oppression or their liberation strate-gies. In the meantime, women of color continue to organize. For more than a quarter century, U.S. women of color have been actively in-volved in the issues of immigrant rights, Indigenous peoples' water and land rights, women in prison, militarism, reproductive rights, domes-tic violence, gang intervention, police brutality, queer youth support, and more.

Women experience oppression distinct from men; but, like men, we always experience oppression *within* the context of our racial and ethnic identities. As Angela Davis queries, when speaking of violence against women of color, "how do we develop analyses and organizing strategies . . . that acknowledge the race of gender and the gender of race?"[13] This question is especially salient when considering the race- (or ethnic-) based political movements, or cultural nationalisms, initiated in the 1960s and reemergent today.

For a number of years, I have been looking at question of cultural nationalisms in the face of environment loss, globalization, and so much warfare in the name of tribal, ethnic, and religious affiliations. The civil war in Bosnia of the nineties and the human rights violations executed by the Taliban regime, especially against the women of Afghanistan, are only two examples. In some ways, the violent manifestation of tribalism we are witnessing today is a reaction against efforts by Western nation-states to dominate the world economically, justified by a kind of moral (Christian) superiority where the "winners" are the blessed and the "losers" the damned. This is an obvious reversal of the Islamic fundamentalist's view of the West as the land of "infidels." Both perspectives are equally useless in achieving a tenable peace among divergent cultural and ethnic communities. Still *tribe* in itself is not a dirty word,[14] not for Indigenous peoples struggling for self-determination within occupied nation-states of the West and the Global South. The international campaign for Indigenous rights is as integral to the liberation of women of color globally as are, for example, the anti-violence movement to defend the rights of women in Iran or the domestic worker reform movement here in the United States.

As survivors of cultural nationalists movements of the sixties and seventies, which severely restricted women's freedom of movement and expression, as survivors of rape perpetrated in the name of nation, as widows of race wars and the mothers of mass-murdered children, women of color are in a critical position to redefine what "ethnic nationhood" may mean as a living practice toward not only the survival but the flourishing of our peoples. But as women we remain barred from most sites of political influence.

In recent years, Indigenous women throughout the world have begun to find their voice through the United Nations Permanent Forum on Indigenous Issues as well as through hemispheric gatherings such as those of Enlace Continental de Mujeres Indígenas de las Américas (the Continental Network of Indigenous Women of the Americas). Xicanas, although often displaced from our native Mexican herencia by many generations, have been brought to the table of these encuentros. For us, the Indigenous movement in América remains the one viable politic for ensuring a radical oppositional consciousness and practice against the genocidal policies of the United States and México.

Still, Indigenous-based struggles, like other political movements, create no easy alliances, especially when transnationally Indigenous peoples attempt to identify themselves through and in spite of a bitter colonial history of government-imposed definitions of what is "Indian." Further, as a queer Xicana, I recognize that it is still dangerous to speak publicly of lesbianism in most (North and South) American Indian gatherings, even among women. But queer identity cannot remain a private matter when it is not publicly protected. The censorship of queer issues (including sexuality and transgenderism) continues to be prevalent in most ethnic-based political struggles.[15] The idea that all aspects of human freedom are intimately interdependent may be given lip service within our politically active ethnic communities, but it is seldom practically implemented.

What these personal meditations attest to is that there is no safe place for any of us in revolutionary work. We make and break political alliance as we continue to evolve and redefine what is our work in this life. As a Xicana, I find the deepest resonance in that evolutionary process with my "sisters of the corn," as Toni Cade Bambara called Native women.[16] Indigenism (north and south) gives shape to the values with which I raise my children; it informs my feminism, my sense of lugar on this planet in relation to its creatures, minerals, and plant life. Ideally, it is a philosophy, not of a rigid separatism but of cultural autonomy and communitarian reciprocity in the twenty-first century. It is my sure-footed step along that open road of alliance with my "sisters of the rice, the plantain, and the yam."[17]

Toni Cade Bambara believed that we women of color have not forgotten, not in that cave of memory where the freest part of us resides, the basic elements of our lives: the mother-ground that brings sweet sustenance to the world's children; the mother-ground in which we finally lay down our bones and brain to rest. A women-of-color move-ment is a movement in the act of *remembering earth*. Ultimately, our politic remains beholden to it. To her.

NO LONGER YOUNG

Reflecting on the twenty-year passage of time since the first edition of *This Bridge Called My Back*, I wanted to write what was never told to me as a young woman: that one's world and the possibilities for it—be it a change of heart or a change of address—look very different when one is no longer young. I am no longer young. Neither am I old, but soon enough old age will come, as the fragile eighty-seven years of my mother constantly remind me. We are born and die within a particular epoch and within that era we may affect, through small or grand acts of courage, whatever changes we can upon this pitiful planet. Maybe to the young ones, I simply want to say, "Work tirelessly when your bodies do not yet ache at night. Do not waste your lives, your good health, strong bones, and resilient muscles. Use them."

I remember being so scared as a young woman with an emerging consciousness amid the political turbulence of the late sixties and early seventies; scared of dining-room political debates where my "college-indoctrinated radical ideas" alienated me from my loved ones; scared of the faces of Chicanos, who could be cousins, on the evening news, pro-testing the racial discrimination from which my light skin and Anglo surname had shielded me.[18] I also remember being afraid, to the point of paralysis, of coming out as a lesbian to that same familia and com-munity. I did come out, finally; and in the act drew from a courage that would sustain me for the numerous battles of conscience that lay ahead. What I had not realized at the time, however, is that consciousness births consciousness and that the state of embattlement, which emerges through principled engagement with the world, never really lessens.

I see the World Trade Center falling before the eyes of my parents, my father a veteran of the Second World War, my mother born during the period of the Mexican Revolution. They are U.S. citizens and in the latest hours of their lives, they watch symbols of U.S. power crumble like castles of sand. Would that those buildings had been sand castles, structures built in full creative knowledge of our ephemeral life spans, our vulnerability to the righteous forces of nature. Call it karma, if you will; moral debts are being paid.

For the first time I fear for my children and the world they will inhabit after my death. For the first time, it occurs to me that as residents of the United States we are finally subject to the global violence we have perpetrated against the non-Western world. What has also shifted is my sense of time. Maybe the revolution I had hope for and feared *will* be realized in my lifetime. Or maybe I will only live long enough to witness the dreaded violence that anticipates revolution and the erosion of the real quality of our lives.

The real quality of our lives. Pulling my son out of the bath, I urge him, "Hurry, put on your piyamas. Come outside and watch the thunderstorm." And in the twenty minutes before a relentless downpour, he, his sister, Camie, and I pull out the folding chairs and watch the better-than-fireworks lightning storm. The sky splits open. Crack! The kids jump up from their seats, grab hands, and dance to bring the rain down. Nobody's dollars bought this moment. The sky's for free.

Maybe a new world is emerging as my son feared. I've got a full belly and healthy kids who still dance under the rain clouds. Es un momento fugaz. How long can we even claim this small spot of peace? It is a privilege threatened by war. And war, at its most elemental, is death for all of us. "Not in my back yard" no longer exists, America.

In her novel *The Salt Eaters*, published in the year before *This Bridge Called My Back*, Toni Cade Bambara proffered this question to women of color: "Can you afford to be whole?"[19] It is a question to ask myself, it is a question to ask my country.

The United States does not need to be defended; it needs to be cured. The collective denial of guilt in this country weighs so heavily upon its national psyche that soon the day will come when not one scapegoat (neither Muslim fundamentalist, Mexican immigrant, nor lesbian of color) will be able to carry it.

I work forward to that day.

An Irrevocable Promise / 2002

STAGING THE STORY XICANA

The ceremony always begins for me in the same way . . . always with the hungry woman. Always the place of disquiet (inquietud) moves the writing to become a kind of excavation, an earth-dig of the spirit found through the body. The impulse to write may begin in the dream, the déjà vu, a few words, which once uttered through my own mouth or the mouth of another, refuse to leave the body of the heart. Writing is an act prompted by intuition, a whispered voice, a tightening of the gut. It is an irrevocable promise to not forget what the body holds as memory.

Writing for the stage is the reenactment of this ceremony of remembering. Experience first generated through the body returns to the body in the flesh of the staged performance. In this sense, for me, it is as close to direct political activism as I can get as an artist, for theater requires the body to make testimony and requires other bodies to bear witness to it. The question remains: bear witness to what? It is a question all Indigenous artists, the survivor-children of Euro-American genocide, must ask. And so I too ask myself most simply: what *is* the story Xicana?

As a teacher and maker of theater, I still consider the importance of the Brazilian teatrista Augusto Boal's ideas on the ways in which mainstream theater is used as a tool for political and cultural domination. In his *Theater of the Oppressed* from 1979, Boal calls for a theater practice welded and wielded as a weapon of political resistance. For me, these early writings assume even greater importance in the face of the growing cultural amnesia in América, aggravated by global capital.

I have always viewed my work as a writer in general and a playwright in particular within the context of an art of resistance or a literature toward liberation. *Toward* is the operative term here, as Xicana art and its forms are hardly free. In fact, if anything accurately describes the Xicana story, it is the site of conflict and resistance; revolt, but not revolution. Not yet. Or not ever, as at times it feels that, with the growing commoditization of Latinidad, we are moving further and further away from that requirement of resistencia in our art. Still I have never questioned the revolutionary potential in bringing the Xicana experience full-bodied to the center of the stage (and page). What I do question are the forms, the shape and structure in which that staged storytelling might be rendered. What languages do we use? What physical action? What objects are called forth? What voices? Help me remember, I ask of my dioses, what I never read and may never have witnessed but somehow know. This is the mantra of my own writing process. Help me believe I have the right to remember *and know* what at times only my troubled heart tells me to be true.

AGAINST AMNESIA

For over fifteen years now, I have wielded theater as part of my arsenal of cultural resistance as both an artist and teacher. It is not the single nor necessarily the most effective weapon I carry, but since lifted, it has impacted all the genres I endeavor, as well as my role as an educator. I came upon theater organically, out of the *spoken* voice of my first truly fictional character. I remember the day, exactly, when what had always been autobiographical writings first etched out in my journals suddenly transformed into the barrio tongue of a teenaged "cholito-style" blade-packing Mexican American girl.[1]

To say my work emerged from the oral tradition of my MeXican-ismo is to tell you a simple truth: that my writings have always had bodies and as such are best rendered through the physical space of staging, even if that staging is no more than my body speaking aloud behind a lectern. The oral tradition is the only "literary legacy" about which I am completely sure, since books did not hold the first stories that held me. The rest of what I know as a playwright and a writer has been garnered, learned, assimilated. And all of this is what I bring to the art of making and teaching teatro.

Cinco de Mayo Celebration, Sequoia Elementary, Oakland Unified School District, 2002.

I am doing a children's play or so I tell myself. "This is only a children's play," which I have authored in order to provide my eight-year-old son and his Oakland public school with some notion of MeXicano history and culture beyond the obligatory Ballet Folklórico performance; red, green, and white crepe paper draped from the cafeteria ceiling; and tortilla chips with salsa. (My compadre and fellow playwright Ricardo Bracho affectionately referred to this three-month residency at Sequoia Elementary as my unofficial Theater Communications Group grant. What a country it would be if national granting programs actually paid for such work.)

The majority of the kids in my son's second-to-third-grade class are African American, followed by Asian American and Latino. There is one white girl among them (who herself claims to be a quarter-breed Mexican; I don't doubt her). The project of our coming together is clear in my mind: the opportunity to re-(en)vision Mexican and Xicano history from a Xicana Indígena and feminist perspective on stage. I hadn't exactly articulated this to anyone, but was gratified to find that my son's teacher, African American and a lesbian, was only too eager to yield the stage floor to me and my ideas.

In *The History and Future of the People of the Corn*, as this play is called, human beings are created by Grandmother from the ground corn of her metate and the oil of her tortilla-making palms (true to the Quiché Maya creation story). The Spanish are not brave explorers, but foreign invaders. Christopher Columbus wears a suit and tie and carries a cellphone as he encounters the Arawak for the first time. As the play progresses, he will, in the tradition of teatro Chicano, bear a sign that names him "Greed." Greed becomes the enemy and reappears in the body of the Spanish conquistador Hernán Cortés and all subsequent historical enemies of the disenfranchised Indians of México. Greed battles Father Hidalgo, Benito Juárez, Emiliano Zapata, and las soldaderas of the Mexican Revolution. He goes on to encounter César Chávez, Dolores Huerta, and the contemporary Zapatistas of Chiapas. The four-feet-tall female Zapatistas, their eyes peering from above their bandanas like ski masks, surround Greed and he is forced to succumb to the righteous power of revolutionary resistance. They overtake Greed and remove his sign, replacing it with another. "Compartir," it reads, which means, "Share." And, in this manner, one American history lesson is told to right the record, just a bit, and the Oakland City school district's kids of color (which are the vast majority) are just a little less deprived of themselves and their history.

The seven- and eight-year-old actors are having a good time with this interpretation. It is new material for them in terms of their schoolbooks, but it is not new to them intuitively. They giggle out of a subtle sense of the danger in this version. In one rehearsal, we "improvise" the story of the first encuentro (meeting) between Columbus and the Arawak, using gibberish. This is a standard theater game, which teaches participants about the function of subtext; how we understand the meaning of words by tone, gesture, and body language even when we may not know the language at all. I first ask the kids, "What language do you think Columbus spoke?" Some agree on Spanish; some of the more astute ones even venture Italian. When I ask them what the Arawak spoke they respond, "English." Which, of course, to them is the "American" language.

By way of illustration, I call two Cantonese-speaking kids to the center of the circle and ask them to speak their native tongue. They do so, at first shyly, then with pride that they have something special to contribute to this lesson. The rest of the kids—African American, Latino, and Pilipino—respond that the words sound like nonsense to them. In short, it is gibberish. We begin to improvise. Five kids volunteer to be Columbus and his crew and another five an Arawak chief and his tribe. The two groups confront each other, speaking "gibberish"—gibberish that ends up meaning "I came for gold and if you refuse to give me what I want, I will kill you," which is exactly where genocide and greed meet. Columbus and crew raise and shoot their rifles and the Arawak drop dead en masse. They had not been directed to do so. This was an improvisation, which ended our rehearsal for the day and began our first lesson in colonization. And we, the kids and I, have fallen in love with theater's power to teach. Truth. Or lies. You choose, as Boal reminds us.

Days later, in rehearsal again, we move on to the history of the slave trade. In the scene, two Black kids, a boy and a girl, are put on the slave auction block. They have their hands bound, their faces drop into their chests, and after being sold, they are led off stage to the tune of Billie Holiday's "Strange Fruit."

> Southern trees bear strange fruit,
> Blood on the leaves and blood at the root,
> Black bodies swinging in the Southern breeze.
> Strange fruit hanging from the poplar trees.[2]

The Arawak chief symbolically stands alone, center stage, and shakes his head in despair. The first time we rehearse this, the entire troupe of twenty stops cold. We are speechless—maybe only for a few moments—when the silence is broken by the nervous laughter of another child. An eight-year-old female snaps back at him, "It's not funny," and the kid stops laughing.

Of course, it's not funny. Black bodies. Real children's black bodies. I had asked the two kids to show in their bodies "great loss, great sadness." And somehow these children, who are not actors, knew how to enact this story, for there was an agelessness, an old knowledge, in their bearing that indicated to all of us that they remembered slavery on a visceral (genetic?) level. Nicole and Dion are their ancestors incarnate. Nicole and Dion are slave children being separated from their mothers.

And I know and they know we will never forget this lesson in remembering. This is the marvelous horror and promise of teatro. Real bodies. This is what brings me back to theater again and again. The lesson of it. The promise of conscientización, coming to consciousness, through the physical act of art.

In my three-month "residency" at Sequoia Elementary, I was honored to observe twenty seven- and eight-year-olds discover for themselves the infinite political and life-saving promise in the making of teatro. Their bodies did it. They did not enact the "discovery" of América, where the white male is always the agent of superior intellect and moral rectitude. They enacted a historical moment of murder and thievery that continues to shape their own twenty-first-century place in this country, as African American, Xicano, salvadoreño, and Asian immigrant–descended children. The theater project brought home to them, through their bodies, the knowledge that their second-class status in the United States is not a natural-born fact, something I barely began to glimpse before my twenties.

THE BODY'S PROMISE

The violation of the collective body is re-membered in these staged enactments. Here the pieces of ourselves broken by racist and colonial incursions are re-collected and reconfigured through an art of social transformation. Historical oppression is, however, at the same time experienced individually and intimately. This is what makes the scene of the slave auction so compelling: the actor's personal embodiment of that trauma.

About ten years earlier, in working with a pre-teen Latina actor, I had experienced through the staging of a scene, the visceral intimacy of oppression. In this case, the violation was a deeply private one, dependent on secrecy. It was the kind of oppression that happens behind closed doors, seldom recognized through the male gaze of the Euro-American proscenium. For the premiere of my play *Shadow of a Man*, the Cuban American director María Irene Fornes casted an eleven-year-old girl to play an eleven-year-old girl, Lupe, who suffered an unwanted intimacy with her father.[3] Although not explicitly sexual, his habitual drunken visits to her bed for an abrazo after a night spent in the bar evoked the same childhood burden of guilt and shame that incest inspires.

I had written the scene, seen it enacted numerous times in other rehearsals and staged readings by actors sixteen years old and older, but never by a real live girl whose body balanced itself precariously and quite beautifully on the verge of puberty. So when that two-hundred-pound man playing the father dropped his drunken head onto Lupe's blanketed, eleven-year-old belly, I was not prepared for the holy terror of that moment. Although I had written the scene, I had not anticipated my own sense of revulsion, as I felt the audience gasp at the embodied experience of Lupe's vulnerability. It was exactly the effect I conjured in the words of my writings, but it took the Xicana/Latina stage to realize it in just this manner. For women in the audience, such visceral, unromantic staging made public an oppression reliant on its secrecy for its power. And, for me as a teatrista, the "conscientized" enactment of the oppressed body of this girl-child proffered, for a moment, the imagined possibility of an end to such clandestine violations.

The revolutionary promise of a theater of liberation lies in the embodied rendering of our prisons and, in the act, our release from them. I think of my teatro student, eighteen-year-old Daniel—he with the poet's heart, the delicate hands, the sharp wit of a cultural survivor. While rehearsing a performance piece he had written about the one-hundred-year legacy of machismo in his family—from Mexican miner, to revolutionary, to impassive laborer father—Daniel is suddenly overcome with tears. He breaks down right there on the stage floor. A moment later, he has quickly recovered himself, laughing nervously, "I didn't know this was gonna be therapy." But it is not therapy. "Therapy" is a privatized gringo concept that our illness is somehow individual, as is our cure. Daniel performs a history of the formation of masculinity in his MeXicano family. He is its ambivalent inheritor, as are the majority of young men I meet these days. He is involved in the art of unraveling how we all got in this mess—men estranged from women and themselves. His writing and its enactment, even beneath the shadow of Stanford's colonial archways, reflect a contemporary curanderismo. It emerges from an ancestral knowledge that a story told with the body can cure and create great warriors of heart on the cultural battlefield. "Word warriors," the author Denise Chávez has called them.[4]

The bodies of Teatro Maíz (those second- and third-graders), Lupe of *Shadow of a Man*, and Daniel's "queer" portrait of masculinity occupy censored sites of knowing on the Anglo-American stage. But it is more than institutionalized censorship exposed here; it is what the Latino queer scholar Alberto Sandoval Sánchez means by the "abject" body—the body of the enslaved, the violated, the diseased, the queer—performing itself as an act of transgression against the master class. "Performing abjection," Sandoval Sánchez writes, "has the potential to disrupt normality." The abject is "dangerous," it "menaces" hegemonic culture.[5]

In MeXicano terms, women's sexuality has occupied a fundamental site of abjection in the collective imagination since Malintzín Tenepal's fateful rape by the conquistador Hernán Cortés.[6] Abjection: debasement, depravation, abnormality. We are despised from within and without—our bodies, the conquered nation. The perverse irony is that we are further despised, within our own cultural ranks, when we refuse to be vanquished.[7] Is it a secret we women pass on to one another, those remembered acts of resistance, those native rebellions against female enslavement? For Xicanas (and I must add all women of color who walk in a remembered history of colonial rape), the enactment of decolonized female desire is the very locus from which abjection arises.

As active desirers, we become the "monsters" of the Western and patriarchal imaginations.[8] Over and over again, the protagonists of my own work in theater have been these heroic and disfigured monsters: the bodiless Cerezita of *Heroes and Saints*; the infanticidal Mexican Medea from *The Hungry Woman*; and the self-loathing, closeted, and queer killer Josie Zanzibar in *Digging Up the Dirt*.[9] Each reflects sites of abjection that "menace" the lie of colored queer invisibility, MeXicana criminality, and female perversion. We are reviled when we speak up; we are reviled when we act out. We are reviled when we create complex depictions of female sexuality (and not some man-pleasing, minstrel-like, consumerist portrait of women "wanting it"). Whether we are lesbian or heterosexual, as self-proclaimed desirers we become bodies of revolt, bodies in dissent against oblivion. I think here of Alicia Gaspar de Alba's depiction of Malintzín Tenepal in her short story "Los Derechos de Malinche." In it an imprisoned Malinche, in anticipation of Cortés's arrival to her cell, places a nopal con espinas (a thorny prickly pear) inside her vagina. She awaits her rapist. She is the MeXicana menace—a body in dissent against oblivion.

Against oblivion, our bodies refuse to forget our preconquest selves.

As a teatrista, I have thought often of the Stanislavski acting system (and Lee Strasberg's related approach, "method acting"), wherein emotional memory is linked to physical action and the body is explored as the reservoir of memory. The process requires uncovering resistant, resilient, and living memory. If remembering counters oblivion, how does the Xicana artist, especially in theater, draw on memory she has been historically sanctioned to forget? Returning to Sandoval Sánchez's meditations on abjection, he also describes it as a condition of the exiled, those who have been forcibly displaced from their homelands. And, "Death," he tells us as a daily survivor of AIDS, is the "ultimate exile."[10] Then genocide is also the ultimate site of *collective* abjection. This is the Xicana Indígena story: the story of displacement, amnesia, exile, orphanhood, rape, and genocide. This is the story of female desire forgotten. *How does the Xicana artist stage that? And who would buy a ticket?*

I dream I am among Jews in a Second World War concentration camp. (It is not the first time I have dreamed myself there, imprisoned, awaiting extermination.) In this dream, I lie naked in a small hard bunk. Another woman, also naked, lays her full length on top of me. We hold each other. We will be killed for this act.

When I awaken I realize I had fallen asleep afraid. The night before I had been invited to speak by a small group of progressive faculty at a nearby Catholic university. For the majority of the audience, however, my words were hard to hear. It was impossible to ignore the feeling of being silently ostracized, quietly assuming the place of "other." *That dyke, that white-faced Mexican, that lady who talks Indian, she ain't me.* I have no idea what, in fact, those students felt. Only my dreams showed me what I felt, that utter vulnerability in claiming all that we are at once: lesbian, Xicana, hungry for a free nation when the America world tells us we are already free. I am, we are, those women who as unrecognized and unreconciled aging artists in a whiteman's world are one day found scratching out ancient symbols on caves walls with shit and blood for pigment. We are the women on display, the Mexican bearded-woman-circus-freak—the Julia Pastranas of the world[11]—mocked and mummified by a culture plagued by the fear of difference.

HOMEGROWN INSTRUMENTS OF NAMING

The stage is bare, except for several woven baskets. The music is Northern Mexican/Southwest Indígena—antler and flauta. AMADA *enters, carrying a basket under one arm. She tosses dirt from it onto the ground. She wears a serape in the style of a "sweat dress."* POET *digs at the earth with a shovel. It is a closing ritual as the two recall the ceremony offered to Amada upon her tragic passing.*

AMADA: Was there a fire?

POET: Between us, oh yes.

AMADA: No, I mean . . . at the end?

POET: . . . Blazing. I built it myself. And into it, entregamos tus faldas, tus huipiles, tus joyas de silver and turquoise. . . . Do you see it, your honoring?

AMADA: I . . . don't . . .

POET: I am just trying to do something other than theirs on this stage.

AMADA: (*After a moment*) Yes. I see it.[12]

Always in my imagination before I write, the stage is as empty as the page; always I wonder how to fill it. How to tell a story different from what has been prescribed to us: something beyond progressive plot lines, the Eurocentric "arc" of a story, and the single protagonist. Something beyond a literature that entertains Euro-American audiences by describing who we are to them with them in mind.

In the best of my imaginings, the Xicana stage would house an uncompromised story of dissent, one where the axis upon which freedom is conceived spins from a wholly alternate worldview. Spinning tales for the stage, I study I write I research I land upon the words of El Mallku, leader of the Katarino (Indigenous) movement in Bolivia: "Hay que indianizar a los q'aras" ([Whites and mestizos] must become Indianized).[13] Not the other way around, he means. And, suddenly, the ground opens up in the toiled field of my thinking.

A truly liberationist theater is not generated from some neoliberal Latin American notion of mestizaje or North American corporate-conspired definition of *multiculturalism*, nor academic-inspired discourse on hybridity, nor New Age reconfiguration of indigeneity; it is one conceived by those who have been erased by the official colonial narrative. It is *our* liberationist theory assuming flesh on the América stage. It is a living art, requiring tools of our own making, our own objects, our sacred and profane practices; or maybe for us lost, queer mestizos, it is just some clumsy grasping at a precolonial language and history almost forgotten.

I have no nostalgia about some idealized original tongue that we, the thousands of tribes that make up the Xicano nation, once had. Still, I admit that as an artist not born into the educated classes, I am always protecting what may be original in me, not me alone, but the "we" of me. I am suspicious of Western thought, even as I stand here as its product. I do not naively confide in the postcolonial theory created by the colonists nor the liberation theories of my oppressors. I am both the freed slave and the enslaved. I am talking out of both sides of my mouth. I contradict and speak to you in their language, which is my language. And is not. I am the mestiza: Indian and white, more white than Indian. I have forgotten almost everything. I pick and borrow what I can to try and find my way to a manner of expression that will, from the simple vantage of an eight-year-old, stop greed. I want to turn the sign around.

Sometimes, as a writer, I feel my task comes down to the simple fact of declaring, "Sí existimos." We exist and have always been here. I remember the mother in my play *Shadow of a Man*, trying to get her husband to respond to her. She cries, "Manuel, existo. Existo yo." Maybe this is the same refrain in all of my work: an insistence on a presence where the world perceives absence. Maybe this is fundamentally the project of all Xicana work: to announce our presence to one another and the world, but in our own tongue, on our own ground, brandishing our own homegrown instruments of naming. This is where the project of revolutionary teatro occurs: self-defined, self-determined, employing words and images before and beyond the colony.

BEYOND THE COLONY

The language of the Xicana story—if it were to be real—is fragmented, it is the stutter, the garbled utterance caught in the silence between tongues, tongues literally ripped from mouths. It resides in the taboo languages of the body: the vulva pressed unashamedly against a bed of dirt or the body of another woman in the effort to remember what got lost somewhere. It is a paling Odami descendant speaking through the body of Xicana performance.

Día de los Muertos, Oaxaca, Mexico, 2001.

On the last evening of a four-day encuentro between Mexican and Xicana visual artists, Celia Herrera Rodríguez[14] is to perform in the colonial courtyard of Santo Domingo, a massive cathedral-turned–cultural center. I was there among the audience beneath the moon-lit, delicately clouded evening sky. I was there when that pearly disk slipped out from behind a cloud and showed herself in all her full-moon wonder. I was there when Celia threw a petate (a straw mat) the size of a beach towel down onto the cobblestoned ground and said to the mostly upper-middle-class Mexican audience, "This is what's left of my land."

Stunned silence all around. From me too. I had seen this performance several times before, but suddenly, here among the Mexicans, it is different. Suddenly we Xicanas, in one gesture of claiming, become bodies in our own right, citizens of a nation of peoples dispossessed and displaced. We are not caricatures of what could have been, neither malinchistas, nor wannabe gringas, nor vendidas-mexicanas. We are a pueblo in exile from a México Antiguo, that petate said. We are people who made our presence known in the physical body of one MeXicana and Odami woman and one damn "prop," I tell Celia later that day. She responds, "It isn't a prop," meaning the petate. And of course, it isn't. As her "performance" is not quite that. It is something else, not quite performance art, but art and performance at once. It is a story told through a single Xicana gesture and a dozen words. I don't know how she does it. I know it is not scripted, only thought about for many days in advance while washing dishes, hanging out laundry, spreading watercolor onto a piece of amate paper. It is a ritual of remembering, a kind of prayer as in ceremony. It is the Xicana stage. A land and history reclaimed.

Sí, existo. Existo yo.

Seven months later, Celia will perform in Málaga, Spain. She will take La Virgen del Carmen, a revered religious figure in Málaga, and smash the plaster statue with one fatal blow to the head. She will return the favor to Spain, smash their gods as our gods were smashed. The audience gasps, stunned. It is a brief visceral moment of historical reckoning. A truth told. But how hard it is to find that truth and give it shape. Simple. Direct. Courageous.

I am reminded of the Cuban American conceptual and performance artist Ana Mendieta, spirit-sister to Celia Herrera Rodríguez, in her effort to re-member an almost primordial rupture from the motherland. In her series "Siluetas" from the early 1980s, Mendieta created out of Cuban earth, gunpowder, and fire the silhouette of her own burning figure on the ground. Lillian Manzor writes of the artist, who died under suspicious circumstances in 1985, "Her work was an obsessive act intended to reconnect herself with the earth, to reunite herself with the ancestral origins from which she was torn apart."[15] "From which she was torn apart." After the Cuban Revolution, as a young girl, Ana Mendieta had been sent to an orphanage in Iowa as part of "Operation Peter Pan," organized by Cuban dissidents, the Roman Catholic Church, and the U.S. government. She was separated from her family for several years, and from a Cuban life forever.

How do we re-member rupture?

I write. It is a pitiful and necessary gesture toward something unnamed, beyond what we have been schooled to imagine.

> This, the core of the Xicana teatrista's journey:
> the effort to uncover what we don't remember,
> to use the Xicana body as a way to dig up the dirt,
> to find something of what is left of us.

two   The Warring Inside

Maguey Takes to the Road

What Is Left of Us

My tía-by-marriage, Lola, has a surprise to show us. She sits my eighty-seven-year-old mother down into the massive La-Z-Boy in front of the TV set. My mother's tiny bones sink inside it. Her feet dangling in the air, she looks the size of any one of the dozens of third cousins frequenting their bisabuelo's house, propped up to watch an afternoon cartoon.

My tía throws a tape into the VCR. Well, *throws* isn't exactly the right word, as I have to get up and help her find the rewind button, then the stop button, then the play button. We wait. I'm a bit nervous wondering how long the "surprise" might take, since my dad is waiting hungrily for us back at the house. And then the tape starts. Sound first. Glen Miller's "Sunrise Serenade." Then, in grainy black-and-white, images of young Chicanos drinking and smoking. Laughing, heads tossed back. A waist grabbed here, a thigh pressed.

This is Los Angeles post–World War II and these are the most beautiful people in the world, I think, remembering suddenly how I saw all my mother's generation as a child. Not pachuco, but pachuco-esque. Men in loose suits draped across broad backs and languorous limbs. Deep-olive-brown women in sundresses sloping off bare shoulders. Smoking. Drinking. Heads tossed back.

Fast-forward the film to a few years later and the women are round-bellied, now separated from the men by small, below-the-knee-sized children. In the next frame my tío in his early twenties, a Gregory Peck lookalike, stands in front of their South Central house. His two baby girls hook their fingertips into the seam of his loose-trousered legs, my tía obviously pregnant again. "God, tío," I say, "you sure were hand-some." And he still is, as he smiles back a toothless, seventy-eight-year-old grin.

Later this old-school, union-man, FDR Democrat and I will discuss the Palestinian situation, lament the locura of victims becoming victimiz-ers in the case of Israel. He will blame Bush with the same fury with which he blamed Nixon and Reagan and all the presidential fools he suffered in his lifetime.

My elders were a beautiful people in their twenties and thirties, much prettier than I remember my own generation, all beard, serape, and rebeldía. Now it is more than thirty years later and my tío's genera-tion is dying in droves: Tía Vicky, Uncle Charlie, Auntie Ruth and her marido, Frank, all within the last month or so. My uncle knows. Un-like my mother, he cannot pretend to deny and act unaffected by the massive loss. Looking over to the fragile arrangement of bone that is his eldest surviving sister, he says to me, "We just hold on, don't we?"

"Yes, tío," I should have answered.
"We just hold on."

MeXicana Blues

Today I sang the blues maybe

on account I don't know

las rancheras by heart,

like her mom usetu sing

when the cocina's americano silence

y el ajo de steaming

frijol sent longing

a thousand

miles

south.

Blue rancheras
de amores traicioneros
de un anhelo fiel
the way my mother whistled
wordlessly the old tunes,
her vocal chords worn down
to a thin thread
por tanto pleito.

I sing as invention
composing words as I go
my voice flattening
into the bass clef of a body
bent over burlap bag 'n' hoe
in want of a freedom
song.

I sing nostalgia
a plastic pastel green
radio blaring 1960s on the countertop   I sing
cuz'm mad enough
to hurt someone other
than myself.

My voice swells the rafters as I shake
cleanser into the mouth
of the sink 'n' scrub
'n' wipe 'n' holler
belting out an old blues
tune.

I am
that much
american
a colored woman cryin'
in black english
a song that won't hurt
nobody with my bitterness.

I get it now how
they felt alone in the world working
so damn hard
'n' no matter
how hard
you work it aint enough
to catch up with the bills
'n' the interest on the debt
'n' the man that makes it worse
in the pocketbook 'n' you
so damn mad
you won't let him touch you at night cuz
you was counting
on him 'n' he messed up
so damn bad
again.

I get it now how
it is to be a worker
woman at fifty-four
like you gotta thousand pounds of people
weighing on your shoulders
'n' you jus' looking for
a little bit
of some one thing
to carry it. A freedom
song.
Oh, say can you sing?
Maybe. Today

I sing
my heart out
'n' feel it fall from my chest
into my water wrinkled hands,
these dyke fingers so tired
of filling in the holes
of this house.

Weapons of the Weak / 2003

I sit at the restaurant table across from my beloved, our two children at our sides. Smiles all around, the kids laughing over some small silliness. Linda's face, a resting place of pure kindness. It is, for me, a moment of well-being, a fleeting sense of completeness, when you tell yourself, *I could die right now, and it'd be okay.*

Perhaps it was this *idea* of death that pulled me from the moment, when pure awareness turns to "thought" and without warning I am suddenly struck with an inexplicable panic. *Panic attack*, it's such an empty expression—the language of a mental disorder—while the feeling speaks to something so human, so fundamental: our terrified glimpse of the ever-possibility of death. The icy heat of fear rises from the lock-hold of muscle in my gut, spilling into my chest, flooding it.

My face reddens, my heart hammers furiously. I scramble to recollect myself. It is a kind of drowning—the feeling that one will never surface from the wave of this unnamed terror. "Breathe," I tell myself silently, in the effort to take hold of myself. "Stay present." The meal continues seamlessly around me; my panic goes unnoticed.

This sudden unexpected sense of dread and foreboding is not a foreign feeling. It has plagued me since my childhood, since those earliest years of adolescent hormonal change. The "attacks" began at age eleven or so, when my body first transmitted forbidden messages of lesbian desire, messages that threatened all that I understood as familial safety, messages to which I would one day be forced to respond. In the interim, before change was possible, and intermittently for ten years afterwards, fear froze my heart.

So, I ask myself, on this winter day some thirty years later, observing my family around the checkered tablecloth of a neighborhood restaurant, *what is the unexpressed knowing that gives rise again to a child's terror?*

THE BAD YEARS

It is 1971. I am nineteen years old. I dial the phone from my father's backyard garage-converted-office. I am spinning down deep again into that vortex of an immobilizing fear. The material word around me dissolves into a kind of waking dream. My body emits a toxic dread blazing through limb and organ. How could such panic-driven despair ever be preferable to change? But to simply "come out" was not so simple for a Mexican American girl child of the 1960s.

The psychologist tells me through the phone line, "What do you see around you? Name the things you see in front of you." She is trying to bring me back to the concrete world, the world that is not supposed to be a dream. And I name pencil and paper pad and MJB coffee can. This is what I now remember. But was the can a pencil holder or plant pot? I remember my mother using coffee cans for plant pots. I remember the geraniums sprouting from the hard sun-baked dirt held inside the mouth of the can. But I remember this from earlier, happier days, days free of the complications of heterosex and the suppressed longing for women.

Now, looking back, I think of those times as the bad years I suffered on the freedom road, wholly unremarkable. No mass protests, no taking to the streets, no presidents burned in effigy. Mine was a silent body's protest against the prison found in arranged marriages and virginal contracts. I woke each morning, fearing my own madness. That much I remember, desperately holding on to a "me" that could survive the trauma of the forced occupation of my body by men's and mother's messages. "Breathe," the psychologist tells me. "Breathe," I tell myself again, looking into my beloved's face at an Italian restaurant in Oakland, California. It is thirty years later. The panic passes. For now.

NEAR DEATH

Weeks before, I had read my friend Lata Mani's book of grand and simple reflection, *Interleaves*. I am riveted by her description of the Divine Mother coming to her aid, Lata's body pressed between the crumpled steel of a totaled automobile. She does not know how long she lay there waiting to die, but recounts the sudden and necessary abandonment of all prejudice and preconceived notions of "reality," purpose, meaning, attachment to this planet. The memoir goes on to describe how this near-death experience completely changed Lata Mani's life, in the same way that her telling of it completely disarmed me. Closing the book, I am without weapon to combat or camouflage my simple, sudden recognition of our earthly, ephemeral existence.

Certainly, it is not the first time I have read of such themes; I have been an avid reader of Buddhism for several years. But I *know* this author. She is Lata, with whom I have sat down to table, shared books and meals and walks in the forest. My friend has been changed by her proximity to death and I am unable to look away from what she tells me she has learned there. It is a work that speaks so thoroughly from within the limitations of the broken body that the body is laid open for all that it is and isn't: the carrier of consciousness, but not consciousness itself. Through the body, we are aware; but awareness also transcends the boundaries and borders of the flesh. And as such, does it also transcend death? In the telling of this truth tale, Lata becomes my spirit-teacher and I am unable to look away from the daily practice of consciousness her book mandates. All the while I grab, hold on tight, seek the mundane for meaning, the personality for permanence, caught defenseless in the impassive heart of this requisite change.

Does change require losing all? This is what I had feared as a child, the loss of my family through the embrace of my lesbianism. Ironically, thirty years later, it is my children's spirited presence and the rise of a genuine smile spreading across my beloved's face—it is this queer familia, which I have strived so hard to have and hold—which reminds me there is no permanence, only change, only loss and found and loss again.

And I am again just a girl who can't lock the doors enough, say enough rosaries, attend enough masses, occupy enough confessionals to ever ward off this utter fear of losing all that I love. Home, familia, sanity, my mother. But today I *am* losing my mother as I have lost lovers to murder and friends to kidnapping, and each "death diminishes me" (Adrienne Rich again).[1] Each black sack thrown over a duct-taped womanly mouth by a thin-lipped enemy in uniform. I fear I can't stand up for them, our martyrs. I am useless because small traumas have shaped me, as my body continues to shoulder a profound aversion to powerlessness.

DEEPER THAN I CAN TOUCH

When in 1993 my baby boy survived a two-and-a-half-pound and three-month-premature birth, along with two surgeries and a deadly infection, I lived each day of the several years that followed with the awakened consciousness of death. Each new day was a gift because it had not been guaranteed for my child. Now I have witnessed the other side of that cycle: aging; the aging that happens overnight in AIDS, the aging of our elders that can appear ruthlessly slow and meaningless.

I watch my mother's desperate attempts to ward off old age, dementia, and the forgetfulness of things small and great. Friends, including her most intimate Esperanza, who have died years before are remembered alive again. "Yes, Espie came to visit last week with her son," she says. And no one "corrects" her. Why? What does it matter really? Esperanza came to visit my mother one way or another—in her dreams, in her memories. Our rigid earthbound sense of the chronology of events is ridiculous in the face of the timelessness of what is after and before death. Is this the change I have feared, this living knowledge that we have no control over the hour nor the manner nor the fact of our deaths? Always, I have worried over the loss of control of my body, suffered great anxiety over confinement, cramped quarters, packed elevators, where I am unable to breathe.

I remember as a little girl my brother stuffing the pillow around my face. It was a game he played. He would only lift the pillow once I started to panic.

He would laugh.

As I age these anxieties increase. I wonder of courage, consider what real spiritual warriorship means when the smallest physical threats frighten me. Once as a child of eight, I stood fearless before a great wall of ocean arching high above me, diving auburn-head-first into its massive and luminous belly just before the wave broke. Today I do not venture beyond the wave's breaking point at shoulder height. I do not venture deeper than I can touch bottom. I do not venture.

Months ago, I finally decide to see a behavioral therapist to help me handle a rising claustrophobia. My anxieties had not accelerated to a state of dysfunction, but I could feel the preoccupation intensify. It seems my fear grew in exact proportion to the requirements of my middle-aging: elder disabled parents; the bruising hearts of my school-aged children; my partner's adult children taking so long to become adults; intimate deaths sudden and violent and senseless; and, of course the "terrorism" and fear of terror brought on by this country's international campaign of warring thievery.

So, I give the therapist a try. A nondescript middle-aged white woman with little emotional affect, she puts me through several weeks of do-it-yourself panic exercises inducing nausea, near-suffocation, and the utter dread of entrapment—all this only to expose myself to emotional responses I have suffered my entire life. The fear seems infinite, ordinary, and deeply, deeply human. I am one of those hundreds jammed into a nightclub in Rhode Island. A fire breaks out.[2] I am clambering for an open exit, stepping on faces to get there. I am one of the faces stepped on. I am she who momentarily considers a trip to the hardware store for plastic sheets and duct tape.[3] "The Terrorists Are Coming! The Terrorists Are Coming!" I am that average of an American.

And then I stop.

I resist the impulse to react as our corporate leaders, who make foreign policy in their own interest, legislate. I drop the behavioral therapist and return to what I already know cures. I sit at my altar and, plain and simple, I pray for peace of heart, while all along I am forced to look at how deeply frightened I am, as if I were a kind of sponge for the hysteria that surrounds us globally. My fears seem so small and pathetic compared to threats of massive bombings, biological warfare, orphaned children. Still they are my fears and maybe through them I can learn courage.

The therapist was trying to teach me how to control my thoughts against death, but we do, all of us, die. And as I spent hours and hours looking at the small place of mind that conjures fear of death, I saw it as not essential to me, but a useless weapon I wield against that most profound and inevitable moment of change for each of us. The fear is so old in the making that it appears to be sinew attached to muscle. It is not. I ended my "therapy" because there was no spirit life there to catch my free fall of awareness, nothing to sustain the boundless knowing of what we are beyond fear.

How does one learn to live fully with an open-hearted, ever-present knowledge of our impermanence? I cannot pretend that death does not exist and in that knowing, cannot invent purpose beyond the simple daily practice of some kind of ethos of justice. Still, I suffer rage and irritation and regret and intolerance most days. Most days I am always forgetting that manda: to simply walk awake in this world and to try and shape a life not directed by fear.

THE WARRING INSIDE

Maybe one of the greatest damages white feminism did to women was to convince us of our own victimization without at the same time requiring us to acknowledge our complicity in oppression and the ways in which we, ourselves, oppress. What feminism did teach women, and what I find of ever-inventive relevance to women of color, is that the personal is political. I have written of this many times elsewhere, not in the effort to extol some rigid self-referential identity politics, but to acknowledge that our bodies and our experiences are that complex site of conflict through which our political work is mediated.

In speaking from that personal place, and in considering the political questions regarding state-sanctioned death and its dealers— urban poverty and its consequent child abuse; the prison of drugs and apartheid-style education; illegal land occupation and war for profit— I am most concerned about my own inability to control the warring inside *me*. My beloved and I speak almost daily about the cost of internal occupation. We witness it from the most mundane to the grandest displays of what the poet Lorna Dee Cervantes calls "that nagging preoccupation of not being good enough."[4] As Chicanos, I see it in the often timidez and assimilationist politeness of our writings. It is evident in our failure to put a Mexican museum in the heart of the barrio of San Francisco, where we all can afford it, instead of bartering ourselves to some upscale downtown project catering to tourism and white folk. I bemoan it in the proliferation of Latino storefront charismatic evangelism instead of storefront political activism, equally charismatic. *We are so colonized*, Linda reminds me. And in this colony, our anger remains intimate, as it remains a disguise for our fear of loss, death, oblivion. The United States counts on the fact that people-of-color anger turns most violently against itself. We know gang and domestic violence, but struggle to find forms for our anger that result in creative organized action against the intersecting oppressive systems of the nation-state that maim and murder us.

Intersections: that juncture where all the roads of our identity— gender, race, class, and sexuality—converge. That juncture returns us first and always home. I make a right turn down the hallway and run into the sound of my son's voice outside, fuming over some perceived inequity in the tetherball game he plays with his other nine-year-old compadres. I hear the familial fury in his voice and remember the frightening tone and volatile pitch of Linda's son's voice, almost twenty years older, hurled at her in a fit of seething rage. Mateo's is a boy's desperate heartache turned to a grown man's violence: the violence of lost sons who find their way back home to blame and bruise us, their forever-never-enough mothers.

"It isn't normal," Mateo shouts, meaning his mother's lesbianism. "No wonder I'm so fucked up!" That was on a Monday. On a Friday night, his sister calls, hysterical, "He has a gun! He's coming over!" And suddenly I have every doubt about the future of my people.

A tetherball fight is a small thing and not a small thing, not in the face of misdirected rage. Later that evening I tuck my son into bed, his head half-buried under the covers. He is the color of leña, an earth-flower surfacing among the blanket of leaves (comforter, flannel sheet, pillow). We talk about anger, about needing some hole to dump all that unnameable inherited grief. I worry too soon for him that one day that hole could turn out to be a woman.

"I'm working on my anger," I tell him. "Will you work on yours too?"

He murmurs a soft "yes."

But I am desperate to convince him to resist this colonial legacy, passed down from one generation to the next.

He had witnessed this inheritance himself only days before, trapped inside my speeding car as I drove my parents home from a family gathering. Was it the glass of wine consumed by my mother's fragile seventy-five pounds that allowed her to pull out all the stops, to show the distorted face of her rage even in front of her youngest, most querido nieto? My son sits quietly next to her in the backseat as she hurls her wild wrath against the easiest target, his grandfather. My father, genuinely blameless at that moment, sits shamed and silent in the front passenger seat. "You think you're a man?" Elvira rages, "You're not a man!"

At eighty-eight, my mother's losses are daily and tremendous and humiliating. They are the misplaced glasses, the husband hiding out in his backyard office to avoid her litany of accusation. They are her baby sister, seventy-eight, who, unable to bear my mother's gradual demise, no longer comes to visit; the younger brother who is physically unable to visit. They are the empty pocketbook because there is no longer any reason to carry anything: makeup, money, credit cards, identification. No one expects anything of her. She knows it.

Violence breeds violence. Anger has always run my life. How do I

teach conscientious nonviolence and whole acts of bravery at the same time?

Our girl-child is fucking up in math. Again. She has forgotten her homework. Again I am in a sudden rage because I am helpless to convince her to care because I know if she refuses to care that she too will repeat some pattern of body resistance: pregnancy, drugs, alcohol— because really and truly we do not believe we deserve better. But my rage cures nothing. I only watch her shrink before the violent volume of my voice, her eyes welling up with tears, and I can't stop myself because my fear is stronger than my compassion.

How can we speak of violence against women of color without also naming our own violent acts? Psychic and physical. How do we become warriors of peace when we do not stop daily to question our gut, out-of-control reactions; when there is little spiritual discipline to our struggle; when we have forgotten to pray daily, as our foremothers knew, not out of some perverse martyrdom, but from a relentless commitment to compassionate action? I raise Xicano children consciously while I try to love my mate in the best way possible, while my mother closes these last years of her life in fits of fury. Some days it is the most work I can manage.

Inside the sweat lodge, my tears fall effortlessly. All that quiets my raging heart is the press of dirt beneath my palm. City dirt, rocky and brittle dry. This is women's country. There is location for me here, here in this relationship with the used and broken, here in the unprejudiced world of the darkness and dirt. I pray the litany of our loss, in the effort to unearth what will not be spoken outside the dark womb of this rite. *Where are the sons of our dispossessed nation?* This question, my lament. How is it that they no longer regard the mother's burden, the grandmother's bulto, the sister's carga of worry? How is it that they no longer know to lift it, if only to the other side of that hill *over there, p'allá*. That hill of another debted day, another dying elder, another orphaned child, cancer'd comadre, another war, another war. They refuse our lessons, reduce the female to the role of nurturer and render all our other sentiments as perverse, abnormal, taboo.

But the grandmother is righteously angered and tired and even queer. And time is running out, as she requires of her descendants pain-ful, conscienced[5] acts of change. Instead her insolent sons respond, "But what does she know? We are discovering this red road, ourselves, for the first time. Her time is over." Is this what the fathers—those aging, tattooed patriarchs—have taught their Native sons through their absence: a fear of and contempt for women's knowledges? Hours later, we emerge from the lodge. My young son, having heard my tears in the darkness, asks, "Are you okay, Mom?" I believe he sees me and holds my pain in a simple honest way. "Maybe you should see the feel-ings doctor."

Yes. The "feelings doctor" would ask me to tell the story of my fury toward the men of my nation. I would answer, pitifully, that I was required to make my brother's bed every day since the day I was old enough to do it and even after that day when I found his sheets stiff and spotted wet with his own silent dreamings. I would say I learned early on that I was put on the planet to witness in him the life I would never have. I did not know how to read the stains in his sheets. I only knew they should not be mentioned but were allowed of boys grow-ing into men and muscles and murder. For it was my death pronounced in those sheets. The death of my own desire, which showed itself in dreams more forbidden than anything that could be conjured in the pre-scripted scenarios of sex meted out to the men and women of my familia.

But that was a long time ago; and, again, it is not so long ago if at fifty I can still suffer the panic attacks of that censured girlhood. What truth will I not allow my body to know now, now that my moon be-gins to recede into a fecund emptiness? The women elders have tried to tell us about it, these ways of knowing that can come with age, but this country, and even the men of our nation have told us otherwise; and so, we refuse (again) to listen to the body's messages. We grow ill. We carry the diseases of our anger, our regret, our grief inside our middle-aged and aging women's bodies. Our bodies are built to carry life. We imagine we can carry death too without it killing us. We can't.

PRECIOUS JEWELS

I have a beautiful diamond-shaped stone growing inside my kidney. It is more than a full centimeter in diameter. After spending many weeks trying to dissolve my precious stone through "alternative" medicine, the medical doctors will blast it with a laser. I consider the warring inside me that gave birth to my precious stone, a warring of such intensity it takes a sonic laser to crush it. There was no good reason for me to grow a stone in my kidney. I am a conscientious eater: little processed foods, no caffeinated sodas, a reasonable intake of coffee, no drugs, very little alcohol or red meat, and so on.

My acupuncturist, Mina Karimabadi, a holistic healer, speaks to me direct, clear words. No evasion. She names the cause of the great stone inside my body. "Your body grieves," she says. "The organs suffer grief." I list my heartbreaks of last month in my own mind: my student Itzolín García's senseless suicide; my friend Sandra Camacho, a die-hard feminist activist who died hard of cancer at forty-two; and my ever-ailing mother. Mina is pure compassion about Sandra, as I have come for a treatment only days after the news of her passing. She goes on to relate to me a lesson learned from a Sufi teacher.

This corporeal life, she tells me, *is just a kind of embryonic sac. It is a short period of existence, a state we reside in briefly until we are born into our real lives, the life of the spirit that occurs with death.*

When I speak of my mother as a daily loss, she responds, "She is returning to being a baby. This is how it is."

I think of the gift that is my aging parents. How I am required to be ever awake with their growing frailty. My mother's dissipating memory entreats, *Remember death, mija.* She keeps telling me, *Remember death. Do not look away from yourself.* This is no dramatic bedside goodbye but a protracted daily reminder, which at fifty has my whole consciousness spinning in a tumult of questions, insights, knowings, and delusions about the nature of my fears. And I cry right there in the treatment room, hearing the word *grief*.

Of course. How long does it take to grow a stone of grief inside you, how many deaths? The murder of my comadre Marsha, followed by the death of her son in prison several years later. The suicides of my Latina lesbian colegas at Stanford University, Lora Romero and Raquel Mendieta. The threat of death hurled at my beloved through the raging mouth of her eldest son. The deaths of a full generation of gay men: Rodrigo Reyes, Juan Rodríguez, Ronnie Burk, Tede Matthews, Arturo Islas, and more. The deaths of my mother's siblings in one great wave of generational loss: Tío Bobby, Tía Tencha, Tía Josie, Tía Vicky, and the eldest, Lolita, nearing one hundred, twenty years now in a "rest home" without a fully functioning brain.

And then there are the other dyings, the ones of which we seldom speak, as they linger in the ghosts of ruptured relationships, the betrayals from which we never recover: those heartbreaking separations from people we once loved with fierce loyalty. (I think of Gloria Anzaldúa here.) In these heart relations, I also mourn the passing of a people, a community we failed to sustain through our envisioned "movimientos."

I do not know I am grieving, but my kidney knows. It hardens against this litany to the dead, while all along I imagined I was handling it; while all along my rage grew in intensity against what I could not control; while all along I foolishly saw my anger as face not mask. I call my stone "precious," because its dull ache ever serves as a reminder that the body wants freedom from fear.

Last summer Linda and I and our two children took a road trip to Chihuahua, México. On the dirt road to Mata Ortiz in search of its exquisite Casa Grandes pottery, we spy an old man sitting in front of his home on the edge of the roadway. A slender ramita overhead provides a little shade from the midday penetrating sun. He is straight-backed, white-haired. He watches us go by. Twenty minutes later, he watches us return; the road up ahead was impassable. He is expressionless or his expression says nothing to me. His posture says all. He waits. He is content to wait, to do nothing but sit and watch. I tell Linda, this is what my mother would prefer to do: sit and watch. And she agrees, the familia would come by and prepare the morning café and frijoles for the day. Sería suficiente, enough for her in these final years, to be home like that, family around.

But no, we are so lost. We have no villages left. My mother puts lipstick on her eyebrows because somehow she remembers makeup, and I'm here in México trying to remember for my mother what came before makeup and Macy's department store and the suburban Cocos Restaurant for breakfast, lunch, and dinner. My mother for two years now has forgotten how to cook.

Trying to remember, we—familia of four—go to the Paquimé ruins, outside of Casas Grandes, Chihuahua. The huge maze of crumbling adobe walls is all that remains of what had been a flourishing urban center in the 1300s. Paquimé was once a city of hundreds of apartments with indoor plumbing and heating, a sewage system, religious and cultural centers, and more. Its museum tells the history of a people who were neighbors to the Rarámuri of the nearby Sierras. Peering through a museum display case, I am struck by a plain-looking necklace, which appears to be made of bone. The posted description of the piece explained that the Paquimé used the small bones of their dead, especially fingers, for personal ornament, rite, and decoration.

Considering this, I wondered how the Paquimé must have viewed death, especially that of their intimates and the close members of their community. If they could hang death around their necks for adornment, how did they feel about each passing relative? Did they wear the finger bones of their parents or dead children or were these the fingers of strangers? The description did not say. They decorated themselves with death, knowing all along that they too would one day become bracelet or necklace for some survivor's pleasure. This told me so much about the culture, one that had the awareness to wear the daily reminder of their own impermanence on their bodies. In this manner, one could never forget one's destiny. In the face of our contemporary rituals of death denial, I see us more lost and ignorant than ever, as generations of people of color move further and further away from the knowledges of our aboriginal forebears.

Driving through the beauteous cañones de Chihuahua, I take our lives into my hands. Mexican truckers barrel through the snaking mountain roads, accelerator pedal to the floorboard. Other vehicles pass dangerously into head-on traffic. I keep a firm grip on the steering wheel, all along considering the fragility of our lives.

We are often roadkill, the victims of the speed and reckless driving of U.S. greed and racist domestic policies. I believe this was so with Sandra, her intestines ravaged from a cancer that grew out of years of activist attention to every woman-of-color suffering other than her own. This is also true for so many MeXicanas contracting cancer in their middle age, having worked in pesticide-poisoned fields as children. I know there are accidents, but so many deaths are state-calculated: the genocide of the poor, disabled, and disheartened. Would that I could wear a collar of finger bones around my neck: the index for the fierce directness that was Sandra, the tallest middle one for Itzolin's grand height, the smallest for my mother's fragility, the crooked one for my father's deteriorated hips. Is their weight a burden? Or are they the precious and brilliant jewels, tokens of our ephemerality, that my ancestors pass onto me?

ON THE STREETS OF "AMERICA"

The more I read Buddhist texts, the more I come to understand fear as this country's national malaise and denial of death as this country's national anthem. If we were not so afraid, maybe we could be free. Nothing brought this home to me as did the incidents of September 11. We allowed our country to go to war, somehow wanting to believe that although we knew Saddam Hussein had no part in the attacks of 9/11, we would be safer with the United States' giant pata over there in Gulf region, a nuclear stone's throw away from its ally Israel. *Good*, we thought to ourselves, two "Western democracies" in that contested region of "colored heathen fundamentalism." Was this not the language on the streets of America?

The more the United States is seen as a imperial monster in cahoots with Israel (which has plenty of weapons of mass destruction, by the way, and is the United States' major role model for an ongoing illegal occupation), the less "safe" the U.S. citizenry is. But we want to believe otherwise, that our country can and will protect us. Because we are afraid. Instead of looking critically at the foreign policy of this nation-state and our complicity in the crimes it commits, we make monsters of the non-Western "other." As a nation we are unable to turn collectively inward and ask ourselves how we are perceived by the majority of the world, outside of the Anglophone nations. It's all right if they hate us, says the Bully in Washington. As long as we can kick their collective butt, who gives a damn what they think of us? This is schoolyard talk. So even when the Bully lies in a deep hole of broken steel and smoke at the tip of Manhattan Island, he thinks himself a rising phoenix. He believes himself a god. He blasphemes.

I began writing this essay on the morning after the recall-the-governor-and-put-another-actor-into-office elections for my home state of California.[6] I did not bother even turning on the TV to learn the latest results, having already accurately predicted them. The morning before, I had walked up an enormous hill (the car in the shop) to perform my civic duty. And, along with other middle-class, thoroughly documented citizens who felt themselves entitled, I cast my vote for governor. I pressed my index finger firmly into the monitor screen. An *X* appears after the name "Cruz Bustamante." It is not a vote of conviction; it is a "ward against the worst" vote, the worst, of course, being the actor Arnold Schwarzenegger. As I press my finger to the screen of my voting rights, I am sentimental enough to feel a kind of sense of civic belonging. I imagine myself a member of that illusive club called American democracy, while down the road, where apartment rental agreements heavily outnumber mortgages, the voting booths are sparsely populated. They know better than I, with my Stanford job and hefty mortgage, the government doesn't give a damn about them.[7]

What would a fearless, compassionate government look like? Compassion is no more than simply one's capacity to empathize and identify with another's suffering, whether that person sleeps on the other side of the bed or the other side of the ocean. At its most fundamental, it rests upon the visceral recognition that none of us can escape old age, illness, or death. A conscienced compassionate life is one in which our daily decisions emerge out of this simple wisdom as well as the knowledge that our existence is integrally connected to the survival or suffering of others. This knowing affects every action we take, every decision we make, even every vote we press into the impassive face of a monitor screen. "It could've been me, but instead it was you . . . ," the protest singer Holly Near laments. None of us is immune.

Today the vast majority of U.S. Americans who do vote, vote with their pocketbooks not their hearts. The candidate that will reduce taxes is the preferred candidate by Corporate America and its dutiful middle class. School vouchers are legislated to ensure that the upper-middle classes can send their kids to the right schools and that the lower classes will fall deeper and deeper into illiteracy. English-only becomes law to guarantee a widening gap in education and employment opportunities between immigrants and the U.S. born. Our state legislators daily create public policy to ensure that the people-of-color and youth population, a growing majority, will be an undereducated, alienated working poor whose economic opportunities plateau at the level of serving the needs of the minority class of propertied whites. But this will not make the propertied class safe inside their gated communities. A majority-disaffected underclass does not create safe cities.

This country's racial bigotry and lack of societal compassion are generated by the very apprehension that the white middle class denies: that it will become a "minority" without power; that it will suffer the revenge of society's discontent; that it will become the victim of terror. It counters this collective anxiety with an image of this country as a kind of dreamland coveted by the rest of the world, while most of its citizens are enslaved by credit-card debt and consumerism; while their elders are isolated and removed from their communities; while their children are not free to play on the streets for fear of abduction; and while youth are alienated from their parents by TV sitcoms, PlayStations, and drugs and gang violence.

I remember after 9/11 I had imagined something had changed in all of us in the stark recognition that as U.S. citizens we could no longer presume our safety. As a result, we would be forced to live with the global responsibility of our shared vulnerability to death, just like the Iraqis, just like the Palestinians, just like the maquiladoras of Juárez. But we soon forgot this. And we grew stupid again, imagining we'll live forever. So we spend our lives lying to ourselves, that we are not afraid, that we can ward off impermanence with mortgages, insurance policies, career goals, and retirement investments; that we can prevent the bombing of our illustrious cities by bombing other illustrious cities;

that as U.S. citizens we are privileged to be on the side of the big guns. Even soldiers of color get to be "white" for a day in Iraq (i.e., card-carrying members of the lie of American superiority); each of them denying that when they come home, their membership cards will be revoked on the streets of Chicago, East Los Angeles, New Orleans, El Paso, and Montgomery, Alabama.

WEAPONS OF THE WEAK

World history is the history of genocide and massive dislocation: China in Tibet; Pol Pot's regime in Cambodia; Israel in Palestine; Pinochet in Chile; the Germans to the Jews; the civil wars in Bosnia and Rwanda; Spain to the Mexican Indian; the United States to Native North America, Native Hawai'i, and the Inuit peoples of Alaska; the African American male between the ages of sixteen and twenty-five; the Amazon forest; and the organic corn stalk. Some days I under-stand the human condition as nothing more than the majority suffer-ing the effects of a minority's grab for power, wealth, and property. This power grab relies on making less than human all those who stand in the way of the object of the grabber's desire. U.S. imperialism is the emperor's refusal to look into the face of the man he robs, while espousing the principles of democracy. But democracy can never be wholly realized within or outside of the United States because, spiri-tually speaking, we are not free while others are enslaved. Was the slave owner a free man?

Our actions are our only true belongings, counsels Thich Nhat Hanh.[8] I cannot escape the consequences of my actions any more than a Bush, a Rumsfeld, a Hussein, or a Sharon can. In the face of death, my illu-sion of being able to hold on to anything is just that, illusion. Life is a dream in that real sense and as we pass through this sueño may we attempt to reduce suffering on this planet. This is the only practice worth preaching. Some days I've called that practice lesbian feminism, on other days Indigenism; some years it was Chicano nation, other years, radical women-of-color activism. But at the heart of each of these movements, perhaps fearlessness was what I sought all along, fearless-ness made manifest in the spirit of solidarity; where for an extended moment, the material world of oppression cannot break us because spiritually there *is* an "us."

Just before the United States decided to invade Iraq, I read an essay by Edward Said in which he noted how, for the first time in history, mass protests were taking place against a war before war was declared. It gave him great hope. He wrote: "Mass action and mass protest on the basis of human community and human sustainability are still formidable tools of human resistance. Call them weapons of the weak . . ."[9]

In this site of "human community," as Said called those with whom we share common cause, our anger and fear are no longer privatized. We are not phobic or hysterical. We do not need therapy, we need revolt. This is integral to our spiritual practice, where collective consciousness is realized in collective respuesta. Even Jesus turned over tables in that New Testament temple, so enraged he was against the moneymakers. To him, they had defiled the house of the sacred. We stand in the house of the sacred, this earth, and it is daily being defiled by the moneymakers. What then is our response to this injustice?

"Weapons of the weak."

Edward Said called us "weak" and named our power.

I think, yes, we march as foot soldiers in the army of the weak: the colored the queer the disenfranchised the duped the exploited the raped the incarcerated the betrayed the forgotten the speechless the censored the female the animal the plant the insect the mountaintop the river valley the desert redwood oak grasses oceans of distress signals the indigenous the tribal the landless the landfills the lost souls the godless and god-fearing the veiled and the disrobed desnudas y desgeneradas assuming collective power.

The story I write here is told by one of the weak ones. It is my story, but it could at its heart be every woman's story (as every man's). I tell it in language intended to transgress the boundaries of genre and gender and generation, while all the while I remain a woman of fifty, born in the middle of the twentieth century, a product of the multiple political movements of the sixties, seventies, and eighties in the United States of America. It is a story of fear and the violence that erupts from fear. It is a meditation on cultivating fearlessness in times of war, which is today and yesterday and will be so tomorrow. I am one of the weak ones, I am honored to say, struggling to find language to say that I am on my way to death. That seems like all I can say. There is no greater warriorship than that of us "weak ones" readying ourselves for death. I am not talking about suicide missions, but missions of daily practice to counter avarice and individualism, based on the notion that anything really belongs to us. Land has no owner, our Indigenous American herencia tells us, as no woman has an owner. For while we, in our personal lives, suffer to make property of people and place, we also collude with those bent on doing so on a scale unprecedented in human history.

I had imagined myself special. I am as ordinary as death. I am the unrecognizable remains of that animal splattered across a mountain highway. Roadkill—those unnecessary dyings of heart, spirit, body—is avoidable if we'd only slow down and learn to walk again. All the while we wear consciousness of death—from the useless slaughter to the noble passings—like the fine jewels of our insistent ancestors. This is the fiercest form of resistance I can fathom, a welded weapon of the "weak."

California Dreaming

Last night, my sister put down the top

of her mid-life-crisis red convertible

and we—my parents, she and I—drove

through the Palm Springs desert heat

in the hour just before midnight.

As the town spun neon and artificially

misted outside my window,

I watched the sparsely-starred sky

braced my cheeks against the windy slap

of black asphalt heat

and prayed for an earth that quakes

inside the deepest heartbreak. My mother

nearing-ninety, her bony frame folded
small and silent next to me,
I wrap my Mexican blue bandana
'round her scull of balding permanented frizz.
My sunglasses straddle huge and bug-eyed across her nose,
awkward protection against the elements.
"She's an aging movie star," I tell them upfront.
"Being chauffeured home incognita."
Through the hot bite of a Palm Springs Saturday night.

My mother laughs, not sure of the joke
but then leans over to me and asks,
"Do you have a mother?"
"What?" I had heard the question.
"Do you have a mother?" she repeats
against the hot rush of panic
spinning inside the leather coupe.

My heart quickens at the prospect
of my sudden orphanhood.
But Elvira is not afraid
from where she sits behind the sun-glassed desert
of her own Tucson girlhood,
she remembers being nobody's mother.

"Yes," I answer, "she's you."
And she laughs—¡Qué mensa!
So, I laugh, too. Big joke.

Still I knew she had asked a deeper truth.

Pointing to the sky, I should have grabbed her hand
and begged—"La ves, señora?
P'alla just beyond the neon horizon
p'atras that black bear of sleeping mountain
por 'dentro those scattered stars of memory
There's my mother and yours.

Así que te precocupes, Mamá.
I'll meet you there one day.
And we will be forever
sisters."

Cuento Xicano

There is the story of the Xicano poet, Alfred Arteaga. A story his sister tells; that as they take Alfred from his home for the last time, she walking alongside the gurney en route to the ambulance, the Poet spies a hummingbird. Hummingbirds had often appeared in the poet's writings. Delighted by the vision of this green and turquoise oracle, he declares, "It's magical. Something great is going to happen." That "something great," of course, was death.

In 1999, Alfred spent six weeks in a coma, surviving a deadly heart attack. He went on to live another nine years. Marisol, his eldest daughter, recounts, "He was so happy after that. Just so happy to be alive." This joy was evident in every encounter the Poet had in the last years of his life. That smile—we, his survivors, recalled—that smile was contagious.

And as I add Alfred's image to my ever-expanding ancestor altar, I pray—

> *Change me, Alfred.*
> *Help me to see with your eyes*
> *the joy of living as we die.*

La Cuentista

Indígena as Scribe / 2005

The moon rises. Hours earlier, the sun vanished behind mustard-colored hills. Above us, the sky remains a fading blue. At eye level, darkness encroaches upon the forest. In this hour, the hour of Coyol-xauhqui's return, her triumph over Huitzilopochtli,[1] I uncover the ephemeral that is I. My son, walking at my side, is not my son but his own dream.

The next day he will ask me, as if intuiting my thoughts, "Is life a dream?" I pause before responding. He quickly inserts, "Some people say we are dreaming—don't tell me 'yes.'" I remember fearing the same as a child, teetering on the precipice of my teen years as he does now. *Yes, yes, yes, it* is *a dream we walk, son*. This is what I say inside. Aloud, I give him what he wants. I say we dream at night truths that teach us for our waking life. (And this is so, but only half-so). I do not tell him that last night I walked down to the riverbank with him and knew us so clearly dreaming. Dreaming, remembering. We had been here before. A leaf, a trout, a quail. Woman. Indígena. We had been here before. These visions, primordial ways of knowing, are all of ours since forever: those sudden moments of consciousness that remind us that our time is short here on this planet and that our precious "I" can so easily dissolve into the ancient original world around us—the redwood forest, the darkening sky, the silencing of birds for the night.

THE OLD WAY

The Aztec poet Nezahualcoyotl wrote:

> Though it be jade it falls apart,
> though it be gold it wears away,
> though it be quetzal plumage it is torn asunder.
> Not forever on earth
> only a little while here.[2]

We try to forget these ways of knowing, this way of the "we," that necessary humility and reciprocity in relation to the earth's elements. For so little in our North American lives matters in the face of this way of knowing. Capitalism becomes extinct. Profit becomes extinct. Borders and War become extinct. But, we look away. *So much to lose* we think. Instead, we elect to become extinct ourselves and lose all. We imagine we haven't lost, surrounded by so much stuff. We imagine we are privileged ones, the free ones. And this delusion becomes the measure of our colonization.

I write this from the perspective of someone who has so much, so much more materially than my immediate ancestors. But my privilege belies a profound deficiency, an ignorance, which is taking me a lifetime to undo. My teachers, those figures in my life who have exposed my lack of deep knowledge, are those who suffer constant heartbreak and somehow do not close up their hearts. They are those living very close to extinction that still abide by an old way. Sometimes I find my teachers in a book, sometimes in my own book of daily markings. Sometimes they are a gravelly elder voice on the Indian radio program. And, sometimes they move inside the body of a nine-year-old kid doing a little hip-hop number in my son's school library, who unwittingly remembers an ancestor's call in the squeaky rub of his Nikes against the linoleum floor.

In the effort to teach the Old Way, my Beloved offers medicine, medicine grown from that high desert ground where our ancestors have resided since forever. It tastes of dirt, holy dirt—this sacrament, more familiar than any flat, pale host melting on my tongue. But I am afraid of this way of seeing, of recognizing my own proximity to my ancestors, that collective source of knowing that comes del otro lado. I am afraid of this rite to knowing, as I am of that blessed moment between breaths in meditation where time is of no consequence and the "I" disappears. Such acts bring one back to a profound place of origin and shared identity, where me is subsumed by we, and violence against any part of that we becomes unthinkable.

Writing too is one of these acts. The best of creative writing, so grand in its particulars, is able to traverse great borders of mind and matter. The distinctions disappear. Our present moment becomes history. History is enacted myth. Myth is remembered story. Story makes medicine. I am in daily search of these acts of remembering of who we once were, because I believe they will save our pueblos from extinction. Our preconquest imaginations offer strategies for building self-sustaining societies today, societies that can disrupt the mass suicide of global consumption, engineered by the empire of the United States. I believe the United States intends to disappear its indigenous inhabitants and our non-Western ways of knowing. So, I write.

I write to remember.

I make rite (ceremony) to remember.

It is my right to remember.

THE RIGHT TO REMEMBER:
OUR VILLAGES RETURNED

For twenty-five years, my practice as a writer has been integrally tied to my teaching practice. For those twenty-five years, I've continued to confront in myself and my students questions of authority—our personal authorization to be authors and our right to write. I have worked mostly with students of color, of all ages, mostly from working-class backgrounds, and many queer. Throughout those years, I have observed, over and over again, the ways in which the authors and transmitters of the Euro-American imagination deny us the authority to imagine outside of their cultural constraints. What we know does not matter. How we came to know does not matter. The language, gesture, and voice we use to express what we know do not matter. In the end, we disavow what we know. We come to the training ground of writers empty of knowledge. We spend a lifetime trying to imitate what we never knew. This keeps us very busy and unoriginal. We do not transgress.

This is the war we wage every time we sit before a blank page and attempt to conjure in our own words. We must ask ourselves: *what do we know? We know more than we know we know. What is the way back to knowing?* As the Cuban American performance artist Ana Mendieta put it, "It is always about a search for origins."[3]

In the early 1990s, I organized a community-based writing workshop called "Indígena as Scribe." Over four consecutive years, the workshop brought together several dozen women, ages twenty to sixty, who were willing to locate themselves (how ever awkwardly) inside the word *indigenous* and consider writing from that place. The women who showed up were Xicana, Native Hawaiian, Apache, Navajo, salvadoreña, Lakota, and more. A core of twelve of these women met continuously once a week for the entire four years of the group's existence.

What initiated the concept for the workshop was nothing more than intuition. Nothing more than some notion or hope that if we used ancestral or "home" memory as the grounding point in our journey as writers, then possibly the literature that emerged might serve a stronger countercultural agenda for U.S. women-of-color writers than that imposed upon us through university writing programs.

The requirement of the class was to look back in the effort to recuperate a lost language, a lost sensibility, a lost voice, even as it twisted itself through our late-twentieth-century, urbanized, multicultural, multifocal lens. It was an attempt to practice what the Diné and Muskogee photographer Hulleah Tsinhnahjinnie calls "an aboriginal world view."[4] Oh, we knew we were ignorant and separated from our indigenismo but equally hungry to want something more from our writings than a quick ticket to a New York publisher.

As people of color living in the United States, how do we authorize ourselves to write toward what is aesthetically original in us when the majority culture insists that aboriginal thought is useless, most aboriginal peoples are dead or dysfunctional, and to look backwards is to be backwards? How do we counter a dominant narrative that rewrites our history in the effort to erase that history and its peoples?

Today, using a language reflecting a kind of liberal multiculturalism and parroted by much of academia, the U.S. ruling class intends to de-Africanize, de-Asianize, and de-Indianize its citizens of color. This is not without purpose. While its domestic economic policies ensure even further separation between whites and people of color, the government's cultural project is to convince us, mostly through empty rhetoric and tokenism (Condoleezza Rice is the stellar example) that we are somehow "white"; that is, equal participants in U.S. democracy. Without a U.S.- (read Anglo-) identified people-of-color population, how will it wage war against the "colored" nations of the world?

This nation-state needs very badly for us to believe ourselves "American," by its monocratic definition and define our allegiances by the geopolitical borders it has constructed. The government proffers to its citizens of color the opportunity to feel white as long as we are pointing the finger or the gun at some other "other," scapegoated by U.S. foreign policy. The price for such citizenship is our cultural separation from our relations around the world. The popular propaganda reads: they are the "others," the terrorists and potential terrorists. Today it is the "War on Terror," a generation ago it was the "Cold War." Considering the most recent twenty-first-century acts of U.S. imperial aggression—the illegal occupation of Iraq; the U.S.-supported abduction and coup of the democratically elected president of Haiti, Jean-Bertrand Aristide; CIA strategies to overthrow Hugo Chávez in Venezuela and to justify the invasion of Iran (while all along the U.S. government's keeping its watchful eyes on the final prize of Cuba)—do we think our mandate as people-of-color writers anything less radical than that of the writers from the sixties and seventies? Because COINTELPRO and rampant misogyny destroyed the sovereignty movements of the 1960s, does this mean sovereignty no longer has a place in our vocabulary as writers of justice? Why is that for the most part only Northern Native American writers in this country, including Hawaiians, put cultural sovereignty at the top of their political agendas? Is political autonomy and cultural integrity not a concern for the majority of people of color in the United States? As generations of U.S. people of color move further and further from our nonliterate backgrounds, does our preliterate oppositional consciousness, derived from brutal physical labor, displacement, and profound want, depart as well? Has our education made us stupid, forgetful, and even further entrenched in our colonization?

I am a writer. I have the education and privilege to write, to publish, to teach, but how often have my peers and I stopped ourselves along the way and reassessed what we really know and how we came to know it? This is an especially troubling question for those of us who have arrived at our middle years. Would that we—all of us—did go through a profound midlife crisis, where we stood before the precipice of our descending years and recognized the small and profound ways we have been complicit in our own oblivion. This government wants nothing less than the complete erasure of self-defining indigenous cultures across the planet. As people-of-color writers and artists, our disidentification with those cultures ensures their and our own disappearance into the emerging Anglosphere empire.

As people of conciencia, we are all aware of the obscene appropriation of indigenous traditions and the facile thievery of Native cultural practices for personal profit here in the States and across Europe. Still, in the deepest sense, before God (however you define that) you cannot steal what is not yours. So if we are willing to go through the broken places first, through our own acts of self-sabotage and cultural amnesia, we will find our own authentic way home. We may have to borrow or invent along the way, but we have the right to remember. And I can no longer let the colonizer nor colonized tell me we don't. I believe Chicano and Chicana writers' fear of claiming herencia as Indigenous people—not out of nostalgia, but as a commitment to the recuperation of progressive Indigenous principles and practices in our daily life—has created a half-literature at best and not the insurgent work we are truly capable of producing. At worst, it is a minstrel-like fakery of who we are, served up for the consumption of Euro-America.

The profound project of transgression can only be achieved by return. We know more than we know we know: the aboriginal mind at work. I make no claims to it. I only collect broken shards of memory and try to shape a bowl that can hold the full promise of my want.

The Native California artist and linguist L. Frank expresses it best through her imaginings of aboriginal California. *I want my village back*, her work insists.[5] Our writing can help take us there if we require the most of it and ask it the right questions. Our journey of return is not romantic; it is ordinary. It is the dusty road of our own pitiful colonized preoccupations, which I have come to call the "mundane." The marvelous mundane of our lives, where the barest truths are revealed.

It happened just days ago when I was awakened suddenly in a writing class by a student's voice, soft-spoken but completely unapologetic. I woke up because hers was language seldom heard in the corridors or classrooms of this elite university. I woke up because it was a home language made art, wholly grounded in the nuanced world that is nuestra gente. And, in its simplicity—a story of five Mexican kids packed onto a mattress on the floor and a father reading *Clifford: El Gran Perro Colorado* to his thoroughly-for-a-moment-contentos children—it countered the lie of Chicana invisibility.

So, as the story goes, one of those kids grows up to carry a gun and sleep with it under the sheets, Papi long gone from la familia. But for a moment, the author chooses to recall life before violence, even while gunshots ring outside her remembered window. The author: a round-faced nineteen-year-old Chicana in a snug-fitting Stanford sweatshirt, who, for the most part, passes unnoticed by the mainstream of her university, but I notice her because I need her so desperately. There is nothing imitative about the writing. It isn't trying to be "barrio." It is "crumby suburban," as the writer puts it. It is our "village" returned to us twenty-first-century style. And I know this girl's gonna go somewhere if this country doesn't stop her first. And that somewhere may not be big publishing houses and book tours, but a life of writing against amnesia. She will document a people through an open humility of heart and we will not forget ourselves to one another.[6]

In many ways, I see the project of educating my Xicano and Xicana students in the trajectory the Aztec Calmécac, those institutes of advanced study afforded the privileged classes of pre-Columbian México. Although the children of farm, domestic, and service workers, they are the spirit-descendants of those ancestor-scribes, who five hundred years ago studied the how and why of our existence. Everyone deserves the right to contemplar.

I urge my students que se aprovechen el momento of their college years; to look beyond conventional career-oriented concerns toward something deeper, toward the discomfort and wonder of real conciencia, which comes, as the educator Paulo Freire understood, through a self-determined, self-defined education. I never let my students forget that their elite education wants them to do otherwise, to look away from the pueblo-self as the source of knowing. Through the practice of creative writing, I have found students uncovering glimpses of knowledges heretofore obscured and untouched. As path stones to critical thinking, the works become grounded in the historical as much as the intuitive and can inspire an engaged social consciousness.

> Read aloud what you have the on the page, I say . . .
> *give it voice, give it voice, give it voice enough times until your body takes hold of it and remembers and then you will be able to walk more surefooted in this world.*
> I tell them . . .
> *you are developing strong armor against lies from the economic class of this country that believes only they think and if you want to think you must become one of them, but you are not one of them.*
> I repeat . . .
> *You are not one of them because the body remembers what you have written even when you have forgotten the words or where they came from. Believe in your body, its voice, its movement, its cellular story.*

I am training my students to identify and respect other ways of knowing, to live a life of learning and teaching that do not engage in ever-inventive forms of intellectual colonization. I am counting on those few with the rigor to remain conscious to do so, to make strong and clear choices toward free, alternate, subversive thought that grows out of a living practice of informed noncooperation with colonization. I do not have a prescription for what this looks like, but I know that it is daily work, that it requires hard choices, that it means speaking up when we are called to and deep, deep listening. As a writer with a thirty-year-old practice, I have had to learn to listen, to fine-tune my hearing and reading ear for words that proffer living, useful knowledges versus words that convolute meaning, weaken me, and promote apathy instead of action. Each morning I rise in search of those words, that image, the cuento that might open a small footpath of knowing toward the abandoned villages of our forgotten.

METAPHORS OF MEANING

One thing my friend and brother poet Alfred Arteaga helped me to understand is that our task as writers is to create metaphors of meaning that can shape and change consciousness. His words confirmed for me the task and potential of poetry (and all art forms) in our lives—to use language that matters in a way that matters. As we enter a new century where militarily backed Anglosphere occupations throughout the globe pose a major threat to indigenous cultures, what is the language of change?

A global cultural war is being waged as virulently and disingenuously as the United States' War on Terror and the CIA's War on Drugs. As wordsmiths how do we forge the tools of our trade to effectively counter cultural appropriation and political obliteration? In my near-decade of teaching at a ruling-class university, I find myself viscerally reacting against the academy's use of terms like *hybridity* and its appropriation of *mestizaje*, especially when posited as language that can adequately respond to the deadly conditions of a "postcolonial" world. Although differently nuanced, both *hybridity* and *mestizaje* intend to address the cross-cultural collisions of multiple identities (queer, transnational, gender, etc.) requisite of a postmodern world. But as metaphors, are they brave enough to counter the insidiousness of the U.S. project of a global empire, whose cultural agenda is to erase our awareness of the bitter realities of social difference? Do the terms not assume and succumb to the loss of our aboriginality with no hope for recuperation?[7] Could these words not reflect another attempt by the corporate academy, however furtively, to exploit the rhetoric of democratic multiculturalism and pluralism at home in order to engage our support and services for neocolonial profit abroad and southward?

The measure of the political efficacy of a metaphor is if a radical living practice emerges from it. These times require new metaphors that challenge the idea that, on the one hand, our colonization (i.e., the de-Indianization of América) is complete, and contradictorily on the other, that as U.S. citizens we are no longer colonized. When did we imagine we became free? Through enforced displacement, one's personal capital, or through the institutional privileging of white-mixed-raced people over "less-passable" people-of-color?[8] I am not free if my pueblo is not free. This sounds cliché, no? How pitiful it is that such true words become clichéd before we've ever lived them. Think about the Bush administration's abuse of the word *democracy*.

Maybe the problem here is confusing the language of academia with the language of art and activism. Maybe my confusion stems from witnessing so many language-makers making their home exclusively in the academy and not in the public arena. (In this regard, the loss of Gloria Anzaldúa's public voice of dissent es una pérdida tremenda.) Maybe because of this, we have begun to believe academics are our leaders, our spokespeople, our metaphor-makers for a new world. Maybe they are not.

At the turn of the century, our divergent identities—indigenous and mixed-blood, transnational and transgender—provide critical approaches to knowings that open roadways to radical transformations in our collective progressive thinking. My own queer and mixed-blood identity resides in the crux of contradictory meanings, where I have suffered the homelessness of queer colored womanhood within the constructs of nationalisms that deny us our female bodies, our desires, our renegade spirits. Still, as ancient tribes disappear and the world-views they sustain go with them, I cannot ascribe special avant-garde status ideologically or otherwise to biological or cultural hybridity resultant of colonization, for it too will disappear inside the neo-colony. It too will cease to matter.

Tu Ciudad, a Los Angeles English-language popular culture magazine, predicted as much in a special issue devoted to the "New Angelenos." The subtitle reads, "They're Half-Latino and Changing the Face of L.A."⁹ The angle of the most of the articles depicts the "New Angelenos" as an emergent population successfully adding to the "spice" of the cultural stew of urban centers like Los Angeles all over the country. While retaining just enough Latinidad to influence their choice of clubs and cuisine, the article insists, half-Latinos can and do blend seamlessly into mainstream America.

Is this is all we have left to offer the next generation of Raza raised in this country, a postmodern recipe for the melting pot?

Beneath the shadow of a giant wave of U.S. and Mexican flags I stand among the sea of protesters on the May Day March for Immigrant Rights. I wonder what we are really protesting amid this bold display of bicultural loyalty to the countries that betray the immigrant from both sides of the border. *Immigrant*, a bitter and ironic misnomer when the increasing majority of undocumented workers are migrant Indigenous *Americans* displaced from their lands of origin. They are the first language-makers of this continent: the bricklayer who speaks K'iche', Pipil, Purépecha, Tzotzil, Huasteco, Otomí, Zapoteco, or Náhuatl; the "nanny" whose "citizenship" resides in a two-thousand-year-old land claim.

If the immigrant rights movement, in which so many Chicanos are involved, were to recognize that this migration north is fundamentally an Indigenous rights issue, the very foundation of that movement would turn from reform to revolt, from the myth of integration to cultural sovereignty. As a result of the North American Free Trade Agreement, hundreds of thousands of Indigenous peoples from México have been forced off their lands, unable to sustain themselves while trying to grow crops in competition with the unrestricted import of agricultural products from the United States. Since the federal government does not view economic rights as a matter of human rights, economic refugees from the south have little legal recourse in this country. And yet, the United Nations Declaration of the Rights of Indigenous Peoples, adopted in 2007, states otherwise:

> "Indigenous peoples shall not be forcibly removed from their lands or territories." (Article 10)
>
> "Indigenous peoples have the right to the lands, territories and resources which they have traditionally owned, occupied or otherwise used or acquired." (Article 26)
>
> "Indigenous peoples have the right to maintain, control, protect and develop their cultural heritage, traditional knowledge and traditional cultural expressions." (Article 31) [10]

Although the United States was one of four states to reject the resolution, we Xicanas and Xicanos have seldom aligned ourselves with this country's solipsistic position on the sovereign right to privatization. The fundamental rights of Indigenous peoples as mandated by the United Nations resolution responds to the growing crisis of globalized dislocation. It is a foundational document upon which Xicanas and Xicanos might begin to build a more inspired and politically effective transnational movement. How else as Raza are we to meet the new day of an insurgent Latin America rising on the horizon?

As it has been for more than a hundred years, Xicanos and Xicanas of today mirror the face of the (im)migrants' children, grandchildren, and great-grandchildren of tomorrow. Our strategic approach to the issue of (im)migration will determine whether or not that face becomes bleached beyond recognition or retains the pronounced features of the culture of its origins.

We need our (im)migrant relations.

We need them to help us re-member ourselves.

Without enrollment card, land base, or native tongue, the Xicano road to re-membering cultural knowledges systematically denied us for generations is fraught with self-doubt, derision from others, and the bottomless grief that comes with the visceral recognition of such grave loss. Through re-membering across national boundaries and generational divides, together we can reconfigure the complex portraiture of what it means to be "American." This is what *movement* means, building conciencia from bisabuela to abuela, from mother to daughter to her daughter, and on. "Seven generations," the Northern peoples say. *Act now, ever mindful of the seven generations that follow.* With such metaphors at work, we might very well grow old and strong.

RE-MEMBERING TRIBE

It is a cheesy Mexican restaurant in Riverside, California. A small group of us, Xicana and Northern Native, has gathered for a casual post-conference conversation. But it is not so casual; it is the work we do when we gather in this way. The Rarámuri and Xicana teatrista Olivia Chumacero says over a plate of enchiladas, "Chicanos are a tribal people." I sip from a watered-down margarita and remember the word *tribe*. Remember how it tumbled from my mother's mouth—just like that—*tribe* in English—at those times when she spoke of our extended familia with the greatest pride and cariño. "The whole tribe is coming tonight!" she'd say, feigning irritation. It was a word I would never let go of, one that would return to me in adulthood and become a metaphor for something of and beyond my own blood familia.[11] The child scribe had taken note.

As writers, metaphor comes to us organically. It feels most often that metaphors choose us rather than the other way around. Our manda as writers is to listen to them, follow the road they take us on and see what stories, what visions, emerge from their usage and how they apply to our social conditions. Over ten years ago I described my mother's generation as a "disappearing tribe" of Chicanos. It was a metaphor to describe the cultural assimilation of generations of familia that follow them. But today I mean it literally; they are a people who are literally dying off, leaving hundreds of quarter-breed and sixteenth-breed vanishing Indians in the wake of their deaths. I write to remember that tribe of elders, as their children stand dumb and devastated at their gravesites. *They don't really know why they are so sad, so lost. They never thought this day would come.*

How do I counter the loss of values, memories, ethics, and faith practices that go with this generation of elders? What metaphors of meaning, as Arteaga suggested, can we derive from their massive and individual departure from this planet? One thing I know for sure, they will go out without a protest. Still, there is one relative who stands out, who refuses to settle for oblivion. He is a first cousin, but one distanced from me and my childhood by generation and imprisonment. More than twenty-five years my senior, my cousin Steve spent the same number of years in and out of prison. Now seventy-five, he brings to my parents' kitchen a tattered supposed-to-look-like-leather briefcase.

"I have something to show you," he says. He opens the steel jaws of the case to expose reams of onionskin paper, wrapped in a weakening rubber band. Typewritten and hand-scrawled, there are at least four hundred sheets of writing. "These are my prison years," he says to me. "Can you do something with it? I'm a sick man. I don't know how long I got. I just didn't want to keep it in my house no more."

Of course, he dreams of a publisher, some kind of money that might come from it to give to a sister who survives him and a "lady friend who has been good to [him]." But that's a secondary thought. We draw up some (would-never-hold-up-court) documents to sign, which gives me permission to represent the work.

I tell him, "You really oughta do this with a lawyer."

And he responds, "You're my cousin, I gotta trust you, right?"

"Right," I say, knowing that of the hundred-plus cousins I have with college degrees, middle-management jobs, suburban mortgages, and aspiring gringo or gringa spouses, few of them could have said those words to me and meant it. But this ex-pinto, whom nobody thought much of, except to talk about him like some bad (vato loco) seed, holds on to some basic familial value of loyalty with which we were raised.

I look over to Linda, who has watched this transaction of signatures and promises. Her expression reflects back to me what I know to be true of this moment. Not all is lost. In an hour, she and I will be leaving Southern California and making our way back up north to our home in Oakland. Sometimes I think of Linda and the extended family we have created as our "last chance," our last chance for saving ourselves— my son and I—from a family of forgetfulness. But not all is lost. I have found a blood brother in this battle against extinction.

He is a writer, too.

ORIGIN STORY

I will tell you how hungry my body is to know something beyond the colony. I am she who puts her face in the dirt, my bare knees slipping beneath me. I lay my belly down on the ground. The hard earth is a pillow for my cheek, but I do not rest. I make rite (right) with dirt and fingernail, stone and fire. I eat dirt like sacrament. I tell you, I am just that hungry for just one whole story that feels true to me.

When I speak of origins, of re-membering, it is because the knowings that are most useful to us, as we look toward the coming transition out of this body, come from sites not fixed in time; for we are not fixed in time. We are future and past at once. So how can the re-collection of cultural memory as a strategy for future freedom be reduced to nostalgia? Does remembering not perhaps instead offer the promise of a radical re-structuring of our lives?

In my lengthening middle age, I am beginning to understand that writing is a common rite, the daily practice of placing oneself in the position of remembering in order to arrive at something beyond oneself, something not individual to the writer, but which passes through all the ordinary and remarkable of her to arrive at that something *in common*.

In my lengthening middle age, through a kind of prayerful practice, I am beginning to see the limitations of an intellect unengaged with the body. I am beginning to see that the intellect can only tell me so much as a writer. It is not the smell of sage and sweetgrass, the scent of melting copal and the ancient history it evokes. It is not La Virgen's face illuminated by my altar candle just beneath the winged angel at her feet. "Intellect" is not the dawn's full moon that pulled me out of my writer's chair and out onto the porch to make holy love to that light one morning. When I returned to my desk, my writing had changed, transgressed. As my teachers say it, *Until head knowledge is embodied, it is not really known.*

Intellect is not the fire—the holy fire, sacred enough to capture the spiritual imaginations of even hot dog–roasting camper-Americans. They put down their beers. They grow quiet at the sight of the fire's dance. Even they remember something in the eye of the fire, something unspoken, something humbling and awesome. Something that shuts them up.

Through the most basic and sacred elements of this planet—fire, earth, wind, and water—our intellects are returned to the body and the body enters the act of writing and transforms it. This remains my attraction to performance, its proximity to ritual which requires the elements, the word made flesh. On a daily basis I ask myself what rites I need to perform in order to remember. At times, I feel I have been educated into spiritual dumbness. I write in the effort to lose my mind into that site where a grand openness can teach me something I hadn't *thought* of.

I have always hoped that in my lifetime I would one day write a "free work." By this I mean a work that emerged from a profound sense of authority to speak fully and deeply through a voice no longer directed by me. The work would be one generated from someone or somewhere much more knowledgeable than what the limited chronology of my own mixed-up, mixed-blood life could offer. It would foretell our origin story pure and true, and as a result, skyscrapers would drop to their knees and turn to stone. It's a great thing to want. Sometimes I believe the best I've done as a writer is just to want. Just to keep wanting stories that bring us to our knees, return us to God, humble us into full recognition of our dependence on one another and a flourishing planet.

I need my ancestors of courage: storytellers who understand that their work is not wholly theirs, but that at its best, it is divinely inspired by history and mythic memory. Through (w)riting, ancestors do come to visit and become our informants for a literature of transformation. Toni Morrison didn't write *Beloved*, her slave ancestors did. The most trangressive storytelling, like the traditional myths of our pueblos, are passed down to us through rites of remembering. How do we conjure those stories?

Rather belatedly, in Movimiento terms, I went south, as other Xicanos and Xicanas had before me, in search of my "raíces" and a cultural connection with a contemporary México. What I encountered, instead, was the daily, and often painful, reminder of my own cultural outsiderhood as a U.S.-born Mexican of mixed parentage. But the templos of México—Monte Albán, Palenque, Tulum, Teotihuacan—told me something different.

As I ascended those temple steps, I unwittingly descended into the visceral experience of a collective racial memory that everything about my personal biography rejected, but that my writer's soul irrefutably embraced. It was as much the natural landscape in which those templos were placed as the buried history contained within the structures that brought a shudder of recognition to the surface of my skin: the green moss carpet on the steps of el Templo de la Cruz en Palenque; the crash of the Caribe against the walls of Tulum; the splice of sun illuminating the jewel-colored turquoise and jade of a Queztalcóatl relief in Teoti-huacan. Those templos to the gods were the edification of a history lost to me. Thus, began my (re)education process and my (re)turn to mito in search of a true god and a true story of a people.

Awakening from a dream, Linda tells me, "If we forget our old gods, they will disappear." I am not Mexica, but that herencia was gifted to me through the Chicano movement. The mitos that inform my work today are the outgrowth of that first journeying as a Chicana lesbian writer in the early eighties. It cost me a great deal to find their stories, but without my gods—Coatlicue, the mother of creation and destruc-tion; Coyolxauhqui, her dismembered daughter; La Llorona, the in-consolable weeping woman—without these icons of collective MeXi-cana sedition, my criminal acts as a Xicana dyke writer would have no precedent, no history, and ultimately no consequence.

Through the mutilated women of our Indigenous American history of story—La Llorona, Coyolxauhqui, Coatlicue—I came to under-stand genocide, misogyny, imperialism. And I claimed them sisters, allies in a war against forgetfulness.

I write to remember—is there no other way to say it? I write to imagine, which is a way of remembering, that "we were not always fallen from the mountain."[12]

How willing are we to remember what the Xicana and Odami art-ist Celia Herrera Rodríguez calls "las cositas quebradas," the broken places of our small life and grand history?[13] Sometimes, while (w)rit-ing, the heart breaks open like a flower. At other times, it just breaks. But therein lies the measure of our work: the risk we are willing to take to speak our truth, where its justification may be nothing more than intuition, a simple cellular knowing it is so. No footnotes. There has got to be a place for this kind of writing by heart. In it lies our own fierce morality to speak the truths we owe to our ancestors. It is an act of justice that can generate justice. By (w)riting, we re-create the nation of our deepest hope and finest imagination. And we will not die out.

Nezahualcoyotl writes:

> I am intoxicated, I weep, I grieve,
> I think, I speak,
> within myself I discover this:
> indeed, I shall never die,
> indeed, I shall never disappear.[14]

We will not die out.

The Altar of My Undoing

1

What the Buddhists

repeat as mantra

as daily breath, the Medicine offers

as tortilla,

as daily bread

as a small cup of fermented vine

that knows the desert

as distant relative

as a thousand drops of history

spilled into the parched throat

of an urban hour.

Blood inhaled
through a curandero's straw
he draws
the red liquid back
through continents
to a river's belly.

I imagine it
mud green and swollen
with life I imagine it
tierra lejana mas potente
than my garnered citizenship
in this place
of cracked slate and
head stone.

2

I do not know the face of god but fear
him faceless and unforgiving.
This is to think like a man, I tell myself
as I try
to wrought truth
from the lie
of habit.
I cross over

a small flame
and there is the infant stirring
on the other side
its mother a curled fetus of journeying.
I cup my hand
over the soft down of its new-born knowing.
Teach me kindly, I beg her.
I am not a man.

3

Now with the break of day
do I return to the poem speechless?
Do I attempt to construct language in the cracks
of consciousness between letters
the white emptiness of a fractioned
second between breaths
the fleeting inescapable dawn of knowing
without thought?

I am not a poem, but a broken
written record of obstinacy.
I press letters to the page
tiles of alphabet to fill in that forever
divide between experience
and telling.

Tomorrow something else will come.
Today I write
because I do not want to suffer
for
no good
reason.

Los ayahuasqueros dicen que
medicine visions are the real world.
The Tibetans counsel
the nature of reality is not
as solid as we think
we learn to see the illusory
of our thoughts.

This is the road to ending
suffering, dicen.
Still I carry a great heaviness in my bones
and call it sadness.
For I have met death and cannot forget

its features.
They are not friendly but impartial
and greet me
without the prejudice of my name.

Upon the death of my mother,
Elvira Moraga Lawrence
29 de Julio 2005

three   Salt of the Earth

Calling the Names of the Dead into a Hole in the Ground

"The dead do not like to be forgotten."

M. Jacqui Alexander,
"Pedagogies of the Sacred"

Aguas Sagradas

In this season of my mother's death, I stand on the edge of the ocean's immensity and call her name into the lion's roar of sea. My human voice, a thin current of sound against the thunderous tenor of all creation.

One summer a year ago, I had shown my son the ocean's night, we two clothed stick figures under the full moon's beacon of light. Our thin jackets are flags of resistance whipping in the wind. The waves crash. I tell him, "Look for me there, in the moon, when I am gone." I say this for us both, knowing and not knowing my mother would leave the watery pond of her own body in the days ahead. Knowing and not knowing, I would return to these waters to resurrect her.

Here, the heart expands without prejudice. There is no stinginess to our existence. Every molecule becomes my mother in her grandeur. The salt water of my tears is the same that I bring to my lips from the tidepool cup of my palm. At my feet, the pool is still and translucent amid an orchestra of crashing foaming cymbals and the booming bass of swelling waves.

In such great silence, I tell you, is where the mother is found, where the human voice of words is of no consequence. How is it that she is everywhere and still at once my mother and I her walking ancestor? The chest heaves and swells with so much knowing, then releases.

When the last waters fell from my mother, how were they released?
Through a thin line of saliva falling from her mouth?
A small puddle of pore gradually drying up?
A tear tipping off the cliff of the inner corner of her left eye?
How did the water leave her once and for all?

Hours later, as my sister and I bathed her con la agua sagrada, did the holes of her pores swallow that river after death? Or was it our hands that took in its sweetness and the molecules of drying skin that made up my mother's corpse of pure beauty? I tell you I have never loved like this, without worry, standing upon the browbeaten face of California's coast.

I had wanted to say to my beloved . . . Linda, this is how I will mourn you too, when you go. I promise. I am loving you this great, this grand, this much. But the mundane heart of words closes before the first utterance, inside the sealed doors of Subarus with engines running and neighboring recreational vehicles parked at scenic overlooks.

She describes me as a "galloping horse" running away with my feelings, they are so strong. But what else, except that aperture between ocean and sky, can take in the voice of such broken-hearted invocation?
What else?
But an ocean the color of sky and a sky the color of ocean?

Santa Cruz, Califas
2006

And It Is All These Things That Are Our Grief

EULOGY FOR MARSHA GÓMEZ

On September 29, 1998, Marsha A. Gómez, a Xicana Indígena (Choctaw) artist and activist, was tragically murdered by her twenty-one-year-old son. Marsha was forty-seven.

Heartbreak opens the heart.
Marsha taught me this . . . keeps on teaching.

Marsha, do you know—
is it so
that your death was not a murder,
but a sacrifice
a sacrifice for great change,
a change of heart for all of us?

I think of how many times Marsha broke my heart, but in each rupture there was an opening, a vista of one's self, brutal, unforgiving, and true. I learned humility in my loving of Marsha, always slightly unrequited, always my love returned to me like an opaque mirror, her breath clouding it. It took terrible courage to raise my hand to wipe that mirror and see my face looking back at me. That is the great blessing of lesbian loving, Marsha's loving: the mirror our desire becomes in the bodies of the women we dare to love.

Driving back from Alma de Mujer[1] with my comadres, we speak of Marsha, trying to receive her offering, to make meaning of her death; to comprehend the kind of mothers/mestizas this makes us. "Her need was so transparent," I say, "and the best-kept secret." They all nod in agreement.

What we offered was never enough. We were never enough. And this is what we mourn today: that she deserved more; that we could not protect her as a mother from her only son, when she had made her life's purpose the defense of the mother, la madre tierra. Forgive us, Marsha, our failure.

Still her death is a gift to us,
even its violence
because we cannot imagine it
because our minds cannot conjure it
because she was so unworthy of it,
we are forced to rethink everything about our lives;
why we are standing on this road, at this hour,
brokenhearted as we are.

The facts of Marsha's murder conjure lies and reveal truths all of us are struggling to unravel, fiber by fiber, separating truth from lie. For my part, I want to believe that at some point, Marsha made a decision toward life, not death; that she released her body to save her son from himself, to save others from the violence de su corazón inquieto.

And it is all these things that are our grief.

Maybe as mothers there's a place in us where we all fear the retribution of our children: la venganza from our sons never mothered enough in a motherless world of missing fathers. Maybe it's too easy to say that; to easy to speak in such grand terms of matricide and genocide. Still, we know those responsible for Marsha's death have faces and do not have faces and that in our own speechless shocked hearts only one truth resounds: her death was not an accident, but the result of a murderous history still in the making.

None of us here is immune to that history. I see myself in Marsha, in her body, in her son's rage used as a weapon against herself. I've seen my own son's anger, only five years old. "Mom, the tears won't stop," he tells me con ojos lagrimosos, slapping his wet cheeks. His tears, already his enemy. "They just keep coming down. Make them stop, please." I bring a tissue or the end of my shirt sleeve to his moist puppy-nose, soaked lashes. He stops crying. For now.

Did Meyaka² ask for anything more complicated than this? *Relieve me of myself, Mom, make the tears stop coming down.* But what you may cure at five, twenty years later is not enough. It is never enough, Marsha. We can never cure them of themselves.

My friends tell me that just after Marsha's murder, Meyaka was looking for his mother. Estaba buscando a su mamá este hombre, todavía niño; someone as infinitely generous as the mothers Marsha molded with clay and fire. But aren't we all looking for the same woman? A primordial all-forgiving mother, like the Virgen de Guadalupe she prayed to? Qué milagro that Marsha found her every time she put her hands into the red earth of her art. This was the gift she gave to each of us through her sculptures; that moment of remembering. We were not always like this, foolish and forgetful.

Go home to your mamá now, Marsha.
Toward that circle of light that is her arms.

Last night, I drove Marsha's family back to Alma de Mujer. Along the way, her father told stories of all the women who came courting after Marsha's mother had passed. He was bragging a little, a little like Marsha; talking big-story, his daughters all laughing along with him. Me too. The youngest sat up front next to me, now and then touching my arm as I drove, laughing along with the cuentos. And the touch felt so familiar, the way Marsha used to touch a person to keep them there in the story, in the joke with her. And her daddy's bravado was Marsha's and her sisters' sister-talk (the telltale slippage into Louisiana bayou), their gestures, all bring Marsha into the small world of that van with us and I'm thinking how much blood matters.

And that's why your family has come here with their wounded hearts all opened up to receive your other family—this tribe of indígenas, mestizas, two-spirited and one wish—that your death will remain a forever prayer in our lives.

Poetry of Heroism / 2007

Pat Parker and Audre Lorde were my lesbian-of-color predecessors, my queer literary forerunners, my age elders (by one and two decades, respectively); but they were also women who could easily have been around with us still today—as Gloria Anzaldúa, Toni Cade Bambara, Sandra Camacho, Barbara Cameron, Barbara Christian, Marsha Gómez, June Jordan, Victoria Mercado, and Ingrid "Flying Eagle Woman" Washinawatok could still easily be around with us today—if it were about the plain math of it. Women who died too soon, some barely looking at fifty.

But it's never about the plain math of it. It's about the complex equations of illnesses that hit women of color harder, the literal heartache of carrying so many warring identities, the poisoning exposures of campesino, reservation, and urban poverty that resurface later in our lives with names like diabetes, heart disease, and cancer inscribed on our bodies. It's about murder familial, local, and transnational—artists literally beaten down dead by their "loved ones," activists literally shot down dead under "mysterious circumstances," revolucionarias literally fired down dead, execution-style—black hood, duct tape, and the works.

We did not invent our oppression nor our fear of retaliation when we speak up against those oppressions. Our deaths are the real consequences of our collective histories, our actions, and at times, our lack of action. Audre Lorde reminds us, "We were never meant to survive"[1] and fear does not ever fully retreat from us, so we might as well advance as warriors, as Audre Lorde and Pat Parker did in their own lives.

I can tell you some small stories about meeting Pat Parker and knowing Audre Lorde. I can tell you that the pure visual of Pat Parker's brave Black butch presence standing in front of a crowd of organizers in downtown Oakland, shouting "Ya Basta!" made me scared for my own, less visible, light-skinned Chicana lesbian life (which told me a great deal about the measure of Pat's courage).

Moving to the Bay Area in the mid-1970s, it was unequivocally the bravery of the likes of Pat Parker and her Oakland comrade in poetry Judy Grahn,[2] that made lesbian poetry possible, just plain *possible*. That there was a story that could be told about our lives direct and true; that the pictures—the pure telling—said more than any evocative metaphor, any lyrically crafted phrase (although their work contained those too). I called what distinguished their work "class" and later came to understand the color of class in my own life. (I have Audre Lorde to thank for this.) Because their works—Pat's, Judy's, Audre's—gave lesbianism a body: a queer body in the original, dangerous, unambivalent sense of the word, a dyke body that could not be domesticated by middle-class American aspirations.

"Call me / Roach," Audre insisted,

> "Nightmare on your white pillow
> Your itch to destroy
> The indestructible
> Part of yourself."[3]

This is a Black *lesbian* poem, one with the unparalleled courage to assume the body of Anglo-America's terror. Audre gave Black lesbianism a body of resistance in the same breath in which she imbued it with desire. We will go to any end, her poems attested, once and for all to get a taste of a woman called us. And that's the secret I recognized in Audre. This is where she and I literally saw eye to eye; that fierce determination to come home to one another in the woman-of-color body. No separatism here, just return. Sometimes the journey home was ruthlessly executed; for it was so hard in those times to find one's way there. Still, the essence of Audre's work was love. "The erotic as power" she named it;[4] the power of that desire to come home to oneself. If we can love she who is despised by others, that sister self, what is there left to be afraid of?

Go 'head! Call me Roach!

In the late 1970s, the lesbian-of-color body of desire was a wounded body, and I watched that wound, over and over again, move from the metaphor of our silences to erupt open-mouthed on the surface of noble warrior-sisters' skins. I met Audre Lorde when she already had only one breast; never met a woman yet who could carry a scar like she did, like a purple heart of honored womanhood. *I am not my parts but the whole of who I am*, her amuleted amputation declared.[5] Audre wrought lesbian desire from the woman-of-color body, beautifully broken and whole at once, and offered it back to each of us to savor. I tell you, I may not have written a line if it weren't for such sisters of courage and merit.

Sometimes I think we are so far away from that moment—that sudden epiphany of a lesbian Movement-in-Black moment,[6] where we didn't worry about the names they called us or having the state recognize our queer marriages. I can't adequately describe to the young people I encounter what it was like *before* that lesbian movement; what it meant to be that queer, that colored, and that invisible, feeling that crazy, knowing your loving is not Radclyffe Hall, nor May Sarton or even *Rubyfruit Jungle* for that matter, because it is less free, more riddled, sexual but not always sexy, "common," like Judy Grahn wrote in "The Common Woman" poems.

Still for some of our little sisters, it could just as easily be 1977 as 2007. It is 1977 when my student comes to me and sits at my desk as she has come to my office over and over and over again for a few years now. She pushes her work across the desktop. Silently submitting page after page of some of the most self-loathing, frighteningly brave, and redemptive Black lesbian writing I have witnessed in years. And after so many meetings and so much denial that this work at all pertains to her *actual* autobiographical twenty-year-old self, I ask her, "What are you so afraid of? Tell me, is it you on these pages?"

And standing behind me—the women who give me the courage to ask—are Audre Lorde and Pat Parker. And twenty-year-old can't answer because she's got a mama she loves who hates her for the answer she's got strangled inside the twisted cords of her throat. Her silence, a great wall of transparent terror. And so I venture to climb over that wall, name the unnameable, because, truth is, in some parts—in her Louisiana Christian hometown, for example, and in the deep parts of so many of us—queerness is still unnameable (for all our so-called liberation).

I say, "There's nothing worse than being a Black bulldagger, right?" And she nods and that nod will be the aperture toward her freedom one day, I believe, because she is writing the stuff down: the fear, the hard black images, the raw desire. And she is not alone because Black lesbians by the name of Pat Parker and Audre Lorde have written before her. And her own Black lesbianism will be hard-won and all the more precious to her one day because of it.

Audre writes:

> The difference between poetry and rhetoric
> is being ready to kill
> yourself
> instead of your children.[7]

Courage still matters. Naming ourselves in true ways still matters.
    "Call me Roach."
No rhetoric here. Just a lesbian poetry of heroism.

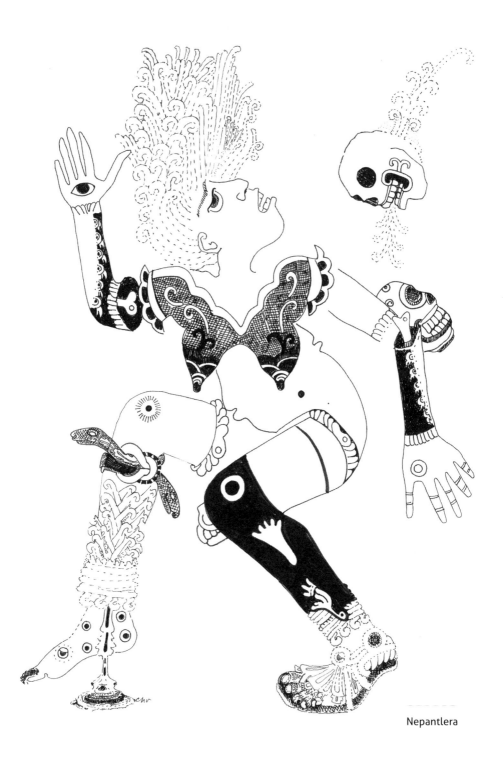

Nepantlera

The Salt That Cures / 2009

REMEMBERING GLORIA ANZALDÚA

> "I write because I want to leave a discernable mark on the world."
> Gloria Anzaldúa, "When I Write I Hover"

It is 1984. Standing in my Brooklyn apartment, the wooden dining-room table heavy and immovable between us, Gloria said she could read the guilt in my eyes. We had been estranged from each other for some time. So much had splintered us: the obstacles in bringing *This Bridge Called My Back* to publication; Gloria's embattled health; new and returning relationships (not always mutually welcomed) that had come into our lives during that time. I weave a broad tapestry here, but such generalities can never untie the complex knot that was my relationship with Gloria Anzaldúa.

By December 1980, with the completion of *Bridge*, I had left San Francisco, the home we shared, and moved East. Because we were never lovers, I never thought I was "leaving Gloria." I also never thought that

THE SALT THAT CURES   117

our relationship had any bearing on her move (also to the East) a year or so later. Maybe that was a naive response or maybe it was an accurate picture of our relationship. Ironically, with the publication of *Bridge* in 1981 and a reinvigorated women-of-color movement taking seed throughout the country, the gap of strained silence between Gloria and me was already widening.

Gloria's fateful visit to my Brooklyn apartment in 1984 finally broke that silence. It also broke us. I can't say I know exactly what happened between us that day. I do know she spoke of "plagiarism." I remember the word, its wounding. I was stunned. She couldn't possibly mean the words coming out of her mouth. *What was it I had taken? A stolen line, concept, image?* She would not say. *We had worked so closely for so many years,* I implored her, *surely some influences were unconsciously exchanged.* But I couldn't change her mind, couldn't stop the history unfolding between us. I flashed back to three years earlier, my bedroom floor in our San Francisco flat carpeted with literally hundreds of pages of Gloria's writings that became her "Letter to Third World Women Writers" and "La Prieta," which she had entrusted to me to edit. I believed I had honored that trust, but Gloria was unrelenting in her accusation.

Despondent, I responded, "I promise you I will never edit a line of your work again." And that was it. The transaction, as I remember it, took less than fifteen minutes; but as we each stood our ground on the parquet floor of that apartment, I knew the relationship was ending. In the days that followed, I would obsessively scan hundreds of pages of my own published writings for evidence of the theft of which I had been accused.[1] It was impossible to recuperate; for what I came to understand years later was that something much more profound than an unconsciously assimilated line of text had separated us. At times, I believe (and more strongly since her passing) that the measure of the distance between Gloria and me reflected the depth of our capacity to really "see" each other. Such exposure is not always welcomed.

Gloria had been infinitely generous with me about her ideas, her knowledge of Mesoamerican thought, her repertoire of spiritual practices, and her living account of Chicano history. How many of us, her younger friends (I was twenty-five when I met Gloria), were introduced to the marvelous prophecies of the I Ching through the small grip of her knuckled fist around those tarnished metal coins? But then, like so many others, I went on to seek oracles elsewhere; found other mentors, lovers, writing partners, other política, other roads.[2]

More than twenty years later, it is another dining-room scene. This time, in the Berkeley apartment of Gloria's lifetime friend Randy Conner. Gloria has been dead for several months. We sit at the table, all manner of spirit icons surrounding us, Gloria's picture among them. I recognize her influence in the world Randy occupies, their mutual exchange over a lifetime of thinking along interwoven spiritual threads. Ostensibly, I came to help him organize a memorial for Gloria on the occasion of her birthday. But it is a pretense. For without saying so, what I seek from Randy is a clue, a trace of truth, some insight into the real causes of the wounding of Gloria's and my relationship.

Without preamble, Randy states, "She was in love with you, as she was in love with me." At once, I know how he means "in love." This is not the story of something as mundane as unrequited romantic love, but just of *love*—a knowing so old and familiar, so naked, that we two— Gloria and I—could not hold it in our shared grasp. Disarmed, I feel his words fall upon me like a great medicinal salve. Tears welling up, I sigh in a profound release of some unnamed carga. *She loved me.* Is this all Gloria and I wanted truly to know about the other, amid the revolving door of girlfriends, the differing política, the chisme and traiciones?

Gloria writes: "I have split from and disowned those parts of myself that others rejected. I have used rage to drive others away and to insulate myself against exposure. I have reciprocated with contempt for those who have roused shame in me."[3] I betrayed Gloria, not for reasons she may have believed or invented, but because I did not love her thoroughly enough. I was not stronger than her cruelties and permitted them to send me away. Still, Gloria was somebody whom I always experienced as familia in the way one loves family members. It is a love that will not let you go.

I have returned with this telling.

EL MUNDO SURDO

Ten years my elder and—like my mother—a farmworker as a child, Gloria was every auntie I ever knew; the way her chin began to collapse into the round fleshy necklace of her throat, the middle-aged thickening panza. "I've had a hard life," she said, laughing, when I first inquired about her age, surprised by how relatively young (in her mid-thirties then) she was. I remember that laugh, how it was just the slightest bit self-denigrating, always the thin edge of sarcasm in her humor. In the best of times, she would tease me ruthlessly in the same way, beckon me to toughen up to it, and measure my Mexicanism by my ability to eat it.

I ate it . . . because she read me like a book—the transparent pages of my Okie-girl hunger, my suburban and second-generation half 'n' half Mexican identity. "You're Chicana, aren't you?" she said upon our first meeting, spotting me within the circle of white female faces. It was 1977, a Feminist Writers Guild meeting in San Francisco. She told me she could tell I was Chicana by how I talked. I had not been hiding my mixed-blood identity on purpose, but so few people had the ears to hear, the eyes to see. Gloria saw. And in that prophetic encuentro, our lives took on a trajectory of shared labor and heartbreak we could never have fully fathomed at the time.

The Gloria Anzaldúa I knew the most intimately was the woman she was in the late 1970s and early 1980s. During that time, Gloria and I were housemates in the Noe Valley district of San Francisco (pre-gentrification). It was, in many ways, the best of times, the best way to know Gloria, when we were both so full of optimism and a tireless energy to create. Inspired in part by Gloria's "El Mundo Surdo" poetry series, we began to organize actively as "cultural workers," bringing together queer folks and women-of-color writers and doing coalition work with the socialist feminist organization Radical Women and the Asian American women's performance group Unbound Feet.[4] It was also, of course, the time of the making of *This Bridge Called My Back*.

Here is a bit of what I remember from those days:

Gloria, bent over one of those huge hard-bound black sketch books we all used as journals at the time. Her left-handed grip fiercely around a fountain pen, she would sit all afternoon at one of the small wooden tables at the Meat Market Coffeehouse on Twenty-fourth Street. Once a butcher shop, the crowded café offered good coffee and reasonably priced foods. It is now an upscale bistro neither of us could've afforded back then. When she was not teaching at the state university, this was where Gloria could be found each day. She needed the noise, the traffic, the teenaged voices on the street—activity all around her—in order to escape into the world of her writing.

I was the opposite, found writing in public distracting and would only swing open the wooden door of that café once I had put in a full morning's writing at home. Gloria slept during the usual morning waking hours—all morning long, often rising after twelve or one in the afternoon. Removing earplugs and sleeping blindfold, she would enter a new day after a long night's metaphorical and metaphysical journeying while the rest of the house slept. The wee hours of the morning were Gloria's most fecund writing time, when the quiet darkness offered her unconscious full reign.

UNA HERIDA ABIERTA

The mirror which Gloria's dusk-inspired writings offered of my Xicanidad awed and compelled me. Twenty-five years later, I read from the galley pages of *The Gloria Anzaldúa Reader*: "La vulva es una herida abierta."[5] I check the editor's note; it states that the work was "drafted . . . around 1990." I do the math and realize that this was long *after* Gloria's and my separation, and yet, somehow the stories printed there are not new to me: the image of the too young Prietita washing out the bloody rags of her menses and hanging them to dry secretly among hidden nopales. I know this story.

My mother, a teenager in the 1930s, had shared with me the same stories of her girlhood, rinsing out the red-stained rags in a bucket. The viscera of Gloria's telling on the page is what brings the story home to me. The same shame imparted from her mother's lips as my mother's, "hedionda," "apestosa."[6] Ironically, my mother also used such expressions with a kind of cariño for us as little girls. In fact, it took me many years to figure out, due to my limited childhood Spanish, that *fuchifachi* was not just one word for "vagina." *Fuchi*, meaning "stinky," was so integral to *fachi* (vagina) that I heard them as one!

I also knew these stories because *Gloria had told them to me* so vividly that they reawakened a shame I too carried as a Mexican female. Gloria was my contemporary, my more-or-less-generational peer, but her stories bridged a gap to that premodern campesina past I could scarcely articulate. I was the once-removed relation (although my dreams told me otherwise), for whom shame expressed itself not in bloodstained rags, but the brown paper sacks that hid my box of Kotex from shoppers' eyes.[7]

In Gloria's writing, there was no hiding, no mask of light skin or suburban anonymity. Gloria was the real deal, exhibiting a relentless courage to articulate the internalized misogyny of what it meant to be female as a brown-skinned Mexican born in the middle of the twentieth century. Most significant was her understanding of how intimately this female hatred is tied to that other site of deprecio, la india. This is what she laments in her "Coatlicue State," the fear of accessing "that voice at the edge of things," the forbidden sabiduría that comes from our Indigenous female antecedents.[8]

Looking at the body of Gloria Anzaldúa's work, su "herida abierta," as a tejana, resided in two sites of equal calling: la frontera y la vulva. In 1987 when Gloria named "as wound" the border dividing the United States from México, she did so not merely from metaphorical imaginings, but because the border had personally wounded her. Indeed, the intellectual and spiritual philosopher Gloria was re-envisioned those wounds as the location for making good medicine for our brokenness, to create por lo menos a metaphorical cure for the legacy of misogyny and racist violence passed down to us through patriarchal colonialisms. Her generously defined vision de "la frontera" y de la "nueva mestiza," were created because she wanted a changed world. But this is not the world she occupied. She desired across the borderlines of race and gender and class, and yet admitted in her writings that she was afraid of intimacy. "I am afraid of drowning," she wrote. "[I feel] resistance to sex, intimate touching, opening myself to the alien other where I am out of control."[9]

For Xicanas, the fissure between the vision and the lived reality is so vast and wide, it is the stuff of our literature. Our ideas and stories are generated from the *actual* experience of *alien*ation; and through our writings, we can take possession of that displacement. We locate ourselves in the geography of a redrawn landscape, where we make a home for the exiled heart in a country of benevolent ancestors. This was Gloria Anzaldúa's "Borderlands." Was this not also Aztlán in its earliest imaginings? Still, the fissure divides. That fault line between what we are able to imagine and our lived reality also drew a line between Gloria and me.

THE POLITICS OF DIFFERENCE

A few years after *This Bridge Called My Back*'s publication, Gloria announced to me that the book did not reflect her vision. As she put it to me, had she been in better health, she would have done it differently. It hurt me to hear this; but again, she did not say more. Still, a part of me had been grateful that in the later stages of the book's development, Gloria had yielded much of the book's direction to me and there had been little debate between us. By 1980, the labor of the book had fallen almost exclusively into my hands as co-editor, while at the same time, without my fully comprehending it, the gravity of Gloria's physical illness (uterine cancer, resulting in a hysterectomy) had fallen upon her. With compromised health, Gloria focused on some of the contributions dealing specifically with spirituality and allowed me loose rein over how to structure and articulate the politic of the book. As I submitted the book to Boston's Persephone Press for publication,[10] I presumed that the feminism of color we had gathered from our contributors and that I perceived as emergent on the horizon was a vision with which Gloria was in accord. In retrospect, I see that this may not have been completely so.

Twenty years later in 2002, with the publication of *This Bridge We Call Home*, edited by Gloria and AnaLouise Keating, I came to a clearer understanding of how Gloria's vision of "bridge" had evolved, which also spoke to what may have been lacking, from her perspective, in the original version. When I learned that the new collection was to include men and white women, I decided not to contribute to the book, not out of a politic that can be dismissed as "exclusion,"[11] but due to what

I perceived as strategic in terms of the further development of U.S. women-of-color feminism. As I saw it, our movement, *in practice*, had not arrived at a place of such inclusion. We were still barely understanding how to effectively move beyond the racial categories and strategies of political resistance and identity politics formulated in response to the 1960s and 1970s people-of-color movements, as well as to white feminism and gay liberation. We had yet to effectively develop a national network of coalesced women-of-color organizing, or a women-of-color theory and practice which might incorporate a new generation of Indigenous peoples and immigrants from the southern hemisphere, as well as from West and East Asia and the Pacific Islands. All this is what I imagined a "new *Bridge*" might address. From my perspective, to be "inclusive" of (even) queer men and white women, at this stage of a U.S. feminism of color, would be to suggest that our movement had developed beyond the need for an autonomous dialogue entrenos. But this was not *Gloria's* politic, it was (and is) mine and what *I* believed we had inscribed for the future in *This Bridge Called My Back*. I had urged Gloria not to use *bridge* in the title of her new book for all the reasons stated above, but did not press the matter.[12]

I see now, with the clarity of hindsight, that a kind of balance may have been achieved between Gloria's perspective and my own with the publication of *This Bridge We Call Home*. By the sheer breadth of its representation, Gloria, in concert with Keating, was able to finally make manifest her vision of how that "bridge called (her) back" spanned so many intersecting communities of thought and ever-permeable identities. Of the nearly six-hundred-page collection, she states: "We define who we are by what we include."[13]

Gloria Anzaldúa's true intention for *This Bridge We Call Home*, however, seems to be neither about inclusion or exclusion, but something much deeper, as revealed in the book's closing meditation, "now let us shift . . . the path of conocimiento . . . inner work, public acts." It is a meditation that is more "transmitted" than written, more rite than write. In it Gloria (w)rites: "'Home' is that bridge, the in-between place of Nepantla and constant transition, the most unsafe of all spaces."[14] As Randy Conner reminded me, "the path/camino [was] home" itself for Gloria.

Of her final collection, Conner states: "[Gloria] recognized that the present was not as she'd hoped it would be and that she was in a way being utopian. She increasingly believed that you had to try to live in the/a future you hoped would one day, and [which you] worked to, materialize. . . .[T]his had something to do with a deep intuitive feeling [she had] that this [book] might be one of her final statements, and she wanted to point toward that which might lie across the bridge."[15]

Fundamentally, my differences with Gloria's philosophies, over a lifetime, have had little to do with the *spirit* of her ideas, which, as the Mesoamerican scholars David Carrasco and Roberto Lint Sagarena rightly note, were like "the dynamic passageways between the human and spirit world."[16] Instead, I remain concerned by how the seeming inclusivity of Gloria's ideas lends them to appropriation and misinterpretation, especially by white and middle-class scholars.[17]

In Gloria Anzaldúa's imaginings, her "nepantleras" would reside as (meta)physical "mestizas" within the matrix of a "new tribalism," a "borderland" free of that wounding "edge of barb[ed] wire" separation.[18] This is a beautiful vision, but should not be mistaken as a *strategy* for resolving the disparities between economic classes, ethnic communities, and women and men within a capitalist patriarchy. From my observation of sectors of the academic, and (even self-ascribed radical) white queer and feminist communities, many are more than happy to subscribe to a politic like "new tribalism," for it rejoins them with women of color and Native peoples purely by virtue of their shared experience of "otherness." In it, there is little explicit requirement for them to look at personal politics (that is, their own life) in relation to the historical and institutional exclusion by privileged whites of lower economic classes and people of color.

As displaced Xicanas and Xicanos, there can be no new tribe without the reparation of the home tribe. Gloria states as much when she writes: "Until the indigenous in Indians and Chicana/os are ensured survival, establishing a new tribalism, a mestiza nation, remains merely a vision. But dream we must."[19] Still, the road to the realization of that dream is different for Indian and Xicano peoples than for non-Natives because our oppression is distinct from non-Natives and cannot be cross-culturally applied. From the perspective of living tribal[20] communities, the idea of a new, ethnically inclusive tribalism may resonate as yet another neocolonial attempt to dehistoricize and weaken the cultural integrity of aboriginal nations. This, of course, was not Gloria's intention, but the danger of such appropriation is not to be minimized.

As the sacred medicines of the Amazon and the peyote of the high deserts of México and Tejas are farmed for ceremonial distribution throughout Europe and Euro-America (north and south), first-world peoples with the economic access to do so grow comfortable with arrogating the ceremonial practices, ideologies, and social structures of Indigenous nations, while few have real interaction with Native communities and their political struggles.

I often wish that Gloria had examined more thoroughly in print the *political* implications and consequences of the philosophical tenets she forwarded as foundational for a new social activism. Her "new tribalism" is especially problematic in this sense. In 1997, Gloria stated that the first stage of her apprenticeship as a writer required "detribalization."[21] Knowing a bit of Gloria's life, I understand this to mean that she had to leave home because its cultural restraints would have killed her—body and spirit. Freedom resided elsewhere.[22] Her autobiographical writings remind us that, as Xicanos and Xicanas, our home tribes are so infected by colonialism—the Indian woman raped, our lands pillaged, our self-governance dissolved—that we are forced into psychic and physical displacement. These acts of colonialism were all sites of visceral knowing for Gloria *and* are a daily occurrence for tribal Indigenous peoples all over this planet. Why then would she write of a "new" culturally inclusive tribalism when the culturally genocidal detribalization of Xicanas and Xicanos and other Indigenous peoples has occurred in part because Indigenous sovereignty has been virtually eliminated from the national discourse on both sides of the border?

Perhaps, in this sense, Gloria and I walked different roads as Xicana scribes; especially in the way in which such political contradictions, for me, often circumvent utopian imaginings. What I have come to believe through my own political and spiritual practice is that as marginalized peoples, we all have to make our way back to the home sites that have rejected and deformed us in order to re-form them.[23] This is the hardest work, especially since the reason we left those homes in the first place may have been a deadening violence. But, ultimately, all of us (white people included) have to go home to our own "tribes"—our home cultures—and make progressive change there specific to our historical cultural conditions. This is the work I "dream" of witnessing among all leftist and feminist communities; that we might meet on the common ground of *shared labor* and in this way, support the reparation of extant Indigenous tribal communities.

Fundamentally, I don't believe that Gloria would disagree with this thinking, although she would (and did), no doubt, frame it differently. Words are so inadequate at times to explore the full complexity and contradiction of what it means to be Xicana in the paradox of a post-modern twenty-first century, while at the same time holding knowl-edges that may predate (and transcend) the modern, the nation-state, and the advent of globalism.

As I review the posthumous collection of Gloria's writings, I see how much política Gloria and I did share, including what Gloria re-ferred to as "spiritual activism" and our faith in art as a kind of medi-cine.[24] Residing at the cultural intersections of women-of-color identi-ties here in the United States we both have drawn from the influences of many immigrant and indigenous cultures to find form for our gods. I sit in a zendo, pray with my African American sisters in the Yoruba tradition, and swallow the bitter truth of that Native Mexican medi-cine when required. On the road back home, pa' otro lado, we learn the new names for things—what Gloria called "spiritual mestizaje."[25] As Xicanas, the same pantheon of diosas and archetypes have haunted Gloria's and my creative and political imaginations for over a genera-tion. The same world tragedies have brought us to sink our knees into the sands of the Pacific and pray. Beneath our distinct languages is a thread of continuity of what it means to be Xicana in this continent, from "La Prieta" to "La Güera."[26]

Maybe age and time and death have brought Gloria and me closer together. What I learned from death is that as human beings we walk the road of *relative* truth—those social constructions of identity—on the way to the *absolute* truth of our ever-impermanence.[27] The relative is the languaged world of thought, the place of injustice we actively confront in the effort to free ourselves and others from such sites of suffering. In the best of scenarios, we live with a kind of necessary "double consciousness"—wherein both truths remain in our awareness as we arrive at each obstacle, each opportunity for change in our lives. This is how I understand Gloria's "Nepantla," that interstice between both sites of consciousness. She was a nepantlera because she saw between worlds. The older I get, I too catch these glimpses.

EL OTRO LADO

I have always known Gloria as someone who had a highly cultivated relationship with "el otro lado," the spirit world. Her desire for alone-ness in order to nurture that most intimate of relationships may have made her the physical lover of no one, even as she was the metaphysical lover of all. There remains a kind of sadness for me in this, that she died alone, in fact. This is the hardest part of Gloria's dying for me—the sense of her aloneness, the price she had to pay to write, to be an artist, to live an uncensored life.

"Poetry is not a luxury," Audre Lorde writes;[28] and no one knew this better than Gloria Anzaldúa, who wrote out of pure survival, who was willing to eat the dirt del valle over and over again to conjure her demons and dreams on the page. She did this as a tejana writer in exile, in a multicultural Northern California, which for all its progressive politics and inclusiveness, included few people who had the capaz to fully recognize Gloria. There was safety in this for her and, I believe, a kind of comfortable insistence on (resignation to?) not being known. She remained elusive, even among her intimates. She testified to this aloneness in her own writings as a source for creative resistance: "Aquí en la soledad prospera su rebeldía. / En la soledad Ella prospera."[29]

I wish Gloria had been less alone in her life. I wish I had been less afraid and more insistent on resolving the profound ruptures of heart between us, what we could not openly admit or when admitted, could not honor. Still, as I age I continue to witness these ruptures, separations from people I once loved in deep and true ways. Loving breaks the heart over and over again. It just does.

I tell you, the warriors are few and far between. Gloria died too early. I don't know how to grapple with this—so much work left incomplete.[30] I acknowledge what has been accomplished: Gloria Anzaldúa's critical role in the birthing of radical Xicana feminist thought, her relentless commitment to enfrentar lo mas difícil de expresar: the censored, the taboo, the wounding silences. What distinguishes Gloria's work is the specificity of her retrato of the Xicana experience, free of the impulse toward cultural tourism, the lens of exoticization, the lie of romance. Still, I am old enough now to recognize that there are knowledges I had no way of grasping in my youth, which took middle age to begin to comprehend, and will ultimately require elderhood to wholly embrace. I mourn the loss of my sister's elderhood writings, and that they will not accompany me as I myself age. I pray that her work will continue in new forms, through new bodies. I pray this not for her, but for us who still walk the earth's surface in need of such uncensored guidance.

Several years ago, after Gloria's death and just before my mother's passing, they both appeared together in a dream. I learn that my mother, stricken with dementia, is lost in New York City. I worry over her, but later in the dream when she appears, I see that she is actually fine, just wandering about but not lost. She is happy. Gloria also appears on the streets of New York, also happy for she is on her way back home. "To Tejas," she tells me. I feel them both in pure relation to each other, as citizens of the dead and dying. There is joy. There is freedom. I am the one tied to the deadly notions of work and worry. I was grateful to Gloria for coming to me in this way, as if she divined what I was so desperately seeking: the continuity between the dead, the dying, and those of us who walk about expectant, carrying that cellular comprehension of our shared location in this universe.

During the first months after Gloria's passing, so many people suffering her loss proclaimed that Gloria's spirit was still with us. But at times I sensed, no. I thought Gloria (or at least that transcendent part of her) was perhaps done here in this realm. Relieved finally of the embattlement of her body, she had moved on to join a pantheon of intelligence far more compelling to her than any of us in our mundane worlds. This is what I would like to believe for Gloria: that she had a great homecoming of the spirit; greeted in death by Audre Lorde, Toni

Cade Bambara, Pat Parker, Sandra Camacho, and Marsha Gómez—all women warriors Gloria had known and walked with in her life; all sisters of awe-inspiring courage. Still, messages continue to come del otro lado and Gloria's visitations compel me to believe she may not yet be quite done with us, with me.

LA APARICIÓN

It is an October Saturday afternoon, a sunny northern Califas Libra day, the astrological sign I shared with Gloria, our birthdays one day apart. Autumn is my favorite season in the Bay Area, when coastal fogs lift to unveil a great metropolis of ocean and skyscraper, suspension bridge and redwood forest; where the contradiction in landscape seems to find a moment of harmony and balance.

That day, driving out of my neighborhood block, I come to a stop at the corner and catch in the periphery of my vision the undeniable figure of Gloria—una chaparrita, built thick and low to the ground. Two small dogs tug at her extended arms as she steps down from the curb. As I slow down, our eyes meet, and it *is* she, the oiled olive tinge to her skin, the round cachetona face framed by a generous circle of black-dyed india hair. She smiles widely, and I back at her. I glance again at the road, my foot still on the brake pedal, then back to the figure, but by then another face has emerged in Gloria's place. Still, I had spotted her, the image lingering in the third site of the eye. And it occurs to me, as I continue my journey up the hill, that perhaps this is the sign I had been seeking—some kind of permission from Gloria to try and write the impossible: a true telling of my relationship with her and of the Gloria I knew in my life.

Gratefully, in what turned out to be the last years of her life, Gloria and I were drawn back in touch with each other again with the re-issue of *This Bridge Called My Back* in 2002. Gratefully, the genuine affection we felt for each other surfaced without pretense. I honor that moment; hold the memory of her cousin-laughter like warm light in my disquieted heart.

"Let us be the healing of the wound," writes Gloria Anzaldúa in the

closing essay of her posthumous book.[31] Today, I read that line differently. Today, I imagine she is speaking just to me, about us.

> *Would it were that our stories*
> *were the waters of the river.*
> *Would it were that they passed over the worn stones*
> *of our hearts and cleansed us,*
> *moving on to the mother sea*
> *in a forgiving embrace.*
>
> *Would it were the salt that cures.*

four   The Price of Beans

The Corn Mother's Return

South Central Farmers

What Tezo taught me

last night standing among the fields

peopled by organic chard

rábano

zanahoria

is that to be

tribe is to be

without property

with land abundant

all around.

"Losing a plot of soil would break us
had we believed it was ours."
How to hold two thoughts
in your head at once
without the heart exploding.

The land is ours and it is not.
They move us off
we return to another
field of food.

This is the poetry of the campesina
who holds a piece (a place) of dirt
fertile and fecund
in the banks of her memory
in the bowl of two hands together.

The Other Face of (Im)migration / 2008

> Migration and Pilgrimage are two of the most
> powerful forces in both human history and human
> psyche.
>> Jace Weaver and Laura Adams Weaver,
>> "Indigenous Migrations, Pilgrimage Trails,
>> and Sacred Geography"

> You took me out of darkness and now I have voice.
> You forced me to speak and so here I am speaking
> and I will not be silenced. From inside my own jail
> cell, I will continue to move my people.
>> Flor Crisóstomo, in sanctuary,
>> Adalberto Methodist Church, Chicago,
>> February 23, 2008

Several years ago I served on an artists' panel at the Jewish Film Festival in San Francisco. The speakers were: Ella Shohat, Trinh Minh-ha, Peter Sellars, and the Palestinian filmmaker Michel Khleifi. When it was my turn to speak, I addressed the Xicano experience of displacement, of internal colonization, of being made foreigners in the land of our own origins, of having borders etched through us like the bleeding "wound" of which the late Gloria Anzaldúa wrote so eloquently, dividing a pueblo, a nation of peoples. I spoke of Aztlán, our origin story that had provided Xicanos with our own land base of political resistance some thirty-five years ago. I spoke of our collective longing to return to a homeland close enough to smell.

Following me, Michel Khleifi spoke via a French interpreter. He introduced his remarks, stating simply, "By changing just a few words in the last story, the same could be applied to the Palestinian people." And in that moment, unexpectedly, hope reemerged for me, the sudden possibility of a truly transnational consciousness; i.e., international solidarity among diverse groups of exiled diasporic peoples who refuse to forget their origins; who find resonance for their own national struggles in the struggles of other nations of peoples.

A few years later in 2002, I would have a similar experience of connectivity, one which would again span the nearly nine thousand miles of geography from my politically embattled home state of California to the warring turbulence in western Asia. At a conference celebrating the twentieth-anniversary edition of *This Bridge Called My Back*, I read an excerpt from my foreword, initially written on the morning of September 11, 2001.[1] It anticipated the full-scale, escalating, and interminable violence that ravages Iraq today. I am no prophet, only a witness (as the West Asian women at the conference especially were) to the writing already on the wall—the wall that divides Palestine, as the wall that divides my own native homeland—north from south. For the United States of America, "homeland security," in response to 9/11, has meant militarizing the border crossings from the south with as much virulence as it supports the militarization of the Israeli border. And in this fact alone resides the potential for viable coalition work among Xicanas and West Asian women in the United States.

WALLS

The other day I read a *San Francisco Chronicle* article about "walls." I learned that the U.S. military has now built a series of "security walls" throughout the various districts of Baghdad, so that all some people see from their home window is about five feet of space. No sky. And in the meantime, the Israeli government bulldozes as many as half a million olive trees, the mainstay of the economy in occupied Palestine, to expand the separation wall in the West Bank.

Growing up in Southern California, I was ever conscious of the divide between the United States and México, regularly traveling to Tijuana and its environs for family outings to visit my grandfather's grave. The desert-dry dirt and cracked stone of the cemetery lay literally within spitting range of the borderline. As children what do we learn from our proximity to walls? *That kids just like you—wearing your own hand-me-down-clothes—will emerge out of cardboard shanty houses to collect the coins your uncle tosses into the dirt road; that the wall makes a difference, marks the divide between the haves and the have-nots.*

Do we grow up to believe in walls? I crossed the Berlin Wall in 1987, passing through Checkpoint Charlie on a highly regulated tourist bus pass. As I observed through the bus window the steel gray and industrial green of post–World War II apartment construction, my "Red Scare" child's imagination saw everything within the repressive dull frame of a 1960s black-and-white Cold War photograph. A U.S.-educated child, I grew up studying the world map as the battleground between "freedom" and communism. During social studies class, the huge map was rolled down like a bored and languorous tongue covering the blackboard. There, the Red threat of China and the Soviet Union blushed across the Eastern face of the world, encroaching—country by country—upon the "free" world of the West. I remember Vietnam, tiny and vulnerable, clinging to its "freedom" on the edge of an ocean at the foot of the ever-menacing Chairman Mao.

This is what we were told in school. The conflation of capitalism with democracy was never noted, let alone questioned. I often wonder what world maps in the U.S. classroom might look like today if fear of terrorism assumed the place of what was once the fear of communism. What color would western Asia be, now that 9/11 has brought it onto the map of U.S. attention? Would it be shrouded in the black color of the burqa?

Two years after my visit to East Germany in 1987, the Berlin Wall fell and within a handful of years, transnational capitalism had destroyed any remnant of it, outside of a few sections preserved for the tourist industry. Currently the same transnational capital erects an impenetrable barrier down the center of the desert heart of the Tohono O'odham people in southern Arizona.[2] The maps keep changing, but one way or another profit, and not principle, is boss and builder and wrecking ball at once.

THE POLITICS OF PARADOX

"¡Ay, Mis hijos! We have to go! Where can I take you?" The mythic cry of La Llorona, the "Weeping Woman," was said to have been first heard in the dark of night in the streets of Tenochitlán, just before the arrival of the Spanish into México.[3] It was a prophetic llanto, a harbinger of the conquest and the decimation of Indigenous peoples to follow. It was the cry of a mother to her nation's children.

Over a year ago, as emissaries of La Red Xicana Indígena,[4] Celia Herrera Rodríguez and I met with Elvira Arellano, a Mexican un-documented worker who was in sanctuary in a Chicago storefront church protesting her deportation and the threat of separation from her seven-year-old son, a U.S. citizen. In many ways, Elvira represented a kind of contemporary Llorona, refusing the separation of families compounded by globalization. This is the current state of the world, her protest announced, in which mothers and children are torn apart through war (in Iraq, Palestine, Afghanistan), poverty (Mexican and Central American undocumented migrants), and misogynist violence (the murdered girls and young women of Juárez).

Last week, my partner and I had a new fence installed in our back-yard (walls, again). The intensive labor of removing sixty-year-old ivy with roots the size of tree trunks was accomplished by two "Mexican" immigrant workers, whose boss was Vietnamese. While I sat at my computer working, I could hear the obreros converse in a Maya dia-lect outside my window. These are Native Americans whose origins on this continent pre-date most of us, but who today serve as hired labor for the settler classes in the United States. For our part, as Xicanas of Indian origins with family members whose class statuses range from off-the-grid poor to corporate lawyers, we live daily inside the politics of paradox. The week before, we had hired Linda's son, an unemployed Xicano father with a teen mother and child at home, to tear down the old fence. He and his half-brother worked hard for a full day's pay. But it was nothing like the intensity of watching those Maya work. And it's all Indigenous workers now. All. Washing our cars and cleaning our houses and pulling our weeds and pouring our patios and building our fences. And yet, *they* are the criminals, as are the other twelve million undocumented migrants living in the United States; as is Flor Crisóstomo, who took Elvira Arellano's place in sanctuary at the Adalberto United Methodist Church in Chicago last January.[5]

Flor's refusal to be deported after a raid in her place of employment continues the protest against the policies of globalization, especially the North American Free Trade Agreement, that forced her to leave her three children in México under her mother's care, and seek work in the United States. She has gone nearly eight years without seeing her family and her homeland. When Flor asks her mother about the land she left behind in 2001, her mother responds, "Mija, el campo no existe. Las tierras son áridas. Es pura piedra." * The lands are rock because the cultivators of maíz are forced by poverty to leave that land in order to build fences for Xicana "maestras" in Oakland, California. I am glad to provide the work; but I am not fool enough to think that the loss of their homelands does not spiritually, culturally, and economically diminish my América and me and my children and the generations that follow us.

At the heart of this political paradox, I wonder:

> *Where can I take you that you might see*
> *yourselves reflected in this other América?*
> *You, whose origins reside two continents*
> *and an ocean away.*

LA OTRA AMÉRICA

Celia had extended the invitation for the temescal and I was to keep the fire. Our neighborhood elder, Samuel, had offered his Fruitvale barrio home to host the sweat lodge. We had invited a local Iranian familia of

* Daughter, our land no longer exists. Everything has gone dry. It is all rock now.

seven and a transplanted Lebanese student of mine, her little sister, and my student's female partner to sit together in this ceremonial way. The offering of the lodge came because the needs of the two families were simple and familiar to us: a prodigal son's return, a first grandchild on the way, a female teen lost in migratory self-doubt, a new queer marriage confronting its tenuous and tenacious beginnings, and the ever-present quiet worry of a mother who can no longer protect the lives of her adult children.

Sitting around the fire, Samuel explains the history of the northern lodge erected of willow and will power there among the encroaching neighborhood yards of apartment buildings, the deep bass of boom-boxes and the passing rev of souped-up cruising engines. "This is native Ohlone land," he tells his new visitors and I know it matters to him as it does to us, to show our friends this part of América, this hidden América, this truer older América that links us as people who remember our origins.

Here is where the transnational movement I seek begins, where we see ourselves reflected in one another across oceans of difference. Days later, my Iranian friend's adult children laugh aloud when, at my son's graduation party, they see the ways they were raised mirrored in our own familia. As Rafa opens his gifts, I whisper to him: "Go and thank la señora. . . . Yes, get up now. . . . Give her an abrazo. . . . Shake his hand. . . ." In the United States, among Chicanos and Chicanas, we've come to refer to this way of raising children as "old school," but it is simply the ways I was taught as a working-class Mexican American girl to behave among my elder relatives, with some basic sense of humility. This is what those thirty-something-year-old Iranians recognized as their own cultural upbringing.

My grandmother was born in Sonora in 1888; my mother, in 1914 California; and my son, in 1993. Can I even describe to you how fiercely I raise him not to forget these ways as intimate to my bloodline as the one-hundred-and-twenty-year-old origins of my grandmother? Can I predict for those of you who, as immigrants, have made the United States your home your own fears of cultural loss raising children in this country? And what of your children's children? Can we share a conversation about retaining culture and critiquing it at once? What is a woman-of-color strategy for cultural resistance against assimilation when as feminists we refuse a blind ethnic nationalism that leaves us silently compromised or, worse, in just plain danger?

Among the diverse groups of the women-of-color movement in the United States, there is the promise of affinity and alliance, but it is a hard road to travel because class privilege and Western feminism remain obstacles on our path to one another. Interviewing Flor Crisóstomo, she disclaims, "I am not a feminist, but . . ." And I wonder to myself, where has feminism failed if a fierce activista like Flor, who identifies her struggle as integrally connected to the conditions of womanhood, dis-identifies with feminism? Because it is a foreign Euro-American concept to her. But a mother's calling to want better for her children is not; nor is the incisive analysis in which Flor, a Zapotec woman, names transnational capital as her nemesis. Maybe language is not really the issue here, but the lack of recognizable aligned political action.

Does the migrant worker choose to be here? Does it matter to us? For many of you, the threat of war and imprisonment, the dangerous volatile politics of your home nation, the suppression of free movement may have brought you (or your parents) to these dis-United States for a time or for a life. So, I ask you, as feminists: *with whom do you hold your conversations?* If you are members of the professional classes in your countries of origin, how do you build a transnational feminism that incorporates (beyond rhetorical considerations) the realities of the poor—immigrant *and* native—here in the United States? I want you to see your own daughters and the stories of your mothers and grandmothers and yourselves reflected in Flor Crisóstomo. I seek a women's movement that crosses nations while it crosses boundaries of class. This is the greatest challenge to creating a truly radical transnational feminist agenda. For the class structure of the United States separates privileged women-of-color feminists from grassroots working-class women-of-color activists, like Flor; and feminism often remains a conversation shared only among the professional and college-educated classes, including white women.

As the artist in residence at Stanford University for over ten years, I have had the opportunity to work with hundreds of students of color, some from as nearby as the barrios of Oakland, others with origins as distant as the Ibo of Nigeria. Many of my classes serve as a kind of "united nations" (with better politics, I hope) where students are required to connect with one another across geopolitical and cultural borders. Still, I notice the difference among them. I see it in my students (primarily women): the timidity of my Xicana first-generation college students, sitting side by side with the already educated South Asian, Iraqi, Egyptian, Ghanian, and Palestinian.

In the United States, especially on California's private college campuses, where affirmative action is still permitted, the reservation Native American, the gang-survivor Xicano, and the once-crack-baby African American have the opportunity to study with the elite members of nations across the globe. Looking at the panorama of faces in my classes, I consider that this may be one site where the next generation of promise for transnational alliance resides, or does it foretell continued separation, division, and ignorance? After all, to what degree can alliances be sustained across class and cultural barriers when they are born within the rarefied context of a ruling-class education?

Still, a cross-fertilization does occur where privileged immigrant students learn firsthand from the once-enslaved-and-still-victimized what the streets of the United States teaches all of them: that class privilege does not provide complete protection against racism in Anglo-America. The violent racist attacks against anyone remotely resembling an Arab in this country after 9/11 brought home this fact with brutal clarity. Still, in these acts also resides my hope: that the racism and cultural imperialism of the United States will not break alliance among women of color, but forge union across class and cultural difference toward the binding activism of a multi-issued feminism. I am trying to figure out how militarized globalization, which has forced a radical migratory shift in the countenance of the United States, can paradoxically serve to create a more politically just country through a highly diverse and expanded women-of-color activism among immigrant and U.S.-born women. Globalization's intention, of course, is to do otherwise: to foster an ever-growing settler class among the economically privileged (even under the name of feminism).

In a certain way, to be here in the United States, as a person of consciousness, you have to care desperately about this country, in the sense that you have to care desperately about its people. As a body, U.S. women of color are not among the fully franchised. We are the *other* face of immigration: the great-granddaughters of slaves and indentured Chinese workers and the daughters of penniless war refugees. We are Merry Maids and Happy Meal makers. We are undocumented college students taking final exams while fearing deportation. We are the Zapotec Flor Crisóstomo, holding a vigil of protest in a storefront church in Chicago. "Miedo?," she states. "Ya no tengo. Lo perdí desde que crucé la frontera."*

As globalism seems here to stay, every defiant disassociation with the violent greed of this nation-state and every renewed association with its forgotten peoples help lay the groundwork for the solidarity required of radical action. Ultimately, if we can create comrades from among the displaced and those whose histories contain the story of displacement, we may be able to build a mass movement from the ground up, composed of the experience we share as members of the "other" América.

IN MY COUNTRY

I apologize for the ignorance of the majority of U.S. citizens. I apologize for our hapless fears. I apologize that we have grown so lazy, so indoctrinated by the lure of comfort that we make enemies of all things foreign. But in our defense, I must add that the majority of us are taught so little of value in our schools. We are taught lies and blind patriotism, individualism instead of solidarity, regurgitation instead of critical thinking. We know nothing of the history of non-European countries. The only anticolonial revolution we are taught to admire is that of British Americans in revolt against the British over the ownership of land that belongs to neither. We know little of political courage, except that which comes in the impulsive response to violence. There are exceptions to all of the above, but I am interested in the rule, the U.S. rule of its docile citizenry.

We are not a thought-full people. Corporate-financed mass media

---

* Fear? I'm no longer afraid. I lost my fear once I crossed the border.

has seen to that. Most of us have traded slavery for enslavement to debt and consumption (Big Macs and big cars). But make no mistake. This is a systemic institutionalized ignorance. The poor quality of public education in this country is intended to ensure that most working-class and poor people of color will not become allies for progressive change. They too will grow up to become, at best, members of the service class for the next generation of assimilated middle- and upper-class Americans, who may very well be your own children and grandchildren. At worst, they will continue to be used as fodder for American wars of imperial aggression or to take their required post behind bars in state and federal penitentiaries. They will not form organized revolt because the leaders of conscience among them are too few and too censored (through poverty or imprisonment) to matter in this lifetime, or they unwittingly espouse a política still miréd in misogynist nationalist agendas that will always fail as a revolution.

But in the intimate country of women, the situation is yet worse.

In my country,[6] young single females are murdered en masse and tossed into garbage bags like so much basura. The violent abduction, murder, and rape of hundreds of maquiladora workers in the border town of Juárez, México, in the last decade grew to be the most poignant marker of the feminicidal effect of globalization on women of color.[7] Mexican Indígenas economically displaced from their homelands travel north in search of work. Peopling the assembly factories of U.S. corporations and those of other foreign nations along the border, these teenagers and young women are reduced to corporeally disposable cogs in the industrial wheel of profit.

*No eres nadie,** México and the United States publicly pronounced to these young women and their families by their bilateral governmental indifference to the unsolved crimes. "The women were prostitutes," everyone from the local police to top government officials proclaimed, as if that were justification for murder.[8] I too grew up inside that mixed message of MeXicana culpability, where mothers want to see their daughters free and fulfilled, while at the same time they make

---

* You're nothing, nobody.

prisons of their young lives in the effort to protect them. The murders in Juárez remind me from what.

"Wipe the streets with it" were the desperate words my mother hurled at the door as my sister and I left in rebellion for a night out; our virginities and marriage-less futures at stake in a Mexican woman–hating América.

And this of course is the most dangerous act in the face of misogynist violence, to free ourselves in spite of our mother's, our religion's, our nation's reprisals. This is what we share, isn't it—across class, across national boundaries, and across cultural divides? Violence against women remains the common ground on which women of color in América can reconstruct a living feminist movement. But we have to see ourselves reflected in mirrors not distorted by the imperial gaze—neither West to East, nor rich to poor.

In my country, the most fearless women I know are the ones with nothing left to lose: the survivors of war and genocide and the pornographic hatred of the female. This is the face of La Llorona, the woman whose cries will not be silenced. This is Flor Crisóstomo, the most radical feminist (im)migrant I can imagine, one who speaks for all of us when she declares to the United States: "Ya me sacaste de la oscuridad. Ya tengo una voz. Tu me obligaste de hablar. Entonces aqui estoy hablando y no me van a callar."* Fully knowing that her protest may undoubtedly earn her prison time, she states, "Dentro este propio carcel yo voy a seguir moviendo a mi pueblo."**

In my country, in a borderless América, Flor Crisostomo is our national spokesperson and the women of Juárez, our national martyrs. In my country, borders are remembered as lines drawn in the sand, erased by the impression of a footprint journeying home. To this country, as a Xicana feminist, I extend you citizenship; for, as the Palestinian Michel Khleifi reminded us . . .

By changing just a few words in the story, the story is also yours.

---

*   You took me out of darkness and I now have a voice. You made me speak. So, here I am speaking and I will not be silenced.

** Even from my own jail cell, I will continue to move my people.

Floricanto

For Simin Marashi

How is it that

her

veined olive-soaked hands

spoon out the lemon's meat

in one fell swoop of stainless steel

bitter juice spilling

onto the bed

of lettuce leaf

and tomato

and

I am returned

to daughter, how?

My orphanhood eclipsed by the bright
midday light of possibility
in the crossroad
of generation
and geography,
the familiarity
of kitchen
of husband 'n' wife banter
of a politic forged from bodies
where choices were few
or none.

He, too, calls me back.
Her thin man, the doctor
whom she scolds
como un niño necio.

These "foreigners"
my relative exiles
for whom my mexican tongue rises
in a wild flower field of farsi.

Modern-Day Malinches / 2008

Malinche, my sister-translator—who imagined those ships on the horizon contained a new day. Only to reveal through history that they proffered the demise of all that she had known as a people.

It has taken me years to figure out that my resistance to many academic considerations, especially the framing of ethnic studies exclusively within the context of postmodern theories, is that so many people of color, especially women—even here in the United States— have never been full members of *modern* society; that many of us were born or raised with some other source within us that summoned us to the page, the poem, the politic, and the protest; that we held other ways of knowing that modernity did not reflect; and that we were without the "formal" language to articulate it.[1]

By the mid-1970s, women-of-color activist-writers began a search for that language, a way to create theory out of the conditions of our lives in the plain effort to improve women-of-color lives. We were responding, critically and in political practice, to the impositions of a post-industrialized, (post)modern nation-state that we knew instinctually and experientially did not completely locate us.

Then something got lost for us along the way, I think. I, for one, lost a thread of connection somewhere along the way. Perhaps for a time I too was one of those, who, as M. Jacqui Alexander puts it, "had journeyed far in the mistaken belief that books were the dwelling place of wisdom."[2]

As a young woman, I had once imagined a newly emergent body of radical feminists-of-color activists-thinkers in the teaching fields of América. But now? Now I have come to believe that the majority of "minority"[3] scholars are primarily in conversation with the imperial West, even in their valiant efforts to distinguish themselves from the West. A paradox most academics may be forced to suffer.[4]

I confess for a time I stopped reading anything the academy might consider theory. I wandered, often alone, or with a handful of others, in search of ideas outside the (mentally) gated communities of the university. I found them in the writings of the repressed bodies of young people, in the mad sculpture and paintings of a Xicana Indígena lesbian, in the impossible sacrifice of mothering, and in the pronouncements of tribal leaders, as much as in my own mother's lucidity in the torment of dementia.

This was *This Bridge Called My Back*'s hope, to make theory like that, from the flesh of the "discontents" of modernity. I am still a citizen of that place. For us, there is no postmodern, no postcolonial—in the literal sense of those words—for we remain so colonized from within and without, and especially and specifically as mujeres. We unwittingly continue to do the White Man's bidding. Not all of us, no. But all of us have to struggle against a profound internalized colonization.

Of her own journey as a writer Alexander writes, "She could no longer rely on what was written in books to convey or even arrive at truth."[5] Indeed, the lessons we learned from a world without letter— that female and "colored" inheritance—are almost lost to us, as we continue to put more empty words between ourselves and memory.

Perhaps as Xicanas who walk along the cobblestone corridors of the university, no longer on our knees with a rag in hand scrubbing those very same stones as we did in another lifetime, perhaps we remember the steam of soapy water upon the broad plane of our chata face, the fire in the glint of metal reflecting off a galvanized bucket. Perhaps we reside in that in-between location as interpreters between worlds — the remembered and postmodern — we, the Nepantleras of Anzaldúa's imaginings.

Maybe we *are* modern-day Malinches. Not traitors but translators, women who tread dangerously among the enemy, driven by a vision of change that may only be intuitively known. This is what is said of Malinalli's vision.[6]

Still, a word of caution:

When you "sleep with the enemy," the next thing you know you've birthed a mixed-blood kid named Martín, who is sent across the sea to fight against the Moors, then dies, without rank, in the name of his imperial father.[7]

He is never returned to the Indian mother.

The Indian mother is us.

What's Race Gotta Do With It? / 2008

ON THE ELECTION OF BARACK OBAMA

My fifteen-year-old son doesn't like to hear of my doubts about President-Elect Barack Obama. He just wants for once in his young life to feel good about his president and his country. But had I been among that Grant Park Chicago crowd at Barack Obama's election-night victory speech when he announced, "If there is anyone out there who still doubts that America is a place where all things are possible . . . ," courage would have required me to raise my hand as one of the doubters.

But I was not in the crowd that night. Instead I was home with my partner and our teenaged kids, along with the "he's-not-my-boyfriend" boyfriend of the elder teen. We had arrived back at the house just in time, ordering pizza en route, to arrive in front of the TV set as voting sites closed across California.

Initially, we had tried to find a "crowd" with which to celebrate Obama's election, but our brief trip to a party at an art center in San Francisco ended abruptly. On entering the center, two giant screens displayed the CNN coverage of the elections and our son immediately gravitated to one. Once the rest of us found our seats, however, the other screen began to display a series of "colorful" images of unspecified Third World peoples performing various ceremonial rituals. Especially astute in manners of cultural appropriation, my partner, Linda, whispered into my ear impassively, "What does this have to do with the election?"

Nothing as far as I could tell, but this was a Bay Area artists' celebration, which meant "partying" could be anything. That night it urged the crowd of artists and arts aficionados to join a ritualized circle dance. Lakota drum at the center, dozens of (mostly white) people joined the circle, bouncing up and down to a quasi–American Indian rhythm, some yelping out in a manner I imagined an untrained ear might consider primal. And with that, my family and I rose from our seats and left.

"Consciousness spoils your time," I always say to my students; but none of us was having a good time that night, including our kids, who by now are used to these sudden conscienced departures from public events. Even they, certainly old enough to begin cultivating their own political views, were uncomfortable with the circle dance because as Xicanos they were raised to know what Indian is and what it is not. So an hour later, we are back home in Oakland performing our own ritual of pizza and watching the election results on the tube. (Yes, we still have a television with a tube.) I am not eating pizza, as I am on the second day of a fast in solidarity with the "Fast for Our Future" protesters down in La Placita in Los Angeles.[1]

"Good. More for me," my son says irreverently, grabbing another slice from the box. He loves it, just a little, that fifteen-year-old boy rebellion against his mother's politics. Then the moment we had been waiting for arrives, the announcement that Obama has secured enough electoral votes to win the election, as the landslide figures come tumbling in. The kids are ecstatic, although the nineteen-year-old girl shows more reserve in front of the "not-boyfriend," her feet snuggled under him on the couch. I get a call from my sister first and then my dad, but it's my dad's words that hit me. "I haven't seen anything like this since 1940 and FDR's landslide." *This Depression-era Democrat hasn't been this optimistic in sixty-eight years*, I think, with a brief reprieve in 1960 with the election of John F. Kennedy.

Happy days are here again.

Hearing Obama's words—addressing anyone out there "who still questions the power of our democracy"—the most "doubt" I feel free to visibly express, even in my own living room, is the sidelong glance I give to Linda, who rolls her ever-critical eyes into her forehead as if to say, "I know." Somehow neither of us wants to bring down the kids' electoral high, their sudden sense of public membership in mainstream politics of the day. After all, as family members in our Xicana-lesbian–headed household, they swallow the issues of political marginalization with their daily breakfast. But in many ways, Linda's and my doubt responds to the same inequity that made staying at that San Francisco artist celebration impossible—a multiculturalism that is not truly multicultural in that it is imagined and defined by whites. The same could be said about the 2008 presidential campaign.

Throughout Obama's campaign, the needs of the urban poor, who for the most part are communities of color, were completely erased from the national debate. To speak of poverty and the working poor in the United States, Obama would have had to face the barbed-wire wall of racist, inhumane immigration policies and the entrenched violence and resultant ever-expanding prison system that has emerged from the government's full-scale abandonment of the inner city. In short, he would have had to bring "race" into the national discussion. Since much of Obama's campaign had been directed at reassuring middle-class white Americans that although a Black man, he represents their interests, Obama could not afford to address these issues directly and expect to win.

Obama's "A More Perfect Union" speech, delivered on March 18 of this year in Philadelphia, was the notable exception. It came in response to the right-wing media's sound-bite portrayal of Obama's former pastor, Reverend Jeremiah Wright. Accused of being anti-American and a terrorist sympathizer by association, Obama was required to speak on the subject of "Race in America" (and he did so with uncanny honesty). The speech was in many ways a truly noble and compassionate attempt on Obama's part to educate whites about African Americans' justified anger and dis-identification with the U.S. government. His words in many ways proffered to white America a rare opportunity—to be gently spoon-fed the bitter pill of American racism by an individual who had been reared within the context of middle-class white America, and therefore holds great empathy for it (and, most poignantly, even for its prejudices).

At the same time Obama understands what it is to walk the "main streets" of this country marked by the color of his skin. This, in turn, served to build in Obama a politic as a self-identified Black American, for whom racism factors integrally into questions of democracy. Obama's ability to speak bilingually in this way (the language of both white and Black America) is not a product of his biraciality per se. Had his background been the reverse, had he been fathered by an absent white man and raised within the context of an African American working-class maternal family, Obama would not have been allowed the same intimate entrance into the white world and could not have emerged versed in the biculturalism needed to respond to a culturally segregated America.

Obama's own memoir acknowledges that, without familial role models, he had to learn to be a Black man in America. His teachers were African American elders, students—men and women alike—as well as a cadre of Black political figures, community-organizer mothers, and in their hopelessness, even those young men in the hood hanging out on street corners of Chicago. His teachers were also found in the Black Church, most notably in the person of Reverend Jeremiah Wright.

The media circus surrounding Wright's sermons illustrates that white Americans do not want to know how angry people of color are in this country and certainly do not want a president who in anyway relates to—or worse, shares a politic with—the raging discontents. Many of us "discontents" secretly hoped that Obama really did agree with Wright's critique that U.S. foreign policy served to create the conditions for 9/11; and we excused Obama's ultimate disavowal of Wright (as we did much of Obama's politically moderate and conciliatory positions) with the mantra "he is just trying to get elected first."

The jubilant response to Obama's election tells me one thing above all else: how disheartened the citizens of the United States have been; how eight years of the George W. Bush regime has shattered a deep faith that the government of the United States truly represents Middle America's economic interests. For it was the shattered economy, as impacted by the unconscionable spending in Iraq, that ultimately tipped the electoral scale in Obama's favor. Unfortunately, race—that is, a true national reckoning with racial discrimination—had little to do with it.

Ironically, this seems to have been the best-kept secret among liberal Democrat supporters who, throughout the campaign, promoted the idea that Obama's election as a Black American would mean the guarantee of a whole list of progressive political changes on Capitol Hill, especially equity for people of color. Young folks, Latino and Black political organizations, and most of those two million on Obama's now infamous database jumped on the bandwagon of this hope.

Days before the election, I scanned YouTube for images of the campaign, especially among Latino and Latina voters. There were trios of músicos and mariachi groups singing corridos in Obama's honor ("Obámanos," la Raza cries!); images of the candidate sporting a ranchero-style cowboy hat; sixties-esque black-and-white Chicago street shots of Obama during his community organizing days. In several videos, Obama appears in shirt-sleeves, shaking hands with the populace; this image is spliced in with pictures of a serape-cloaked César Chávez at a United Farm Workers (UFW) demonstration, looking gaunt and Gandhi-like after an extended political fast: all these emotionally evocative images for a candidate who has been virtually mute on the question of immigrant rights. There were dozens of other videos as well—especially those directed at young voters in MTV hip-hop format. Over and over again, the same tape replays—Obama pictured addressing crowds of thousands with Martin Luther King Jr.'s "I Have a Dream" speech reverberating in the background.

As someone old enough to have actually witnessed the civil rights and farm worker movements, the juxtaposition of the often politically moderate Barack with César and Martin, two figures of proven heroism and political courage, stunned me. The images are meant to suggest that Obama is a man of the people, of the poor, of the disenfranchised—assertions which remain profoundly untested. On the one hand, their vacuity reflects the measure of our desire for political change; on the other, for someone who cut her suspect-the-government teeth on books like George Orwell's *1984* and Joe McGinniss's *The Selling of the President* (Richard M. Nixon), they expose the alarming susceptibility of a generation of people (consumers) accustomed to viewing the computer monitor and television screen as real.

True confession: I want to believe, as Obama prompts, that "yes, we can." Or as coined by Dolores Huerta, vice president of the UFW, who originated the political slogan during César Chávez's 1972 fast, "Sí se puede."[2] Since the election of Obama, I have been keeping a file of emails from all the constituencies that have "hopes" for the president-elect. They are my sister, who as a public school teacher and then principal for over thirty years, waits expectantly for Obama to reverse the discriminatory effects of George W. Bush's No Child Left Behind Act. They are artists eager to see extinguished the censorship inherent in the increasing privatization of the arts in hope of a new era of expanded artistic expression through publicly funded support. They are generations of Cuban Americans and their allies anxiously awaiting the end to the economic embargo against Cuba. They are environmental groups, hoping to reverse the Bush administration's efforts to dismantle the power of the Environmental Protection Agency. They are California Indian tribes struggling for federal recognition; as they are the more than one hundred Xicano youth who held a twenty-one-day hunger strike in front of La Placita Church in downtown Los Angeles to urge Latinos and Latinas to vote. Their hope? That the president-elect will halt through executive order all U.S. Immigration and Customs Enforcement raids.

I was heartened in the final weeks before the election to finally see Raza organizing along their own list of "hopes" or, better stated, "mandates" for their would-be president. Maybe one of the greatest disappointments to me in the 2008 presidential campaign was how the national dialogue reduced race and racism to a Black and white issue.

The specific concerns of East and West Asian Americans, Latinos and Latinas, and Native peoples were seldom specifically addressed in campaign speeches. Instead our communities were relegated to a kind of roll call of generic "others." The campaign in many ways laid bare what most non–African American people of color already know, but seldom acknowledge publicly: that when this country thinks about "race," it thinks Black and back, but not back far enough because it never gets to what Indian people remember. The bitter history of Black slavery that shaped what Obama has called that "imperfect" union still haunts the collective psyche of white America. Ironically, Black people represent white America's greatest fear and loathing as well as its greatest hope for moral redemption. Other people of color as a whole remain invisible or are perceived as of little political consequence, except as the scapegoats for economic and national-security anxiety.

How can the national consciousness of a country profess to detest its history of slavery while slave methods continue to exist just beneath the radar of civic awareness? How else to explain a political leadership and a majority citizenry that allows undocumented Indigenous American workers (from México, El Salvador, Guatemala) to be hunted down like dogs in the night, when all they are trying to do is to free themselves from the slavery of U.S.-induced poverty? How is it that ordinary immigrant Muslims are still held in detention camps as never-tried, would-be or could-be terrorists? How to account for a genocidal death rate within Native America, where a man of fifty-five is considered an elder within his tribe because statistics predict he's not likely to see sixty? How does Anglo-America allow a detained and pregnant undocumented worker to wear an electronic ankle bracelet on one leg while her children still cling to the other? This is the racism that falls between the cracks of the Black and white divide. This is the crack in the world that runs along the southern border and within the broken-treatied territories of a very flawed United States.

Throughout Obama's campaign I have been thinking long and hard about his theme of the "audacity of hope," which he used as the title of his second book and drew from one of Reverend Wright's impassioned sermons. It is a beautiful phrase, really, suggesting that the conditions of our times are such that it takes great daring to still believe that this country really belongs to its people.

There is no denying the power of Barack Obama's oratory, both in style and in substance. In many ways, Obama is the poet that our American author-laureate, Toni Morrison, professes—a man who understands the art and power of language eloquently and precisely rendered. Where the Republican Party spoke generically of "Joe Six-Pack" and "Joe Plumber," Obama—with the support, of course, of skilled speechwriting craftspeople—utilized the one story, the intimate detail, the nuanced single life, as a way of entering the collective heart of millions.

This is real political genius, as is the story of Ann Nixon Cooper, the 106-year-old African American woman, whom Barack employs as the cornerstone of his victory speech. If in one lifetime, a single person can emerge from origins wherein she was denied the vote—as a woman and a Negro—to arrive at a moment in history where her vote helps elect the first African American president, her story tells us that hope for change in this country can be realized for each and every one of us.

This is how we are meant to understand her story, that we too will be uplifted by the resurrected moral character of this country. Through the story of Ann Nixon Cooper, the issue of racism finally reemerges in Obama's campaign, but this time we have triumphed over it. Through the election of Obama, all of us—Black, white, Asian, Native—are absolved of the United States' past inequities, its unspeakable violences, its victims' requisite rage. The power of Obama's rhetorical style, even this mandate of hope, is not original to him, but nonetheless skillfully executed. It emerges from the best of the radical tradition of the president-elect's greatest oratory teacher, the Black Church—the church of the emancipated American slave—with just the right touch of twenty-first-century cool.

Had I been present at Obama's victory speech, I would have had to raise my hand as a doubter because the truth is, despite the United States' rhetoric of democracy, despite a federal house of elected representatives, a "free" public school system, a system of checks and balances, a bill of rights and a constitution inspired by the Iroquois; despite that ever-argument "well at least in America you have the right to speak up," this country is riddled with societal inequities. It teaches consumer citizenship over social responsibility; espouses the pursuit of profit as an American ethos; morally justifies privileging the lives of U.S. citizens over non-European "foreigners" domestically and abroad; and still operates as if it had time and options about global warming. I would have raised my hand as a doubter because Barack Obama was not elected by an organized *movement of people* with an organized strategy for social justice. He was elected through "hope" that *one man* could change a intricate system of discrimination, a system that has never represented the needs of the most disenfranchised in this country—the non-citizen, the Indigenous, the property-less, the impoverished, the ethnic or racial minority, and the disabled. *One man cannot.*

Years ago in the late 1970s and during the brief and minor-scale heyday of the women-of-color feminist movement, my political activism was in many ways inspired by a small group of Boston-based Black women, many of them lesbians, called the Combahee River Collective. In 1977, they produced a manifesto on Black feminism, one line of which clarified for me the purpose of progressive political activism in this country. It read, "If Black women were free it would mean that everyone else would have to be free since our freedom would necessitate the destruction of all the systems of oppression."[3]

This idea that the litmus test for democracy is not measured by the rich, nor the "majority" middle class (which Obama's campaign suggested), but by the condition of the disempowered poor (especially women and children of color), has carried me ideologically through the last thirty years of political activism. All along I (we) have witnessed the passage of anti–affirmative action and English-only measures, legislation against reproductive rights for women, the increased criminalization and dehumanization of undocumented immigrants and the militarization of the border, the virtual disappearance of a whole generation of young men of color to gang warfare and the prison industry, and the illegal invasion and occupation of a foreign sovereign nation resulting in more than four thousand U.S. military deaths and nearly one hundred thousand documented civilian deaths.[4] The list goes on. Still, to quote the slogan of my NBA home team, the underdog Golden State Warriors who battled their way to the 2008 playoffs, "We Believe." But a life of political engagement is not a basketball game nor is the presidency about rock stars; it is about political *practice*.

"Juan Crow" is what the journalist Roberto Lovato has called the current Latino experience of the same segregationist policies exhibited during Jim Crow. What brought an end to Jim Crow in the South? Protest. As protest also brought an end to the Vietnam War, the resignation of a U.S. president (Nixon), the formation of the United Farm Workers union, and the birth of ethnic studies programs throughout the country. Ironically, more youth turned out to vote in this election than they had since 1968. But in 1968, that youth vote required an end to the war and a government responsive to growing demands of communities of color. This was the period of the Black Panthers and the American Indian and Chicano movements. In 1968, Democrats lost the election to Richard Nixon following the assassination of their lead candidate, Robert F. Kennedy. Two months earlier Martin Luther King Jr. had also been assassinated. King's death sentence was written the moment he connected the civil rights struggle to the anti-war movement, and specifically to the corporate profit being gained through the Vietnam War.

So, if you ever wonder what the price of radicalism is in a corporate "democracy," it is death; the death of our most fierce and courageous leaders. In that respect, maybe Obama is wise to have played it safe thus far. But we all know he is not safe. His visibility as a president who can singularly inspire and perhaps enact social and economic changes that threaten Corporate America's pocketbook puts his life in danger. That combined with a fundamental racism that still pervades the institutional structures and private mindsets of many a red state creates a lethal prescription for sanctioned assassination. There is no question about the courage required of Obama to step into such a vulnerable site of international exposure.

Possibly the knowledge of such fragility—that a single life is just that, one life that can easily be extinguished—brought an air of soberness to Obama's victory speech. There was a profound sense of the deep burden he was about to assume as president of the United States. There was little elation on his part, as he stood before thousands with what appeared to be real humility in the face of the awesomeness of the task before him. Long gone was the cowboy, "good-old-boy" bravado to which we had become accustomed through his predecessor. All this gave me some measure of confidence in Obama and indeed, hope. But mostly what gave me hope was that the president-elect gave the "victory" back to us, reverberating what he had said at the Democratic National Convention; that his election was not about himself, but about us. His effectiveness as a president ultimately depends not just on the electorate but on the people of the United States—all of us who make our lives here within these borders—what we require of our leadership and of ourselves in the effort to change the very meaning of U.S. "citizenship." One life can be easily extinguished, but a movement of many cannot.

As a teary-eyed Jesse Jackson stated after Obama's victory speech, his election was not a singular feat, but the result of the enduring and courageous efforts of those who had come before. He mentioned Thurgood Marshall and Martin Luther King Jr. To that list of courageous predecessors I would add Jackson's own name, along with Shirley Chisholm and, of course (the unmentionable during Obama's campaign), Malcolm X. "Because they broke down walls," Jesse Jackson added, "Obama is able to build bridges."

It is the tenacity of shared hope that prevails. This is what can make a grown man cry: an insistent faith held by entire generations of people who preceded Obama and who today, in small numbers, continue to demonstrate the courage of protest. This is my hope, that amid this symbolic act of change—which is all we can really say for sure about the election of Barack Obama—those numbers are, at last, growing; for hope is tenacious and contagious; and cynicism, ultimately useless to our children and those who follow them.

A few days after the election, my fifteen-year-old son approached me with a question: "Do you still have that book about Obama?" I had read and recommended *Dreams from My Father* to him several months earlier. My son, brown-skinned and middle-class, living a short but complex distance from his hometown barrio, may very well suffer some of the same questions about racial identity that the young Barack experienced. I thought the book might be good for him. At the time, Rafa had politely declined my offer, always preferring a basketball to anything remotely resembling a book. Months later, he stands at my office door requesting to read the man's words.

Cynicism aside, the gesture gave me hope; that my son—and by extension a new generation of youth of color—may be interested in finding a language of self-reflection for their own rocky road in a twenty-first-century America. "Post-race" we are not.

"We'll see what he does once in office," I say with predictable critical caution, as I hand him the worn-edged paper edition. "You're so radical," he responds. Still, I swear I detect a hint of familial pride in his smile as walks out the door toward his future.

This Benighted Nation We Name Home / 2009

ON THE FORTIETH ANNIVERSARY
OF ETHNIC STUDIES

Forty years is a long time. Forty years ago, here in the United States, there were true activist visionaries and mass movements to enact those visions. Forty years ago, there were the recently murdered Martin Luther King Jr., the also assassinated Malcolm X, the emergent Black lesbian poet Audre Lorde. There was a César Chávez and a viable farm workers' movement, propped up by the agit-prop of a teatro para un movimiento campesino. There was soon to be the Stonewall rebellion (forty years old in June 2009) on one coast; and a year later on the opposite coast, the Chicano Moratorium, which culminated in the murder of the journalist Ruben Salazar by the Los Angeles police. At the same time Pilipino Americans held firm in a nine-year anti-eviction campaign in support of their elders in San Francisco's Manilatown International Hotel. Forty years ago, there was a military draft, which people of conscientious objection to the Vietnam War could resist, not the mercenary military apparatus we see today. On November 20, forty years ago, the American Indian movement began a nineteen-month occupation of Alcatraz Island.

Forty years ago, revolution was on the minds of everyone in the country, even the most timid and conservative. How could it have been otherwise as revolution reflected off brown faces, shouting, "Boycott Grapes!" beneath protest placards on every other Los Angeles street corner. It exploded in Agent Orange Technicolor and in the napalm droppings onto Southeast Asian jungles and villages displayed on evening news. And, it slept in the burnt rubble of ghetto liquor stores after a black night's Black rebellion.

Like so many of my generation, coming of age in those times, I had imagined that by 2009 the seeds of radical transformation that had been sown in the fields of such struggle would have by now sprouted into fully coalesced, people-of-color self-sustaining communities—con voz y vota—throughout the United States. Of course, forty years ago we could never have accounted for a technological revolution, which helped elect the first Black president. Nor could we have anticipated the current state of globalization and the corporate privatization of the planet, including its most precious resource, water. We did not predict global warming forty years ago. Pity that we did not.

BACK IN THE DAY

I am sure students are tired of hearing about "back in the day"—from their aging professors and their still-bearded Uncle Chato, with a beer in one hand and the television remote in the other. But I do not wax nostalgic about forty years ago. I use it as a point of critical departure in order to ask, *What happened to the people-of-color movement?* I echo the words of the late Richard Aoki, a Sansei Black Panther and activist in the Third World Liberation Front, who stated: "We didn't lose in the sixties, we just didn't finish the job."[1]

Recently, I was present when the veterano teatrista Luis Valdez, his voice swelling with rage, lambasted this country's continual denial of its entrenched racism.[2] He indicted a deluded United States that imagined that with a Black man in the White House the country had eradicated racism, even as we stand by and witness the most flagrant human-rights abuses leveled against the Mexican immigrant. Anti-Mexican sentiment is justified in the face of a weakening economic system and threats of international contagion.[3] But what disease is the Mexican immigrant passing across the border except the illness of impoverished dislocation, engineered by the corrupt treaties between governments fueled by corporate interest? We are certainly no better off than we were forty years ago in terms of the racialization of poverty.

So, what happened to Black liberation, El Movimiento, and the American Indian movement? Certainly the need for race- or ethnic-based struggle has not disappeared. Through critical hindsight, many recognize that sexism and homophobia weakened the integrity of our movements and obstructed the potential of key leadership positions. Certainly COINTELPRO did its part to divide our movements from within,[4] with the assassinations, the incarcerations, and the betrayals that came as a result of such infiltrations. But how was it possible that by the 1980s and the election of Ronald Reagan to the White House, the political climate took such a sudden and dramatic shift that progressive grass-roots political movement (with some exceptions)[5] virtually disappeared from the streets of this country? Reagan, who as governor of California in 1969 called in troops to repel the Third World Liberation Front student strikes, initiated "Reaganomics" as president a decade later. By the mid-1980s, Reagan's actor smile and easy oratory eloquence had won the hearts and minds of Middle America, and laid the groundwork for the corporate welfare state we suffer today.

Two years before Reagan's election, Proposition 13, a precursor to Reaganomics, was passed in California. It capped property taxes at 1 percent of their value and signed into law the requirement of a two-thirds majority to increase state-tax rates. The unconscionable financial disaster the State of California finds itself in over thirty years later (which is far worse than the national picture) can be directly attributed to Proposition 13.

In many ways, the passage of that proposition in California anticipated the changing terrain of U.S. values, where freedom became un-

abashedly conflated with free enterprise, and corporate profit (with reduced taxation) became the solution for all social inequities. According
to Reagan's plan, greater corporate gains from augmented tax relief
would somehow magically "trickle down" to even the lowest rung of
society's ladder in the form of jobs and dollars exchanging hands. If
somehow you missed the buck, it was because you were lagging; that
is, not competing effectively. Racism, sexism, and historical poverty
played no role in one's ability to succeed or not. After all, there was
always the token "exceptional" person of color to extol as evidence of
the plan's virtue.

The economic policies Reagan initiated in the 1980s would come
to full realization twenty years later during the George W. Bush years.
Anything or anyone interrupting profit by utilizing tax revenue for social welfare became an enemy of the state, including the single mother
needing assistance; poor and working-class youth of color seeking an
equitable public education; the impoverished elder needing home care;
and, in general, the discontented public demanding a socially just economy. Again, California would anticipate the political climate of the
nation. In the 1990s the state's strategy to eliminate "the needy" was
to criminalize the poor through legislation, which gave rise to some
of the most virulent racist legislation in the state's history: the "three
strikes you're out" statute (Proposition 184), the Gang Violence and
Juvenile Crime Prevention Act (Proposition 21), and anti-immigration
bills, like Proposition 187.

Prisons, after all, are still good for business.

NEITHER SILENT NOR MAJORITY

Ironically, what the reactionary laws of that decade and after could not
completely accomplish[6] is now being achieved de facto through California's budget crisis. In a state without funds, discrimination against
anyone dependent on state funding becomes justified through budget
cuts. Hardest hit, of course, is California's educational system. It is not
accidental that the state's willingness to sacrifice the education of the
next generation comes at a time in California history where people of
color are now the majority. For most people of color, education is the
only avenue for gaining the skills, knowledges, and training to attain

a leadership role in society. Now that road is effectively blocked, with community college programs being slashed and some California state universities refusing to accept transfer students from those same community colleges.

It *is* as insidious as it seems. California serves as a harbinger of the political future of the nation. No one's saying it (not with a Black man in the White House), but "white-minority rule" is being systematically institutionalized by right-wing Republicans, in collusion with "moderate" Democrats. The phenomenon of the Tea Party movement and the unfounded resistance to Obama's defanged healthcare plan speak of something sinister afoot in this land. In their misguided response to a failing economic system, white (Middle) Americans—that "silent majority," now neither silent nor comfortably the majority—are actively organizing to regain their country as their forefathers designed it, where people of color remain on the margins of the public life.

I haven't always held such brutal pessimism about my "countrymen's" motives. I confess that my optimism (or naiveté) paradoxically resurfaced in the last months of the George W. Bush regime, when I had hoped—as I had after 9/11—that the United States' imminent economic collapse would provide our legislators and us with a *second* chance at national self-reflection. Was it too much expect that the most militarized, profit-hungry nation in the world might take a few weeks, months, or even years to reevaluate the fundamental problems with a unregulated globalized market economy? One might have begun the inquiry by asking a Mixtec day laborer in front of the Kragen Auto Parts in the Fruitvale barrio what had become of his plot of maize in Oaxaca since the implementation of the North American Free Trade Agreement.

Hypocritically, right-wingers called Obama a socialist, even as the Bush administration nationalized the losses of Corporate America. Still, Obama made no protest against the "bailout." Along with the rest of our national legislators, as a U.S. senator he picked up the congressional shovel to dig the rich man out of the grave of his own greed, while all along we were told that the death of capitalism would mean the death of us. But wasn't this the economic collapse for which we critics of Corporate America had been waiting? The threatened failure of the U.S. economy sent first-world and dependent Third World economies into an inevitable downspin. Karl Marx had predicted as much. Did not this international earthquake in the fault line of transnational pirating offer our nation the opportunity for foundational economic reconstruction?

The cure-all notion that the way to save the economy is to get Americans "buying" again—at all costs—is at its base, antithetical to any common-sense understanding of long-term economic and environmental sustainability. One might remember that after 9/11 we were told the same thing—that buying was the most patriotic thing we could do. Still, even after the bailouts to the financial industry that were intended to stimulate the economy (a goal which would have been better achieved by viable employment projects), economic relief has failed to "trickle down" to Main Street as promised. Meanwhile, Wall Street recovers its losses and ruthlessly continues the business of profit as usual.

We don't need more cars, more vacation homes, more suburban four-bedroom-plus-family-room-plus-three-car-garage-single-family dwellings devouring what little green space is left surrounding our major cities. Nor do we need the impossible mortgages and debt that accompany them. We need truly effective mass-transit systems linking metropolitan areas and railways linking regions. We need affordable, built-to-last, fuel-efficient housing for everyone, which makes renting and group ownership a stable and attractive alternative to the individual property mortgage. We need a national healthcare program and a reconstituted public education system—from preschool to PhD. In short, we need to reconstruct the American Dream so that it is environmentally responsible and ethically sound, built upon the idea of reciprocity among community members and their environment, instead of alienated individual consumerism.

What happened to our movement? The current economic crisis makes it patently evident. It was literally bought off.

Today's graduates have come of age in a time when, for at least a quarter century, consumerism has been unequivocally conflated in the popular imagination with citizenship. We have gleaned no other message from the mass media, except that in order to maintain our individual freedom we must maintain the "free enterprise" of those who have enslaved us to this new American ethic. What the Declaration of Independence described as an unalienable right—"the pursuit of happiness"—has been reconfigured for the populace as the "pursuit of purchasing power." Even the so-called public university system, which costs considerably to attend, is being sustained by corporate interests and the ethics of competitive privatization. So, in many ways today's young people are not to blame, but they are *responsible* because it will be up to this generation and those that follow to literally stop passing the buck to the rich guys.

A SOVEREIGN EDUCATION

Every twentieth-century liberation movement has proven that the possibility for real equity is only achieved by first gaining political autonomy. Historically, most radical political movements that remain viable eventually evolve into some form of political compromise; but the degree to which social reform is achieved is measured by the radicalism of the starting point. Begin at the far left from an informed position, I tell my students, so that when the middle ground is reached, it remains progressive.

As people committed to social justice, we must know the difference between reform and radical action, develop a politic based on the strategic employment of both, and recognize how each continues to shape the political landscape. Barack Obama's conciliatory politics may have won him office, but they have yet to win advancements in social equity for the neediest in this country. The same could be said of the present state of the university system. A culturally equitable program of study for people of color has yet to be achieved, because equity as defined by the university means *integration* into the dominant culture, without altering the culture of Euro-American dominance within or outside the University.

The fact that forty years after the Third World Liberation Front strike, the University of California, Berkeley, catalogue now lists hundreds of courses dealing with race is an impressive achievement, but it does not mean the job was finished, as Richard Aoki noted, because the power differential in the university system has not shifted, as it has not shifted for our communities. Neither more race-related courses nor more people of color occupying the academic hierarchal positions traditionally allocated to white men indicate equity within the university system. What is required is the equity of *ideas* that impact people and public policy.

We do not forget that "ethnic studies" was the *compromise* to the Third World Liberation Front's demand for the establishment of an autonomous "Third World College." As people living in what Rodolfo Acuña called "Occupied America,"[7] we never wanted mere inclusion in the education systems of Euro-America; we wanted to create curriculum in which our ethnicities' histories, philosophies, religions, sciences and technologies, cultural values, and aesthetics served as the grounding point for the interpretation of, and intersection with, Europe, Euro-America, and other cultures of the world.[8] Without a fair playing field, which can only be realized through a sovereign education first, what foundational gains does integration achieve?

The original founders of the concept of a Third World College might very well have predicted the ultimate outcome of the compromise in establishing an ethnic studies department: the gradual erosion of the cultural integrity of our studies, a less than complete investigation of own ethnic and culturally based theories of knowledge, and the institutional devaluation of "street knowledge" honed from direct social activism. Ethnic studies did not mean merely training ourselves to be translators between our home cultures and the U.S. academy; and yet, perhaps that is what it has become.

In many ways, ethnic studies today holds a kind of contradictory position in the academy. Even as it falls prey to Westernization, ethnic studies often provides students of color with a physical and intellectual home on college campuses. For me, the ethnic studies classroom remains a small piece of unclaimed territory—this ten-week dialogue I have with my students—a kind of extended "si fuera posible" moment. *If it were possible*, what questions would we ask of our elders, our storytellers, our ancestors, our scribes and scientists? I also know that the ethnic studies classroom has failed to successfully integrate other forms of knowledges that are not quantifiable by academic standards. Our artists and artisans (if a distinction should even be drawn between them) and Indigenous holders of knowledges (those that remain) have been given little place, outside of token appearances, in the college class-

room, and the classroom has seldom found its way into their community of ideas and cultural practices.

Even as I write this—using words like *elder* and *indigenous*—I worry
about how we tend to interpret such concepts too literally. In defense of
our embattled cultures, we do not often allow ideas to grow within the
context of an evolving community base, to live within the site of political contradictions, to abnegate our own need to control knowledge in
the plain effort to listen on the road to learning. I find this especially the
case with some young men who continue to find ethnic studies mentors
who imagine they can achieve a true understanding of our ethnicities
and cultures without (at least in earnest intention) embodying the eyes
of the impoverished, the aged, the female, and the queer.

I sometimes wonder if perhaps non-cooperation with the academy may
proffer a more effective approach toward building a truly "decolonial"
educational system for people of color of all classes. At least, I know
that this has to be one prong in our approach to education; to ensure
that "teaching"—the exchange of skills and knowledges—continues to
occur outside of public education, even as we work to transform the
public education system from within. In the 1970s, many of us took our
college educations and developed free schools and universities (outside
of academia) where teachers were selected not on the basis of degrees,
but for their recognized living practice as community educators. Those
free schools, however, always emerged from within the broader political framework of people-of-color, feminist, and gay movements. Certainly, without community-based campaigns for the radical reconstruction of our public schools and our public health and welfare systems,
supported by an equitable tax system, we are just playing at the rhetoric
of "de-colonization." Free the mind and the body will follow. But free
the body, and the mind will have a *chance* to follow.

FREE THE BODY

You tell me what has changed. You tell me what a Black president
means for the average Black American. Tell me how it is humanely
permissible to hold undocumented immigrants in detention camps,

outfit pregnant women with electronic bracelets to track their where-
abouts, and uphold a war where indebted monies continue to be spent
on the violent militarized occupation of foreign countries, instead of
indigenous-originated programs to rebuild the broken infrastructure
resulting from failed regimes. As the late historian and social activist
Howard Zinn states, "If you want to end terrorism, you have to stop
being terrorists."9

This includes terrorism at home. On New Year's morning in 2009,
a nervous, trigger-happy, white transit cop in Oakland "accidentally"
murders Oscar Grant, a young unarmed African American male. In
videos, Grant can be seen with his face down in the cement and hands
behind his back when the shooting takes place. The twenty-two-year-
old's death should tell us a great deal about the state of our ever internal colonization in white America. In 2009, all over this country the
average "Joe Six-Pack" cop still commutes into the inner city from the
suburbs to police people of color. Forty years after the radical activism
of the sixties, people-of-color communities still do not have access to
the skills, training, and funding to govern our own communities.

A few months after the murder of Oscar Grant, four white cops are
lauded as heroes after being killed by a fleeing Lovelle Mixon, an African American parolee, who was also gunned down in a final shootout.
Grant's death by a white policeman was suddenly eclipsed by the murder of the four policemen by a Black man. Somehow the murders were
connected in both the Black and white communities' eyes, but from
very different vantage points. At the memorial service for the policemen (with several state dignitaries present) Black officials kept a notice-
ably low profile because the (unofficial) subtext was that Oakland's
Black community was foundationally culpable for *all* the murders, like
Mexicans are foundationally diseased, and they will, no doubt, infect
us, if we don't remain vigilant and keep that border between North and
South and Black and white closed.

My fifteen-year-old son complains to his parents, "Not everything
is political." I know he is burdened by our relentless quotidian critique
and is trying to figure out how to rebel against the rebel-parents in a
way that will not align him with the enemy. For it is a war, we tell him,
not always so kindly, when as women beyond the half-century mark,

we can testify to the relentless attrition in the United States of the values of a real social democracy for people-of-color communities and the indeed murderous toll it takes on our bodies, minds, and spirits.

SI FUERA POSÍBLE

Ten years from now, on the fiftieth anniversary of the Third World Strike, I would like to be able to say that I had witnessed in the decade that lies ahead of us a radical change in consciousness. I would like to believe, "si fuera possible," that somehow, some way this country's recent college graduates and the generations that follow will subvert the University, make the University theirs somehow; that they will never stop demanding;[10] that they will not settle for integration but instead require distinction of themselves independent of the academy's sanction; that teaching and learning as women and men of color will mean something distinct from the structures that house that learning; that as feminists and race activists, they will remain renegades of the system; that they will become very precise about language, not lazy, and will not appropriate other, more insidious colonial tongues, but draw as fiercely as they can from the languages shaped by their origins and the critical education they acquire along the way toward revolt; that they will remain wide- and eagle-eyed in their amazed perception of the ever-cleverness of colonization, its myriad forever-shifting disguises, its friendly liberal countenance; that they will never relax, but remain always on flexed, always-suspect toes, wary of co-optation; that they will serve as great models of hope for subsequent generations in their insistence on the free life of the mind. *And the body* will *follow, I promise*.

"What does [all] this have to do with the price of beans?"[11] In other words, *Where is your work?* Our communities need engineers, doctors, social workers, policy makers, educators, city planners, environmentalists, architects, biologists, physicists, and more. The university ostensibly provides people of color with the training to assume these roles, if one can manage the financial costs and survive the "mind"-field of a colonial education. But, we equally need students who think outside the system.

What are you reading? To whom are you listening? Who will be your teachers and whom will you teach? How will you put yourselves in those sites where you continue to question systems of power? As you construct your families, to what degree will you challenge the United States' cultural impositions on the minds of your children? To what degree will you cooperate with mainstream expectations about progress, gender roles, coupling in sex and in marriage, a spirituality devoid of progressive activism?

Do not waste your time. Choose life work, not a career, one that grows and moves with you as you evolve. Stop depending economically on your parents. Learn autonomy and self-sufficiency so that you can come home free men and women. If your family is in need, help them. But as hard as it may be to accept, you did not get your degrees to serve their dreams, but to fulfill your own, giving back to your larger family, su pueblo, in the way your conscience and consciousness will dictate.

As people of conscience, we write, we think, we work in the face of death. Some days it seems that it is the only thing worth doing, to counter injustice in this way; for injustice—for perpetrator and victim—kills spirit. We are in search of ideas that can separate the strands of human exploitation and its consequent environmental ruin in order to illuminate the causes of the utter holocaust of the planet's heart. We want to stop the destruction; I imagine that is why we imagine. We proceed with some infinite faith that if we say it, write it, walk it well enough that it will matter somehow—that spirit can be materialized as consciousness can be materialized.

We hope. And this is what I hope for a new generation of conscienced world citizens: that, in this manner, they will begin to re-imagine and reactivate the political project of public education—at all levels—so that it may fulfill its mandate to provide a socially just learning environment. And more.

May we want more than justice.

May we want an education which honors the bodies on the margins—our own and that of our ancestors—as the repository of knowledges capable of transforming this benighted nation we still dare to name "home."

Still Loving in the (Still) War Years / 2009

ON KEEPING QUEER QUEER

I began my first book, *Loving in the War Years*, in 1977. It was conceived in silence and written against absence. To experience one's writing as an act *against* is to say what it means to write within the context of movement struggle: our words, the polemics of a people, become *the language of war*. At the time when I began the work, I had no idea of the full implications of such warriorship; that one writes to refute the vanishing of a pueblo—queer, Native, Mexican, female; the socially orphaned children and demented elders—all those folks hanging on to the edge of the abyss of cultural oblivion. We do what we can to catch their fall.

ANTHROPOLOGY OF DESIRE

Looking back on my younger writer-self, my writings have always been a kind of extended love letter to my relations, not always laudatory but always with the intention of reunion. I am not unique in this. As queer sons and daughters we have so often been the social conscience of our familias, because we are the queer pegs in the round holes of the family structure. Placed on the outside of the mating rituals of the majority, we have had the opportunity to study our families as intracultural anthropologists of a kind, observing the choices (for better or worse) our siblings and cousins and parents and aunties and uncles make within the sometimes chilling embrace of institutionalized heterosexuality. We understood early on that "love" has very little to do with marriage, since even as children we knew our brand of loving would never know a preacher's or a priest's sanction. Of course, I am describing the "we" of thirty years ago, before the national movement for gay marriage.

When I came out as a lesbian, in 1975, it was the freest act I could ever have imagined. What I loved about lesbian love as a young woman was that it seemed to require no conventions. How we shaped that love and how we arranged our blood and heart relations in accordance with that love was not prescribed by societal norms because, as queers, we lived outside those norms. The thought of aligning queer desire to the institution of marriage (or the military for that matter) as a political issue was unthinkable at the time. As a young feminist, I understood my lesbianism as an opportunity to conjure new forms of familial structures, in which desire was not bound by patriarchal marriage contracts or the hierarchical structures of the nuclear family. These were the issues we stayed up nights debating as young radical, Marxist, Third World, and working-class feminists.

Within a handful of years, however, convention took hold of lesbian feminism, and the largely white middle-class movement began to impose upon its constituents its own class-biased version of politically correct lesbian relationships. Butch and femme roles, most evident in working-class communities, were considered sexist, oppressive to women, and politically reactionary. Any non–mutually orgasmic lesbian sex, especially involving penetration, was viewed as violent

and patriarchal, and mimicking the oppressive sexual relations between men and women. Well, that made me and most of my camaradas
(working-class and of color) "counter-revolutionary" on most counts,
as we attempted to construct a lesbian feminism that allowed for a full
range of sexual and gender expressions.

Thirty years later, little trace of those early white-feminist sexual
decrees can be found among lesbian-of-color social communities. Instead, it appears that desire and gender roles are being explored (and
sometimes legislated) more fiercely than ever, especially among young
queers. Butches at the club rival and bond as studs and aggressives,
with plenty of young femmes falling in eager line. Even as a twenty-
three-year-old, I knew that the tenet "feminism is the theory and lesbianism is practice" would not hold up in court or in bed, because de-
siring women does not by definition make a feminist or a radical. But
constructing an ever-evolving feminism of color among young queers
becomes especially problematic in an era when the media reifies hyper-
masculinist depictions of Black and Brown men as it extols the virtues
of capitalist patriarchy. The required additional component of the hype,
of course, is the imagined "always-wanting-it" femme for whom an impenetrable masculinity becomes the irresistible object of desire. I'm not
saying it ain't sexy, I'm just saying it ain't true. It is a "performance"
that can be emotionally murderous for women and men and queers in
love, if we confuse it for true.

What happened to queer freedom?

"Not everyone wants to be free," Linda reminds me. Maybe for a
whole new generation of queer folk, this may be the case for everything from night-club courting to (paradoxically) the courtroom itself.
I never dreamed it, that gay marriage would actually be debated in our
highest courts, and that in the same era, technology might actually afford us the opportunity to *choose* our gender. Still, as these political and
societal "gains" present themselves to us, we have to look more deeply
into what may be truly liberating about non-conformist queer identity,
so as not to confuse "progress" with progressive politics.

SIGN ON THE DOTTED LINE

Since the inception of the gay marriage campaign, I have been dis-
comfited by it. Although I am gratified to witness the reemergence of
queer activism, as a feminist of color I remain disheartened by the gay
marriage assimilationist agenda. I support gay civil unions as an equal
rights issue—state-sanctioned discrimination is wrong—and I voted
against Proposition 8, the California initiative that changed the state
constitution to restrict the definition of marriage to a legal union between opposite-sex couples. I have also personally shouldered the ven-
omous contempt of honest-to-god homophobes who emerged in my
neighborhood when the issue of gay marriage hit the streets.

But endemic to the gay marriage campaign, as it is popularly understood, are two major political pitfalls. First, the national campaign for
gay marriage is a predominately white, middle-class, single-issued liberal movement prompted by the sense of entitlement that class and race
privilege afford. Although there are plenty of queers of color among
its proponents, the campaign assumes identification with mainstream
America that preferentially applies full citizenship rights to the ownership class. The second problem resides in the fact that same-sex marriage does not challenge the fact that marriage as an institution is nor-
malized in our society, while other kinds of relationships and families
continue to be marginalized. Why should the (hetero- or homo)sexual
union of two people receive privileges denied other forms of genuine
kinship? From a queer perspective, given our history of struggle for the
right to create relations that were once illegal, privileging marriage as
an institution should seem counterintuitive. From a feminist-of-color
perspective, promoting marriage as "normal" aligns us politically with
the likes of George W. Bush, who in 2002 promoted marriage for low-
income couples as a way to get single mothers (of color) off of welfare.[1]

The gay rights movement as a whole has seldom critiqued the issues of
cultural entitlement among its constituents nor considered the negative
impact that some gay "rights" have on the "un-entitled." For example,
there is little discussion about the cultural trauma that can be caused in
transracial and transnational adoption, in which white gay people also

participate. The demise of people-of-color urban communities through gay gentrification is another example. The mainstream gay movement has not questioned its own cultural imperialist views of Third World sexual and gender oppression, nor how those same imperialist views allow gay people, "in good conscience," to support immigrant rights for gay couples, exclusive of the rights of undocumented workers.

White middle-class gays and lesbians may be the only queers with the privilege to believe that they can and should be allowed to seamlessly integrate into mainstream America. Internet blog postings during and after the passage of Proposition 8 exposed the cultural arrogance of the mainstream gay movement, as many white queer people blamed the passage of Proposition 8 on the Black community, 70 percent of which voted in favor of it. Suddenly a reactionary racism that had nestled itself conveniently beneath the down covers of middle-class privilege surfaced with great virulence when privilege was denied.

Predictably, racist postings were countered by profoundly homophobic remarks by Black heterosexuals. However, as a queer person of color what most impacted me were not the vitriolic comments—such as "Go back to the back of the bus"; "I marched in the civil rights movement"; "Why don't you just marry a dog?"; or "You never drank from a gay-only drinking fountain"—but the usage of the word *you*. "You white homosexuals / you Black heterosexuals are morally wrong," both sides insisted.[2] The possibility that someone could be simultaneously queer *and* of color never entered the virtual equation. In this sense, queers of color remain queer pegs in the round holes of both white gay-liberation strategies and people-of-color conservatism.

For many queer people of color, the nuclear middle-class family, which gay-marriage proponents seek to emulate, is not the family of our herencia. The paradigm of the domesticated mom-and-mom- or dad-and-dad-headed household depicted in the movement for queer freedom does not always depict us. It is our right to have it, of course (if we want it)—all of us, gay and straight, white and Black—but not without looking away from the truth of our social conditions as people of color. What do our families really look like and is that model deficient or might it not proffer less privatized, more interdependent alternatives to sustaining community?

Ours are extended families of single mothers, nieces and nephews adopted as children, elder live-in aunties, grandmothers as mothers, prodigal uncles returning to father in the father's stead, the show-up-now-and-then twenty-something-year-olds looking for momma, and even a few decent, quite decent, biological dads, not to mention every family's lesbian cousin and her "friend" and queer brother-in-law. As queers of color we insist that our cultures hold some core values and social constructions that we will not so easily relinquish to middle-class America, even when it offers us the "freedom" to be queer.

But while we queer folk defend the cultural integrity of our families as they are, our queerness is not defended by those same families. Instead, the institution of marriage and the nuclear family are extolled by sectors of our own communities as the keys to private membership in upwardly mobile Middle America. Why do communities of color appear to be so oblivious to right-wing efforts to politically manipulate them through the anti–gay marriage campaign? Conservative Christian organizations proffer the lie of fast-tracked cultural assimilation through homophobia and patriarchal hierarchies, while true integration is daily denied our communities by a capitalist-driven "democracy" that discriminates in education and social welfare. Queers of color are not only not immune to such discrimination, but often suffer exacerbated racial discrimination because of our sexual and gender orientations.

Given the plethora of contradictions in the campaign, it comes as no surprise that a disproportionately low number of queer couples of color signed on the dotted line during the brief window of opportunity provided by the city of San Francisco in 2004. For as we sign the gay-marriage contract without a footnote of critique, we also unwittingly sign a contract with neoliberal America, which insidiously relegates majority-people-of-color populations to the socioeconomic margins, where marriages and families are threatened by poverty, forced migration, and the prison system. To reform the institution of marriage independent of these considerations aligns us with a national politic built upon the continued disenfranchisement of the poor and the unjust entitlement of the privatized nuclear family structure. What people of color and progressive communities (Christian and otherwise) should be mandating is a critical examination of the multiple inequities, including homophobia, inherent in the very institution of state-sanctioned marriages.

A ROPE WRAPPED 'ROUND THEIR BODIES

I light the ceremony fire as to light the way for them. I see the courage it takes to stand así mujer con mujer, their hands clasped together before their confused fathers, their weeping mothers, a brother rigid with prejudice. It requires courage for everyone here to change.

But "wife and wife" are the wrong words, it is something else we make with each other. Even as they go through the act—the wedding protocol mirroring their parents'—it is something else we make or so I want to believe.

Perhaps this is why my woman, as officiate, comes to bless this union, wrapping la pareja's twin beauty in a rebozo scented with copal y crítica. Because we will not abandon our queer hijas . . . because something comes after, we hope. She ties the knot . . . something *better* than marriage.

If marriage is a "sacred" institution, as Christians and other spiritual practitioners profess, then the state should separate sanctified marriage from civil unions, for gay and straight folks alike. Religious institutions should be the ones administering "sacred" vows, and anybody choosing to "marry" by this definition would be answerable, not to the state, but to their "God." This holds true in most spiritual traditions. In certain northern Native traditions if you are married in the presence of the sacred pipe, you are married forever, even into the next life. In the Mexica tradition, when the couple is "tied" together in matrimony—a rope wrapped 'round their bodies—that tie cannot be broken. State divorces mean nothing in a spiritual context.[3] The problem is the confluence of church and state.

My mother knew the difference. She was twice married by the state: the first marriage ended in divorce and the second, her marriage to my father, was not consecrated by the Catholic Church until we three children were all in double-digits and old enough to attend our own parents' wedding. As a woman of deep faith, my mother was no fool. She knew better than to bring "God" into it before she could wager that the marriage would last.

Ironically, it isn't queer people eroding the sanctity of marriage, as conservative Christians of all shades profess. If Christians really want to preserve the "holy family," then they should dig into those deep Mormon pockets, take their protest signs, and go down to their local California penitentiary and first demand the release of all the mothers and fathers held captive there, and then figure out how to get them some viable employment. Finally, they need to quit using the colonized to do the bidding for the colonizer.[4]

OCTOBER 25, 2008

On street corners a city stone's throw from my front door, the battle around Proposition 8 is being waged fist to cuffs. Here is a snapshot of the debate: while mostly white gay folks and their supporters stand at freeway off-ramps during return commute hours with signs reading "NO on 8," an equal number of Mormon Tonga families stand on the opposite corner, ice chests and children in tow, to urge commuters to vote "yes."[5] Signs read: "Marriage = 1 man + 1 woman," a slogan generated by yet another "Christian coalition." I drive by, authoring my own slogan inside my head, "Get your f—ing Church out of my State."

Gay-marriage advocates are right: the government does not have the right to discriminate against anyone on the basis of their sexual orientation. Everyone deserves equal protection under the law. Simple. A gesture in the right direction would be a federal bill that extended full rights to domestic partnerships of both same-sex and opposite-sex unions. Who cares if the state calls us "wife" or "partner"? Many. Many care, more deeply than my lesbian feminism could have ever imagined.

No doubt, progressive political activism and strategies for social transformation occur on multiple fronts. No doubt, when discrimination strikes, when a person's civil rights are being threatened, we instinctively rise to the occasion of public protest and asphalt activism—get your f—ing church out of my state. But as Latino and Latina,

Xicano and Xicana, West and East Asian, Native, and African-originated people we do not have the privilege of a single-issue, unilateral political perspective or movement. You might recall that when mainstream America began to care about gay bashing it was through the brutally beaten white body of Matthew Shepard. But does it even know about Gwen Araujo, an indígena, Latina, Bay Area transgender teen who was also beaten to death by several youth in 2002?[6] Sadly, neither white America nor nuestra Raza even sees the body of Gwen Araujo as one of theirs.[7]

ENTRENOS

A full forty years after the writing of El Plan Espiritual de Aztlán, queer rights have yet to be fully integrated into the political agenda of the Xicano nation. We remain the renegades of the movement, even as we work for common cause. Three decades after the birth of the Chicano movement, indigenous belief systems—as a life practice and a radical politic—are applied with new vigor to Chicano activism. Everybody is having babies again for the nation (I did too); but queer familias are not invited to our nation's ceremonial circles without sequestering our queerness. The machas are told to put on skirts and our queer brothers remain in the closet of their nondescript guayaberas.

The privilege and social imposition of heterosexual coupling over queerness is never acknowledged. Instead, Xicano Indígena "tradition" is confused with the heteropatriarchy of colonialism, where male leaders and the women who follow them have forgotten the ways of many indigenous traditions—for example, the role of women elders as council members, of transgenders as necessary "contraries," of females as warriors in their own right. And so our movement suffers from a critical absence it cannot acknowledge, and continues to wonder why it fails.

For queer folk of color, this is nothing new. We did not grow up believing we were going to get everything we wanted. We grew up with some notion of a collective disenfranchised "we," who required, as a matter of good conscience and survival, a strategic oppositional vantage point in relation to mainstream America. This is what informs our politics to this day, because colored queers are not "normative," I am proud to say. And, I remain committed (as old as I am) to keeping queer queer, with or without the law's protection and with or without viable "citizenship" in the Xicano nation.

KEEPING QUEER QUEER

Transgender folk, by their uncompromised visibility in our communities, have contributed to an evolving understanding of how desire, gender, sexuality, and sex interplay in ever-complex ways to create the lovers, and male, female, and genderqueer people we are. In recent years, a whole language has developed to respond to the broad spectrum of cross-gendered experience. For many years now, in order to respect the rights of this increasingly visible, highly vulnerable, and often young community, there has been a reluctance toward open discussions about transgenderism among queer communities of color cross-generationally, resulting in a kind of in-house censorship, wherein to question *any* aspect of the identity, one risks being labeled transphobic.

Well, maybe it is a generational thing because I know I *am* scared; scared that the political agenda of the transgender movement at large, and plain ole peer pressure, may preempt young people from simply residing in that queer, gender-ambivalent site for as long and as deeply as is necessary. I am also concerned that accepted models of transgender, especially for transmen, influenced by a generation of the commodification of Black and Brown masculinity, may not offer young people of color the opportunity or option to draw from their own "unmarketable" cultural traditions and histories in framing their gender identities. I am scared when yet another student comes into my office to announce their planned breast removal over summer break; scared when I read the same student's work and know he is only beginning to uncover how to bridge that divide between desire and dick.

We *are* transgender, so many of us, crossing the male–female divide with our daily rice and beans. It is the rule of our lives and, for some of us, one more dramatically and painfully followed than others. Still, as I watch the generations that succeed me move from butch dyke to post-op man in less than a handful of years and before they are thirty, I wonder of it. I wonder what constitutes queer resistance. I wonder when a handsome Black butch undergrad, suffering under the pressure of her queer peers to identify as trans, says to me, "But, I don't want to give up being my mother's daughter." "Me neither," I say to her. "Me neither." It's an old-school reticence, I admit, shaped on the playgrounds of my early dyke days, where bulldaggers who almost passed as men reflected all I feared and admired because of the great courage it took for them to publicly stand in that dangerous, visibly queer place. In that mixed-matched body.

I remember that as a young person my palpable hunger to be sexual with a woman made me desperately want to have a penis, all the while denying that forbidden want. Had I been born in 1982 instead of 1952, my own childhood perceptions of my gender would have defined me as transgender. Did I feel I was a boy trapped in a girl's body? Absolutely—at five years old and every day for nearly fifteen years thereafter.

In retrospect, I am grateful that feminism (even with all its cultural blind spots) appeared on the political landscape as I came into my lesbianism in the mid-1970s. It gave me a lens for looking at gender and desire outside of the bar and mainstream prejudices and phobias. It offered me a way to live in and with my body of desire as it was; to grown into a woman-of-color lesbian identity on my own terms and within a critical political framework. This was the terrain of the lesbian-of-color movement of my time, which by the 1980s allowed for a viable range of sexual roles and gender variance among born-women without the aid of surgery or hormones. It did not mean that all of us felt "whole" within our bodies, but there was an evolving critical language to house the "parts."

True, there were many things we didn't think to discuss back then: the way we conflated butch identity with lesbianism or the assumption that all femme lesbians desired butches. Thanks to the contemporary and more broadly defined lesbian, gay, bisexual, and transgender (LGBT) movement, desire is restricted neither by gender nor by gender roles, and we begin to recognize that sexuality can be as fluid as gender in its possible permutations.

As a lesbian of color, I write this especially for queers that were born female, because this is the queer world I understand best. I also, admittedly, write this as a kind of outsider in the contemporary trans-gender world. I did not construct my life as a transgender person; the choices (or lack thereof) came to me differently, but I am "insider" enough to insist that my generation of butches of color (dykes) is part of this extended familia. And that if we, all of us—butch, studs, ag-gressives, trans, tops, bottoms, y mas—agree that gender occurs along a continuum, then my generation and I remain your queer elders, even in this aspect of your queer formations. Perhaps there is something valuable to be learned in this mutual exchange among us all as former "mama-boys" who remain dedicated to the liberation of women of color.

Maybe the years have taught me a thing or two. Womanhood mat-ters. I do not want to keep losing my macha daughters to manhood through any cultural mandates that are not derived of our own making. I do not want butch lesbians to become a dying breed, headed for ex-tinction. I do not mean to prescribe for anyone what his or her journey should entail as a queer. I do know, however, that it is vitally necessary to view one's *personal* suffering within a *political* context in order to understand the *design* behind oppression: *Who is oppressed in our society and why? Whom does our oppression serve and to what end? When we want to get out from under oppression, is there a road map to liberation that does not collaborate with our oppressors?*

I know these are questions that many "bois" of color are asking themselves. I learn of their meeting sites from Oakland to Brooklyn. Places where, they tell me, young transmen and butches of every ilk are looking at masculinity through the critical lens of an increasingly racist misogynist Americanism. I am not privy to those conversations, but their contents give me pause.[8] And I suddenly wonder, might not these bodies walking outside the borders of their "born-gender"—whether scarred by surgery or scarred by life—might not *your* bodies, which still carry the memory of womanhood, serve as queer models of radical feminist resistance?

I know of the other stories. I know of the young, queer "tomboys" coming into their school counselors, saying, "I don't want to be queer, I want to be a man." Straight up like that. But who can blame them? Without a woman-of-color feminism to honor the denigrated female that they still hold in their genes, how do they view their bodies in more complex ways?

As the queer and colored pegs in the round holes of the gay movement, I want something else for us. In the Aztlán that *I* imagine, our queer bodies, as they were born, would no longer be marked by society. Or, better said, we would not have to change our bodies so that they cease to be marked. I know such thinking does nothing for a person's pure desire to fully inhabit a body that just feels right, right now. So, maybe I am not thinking of "right now," but of "back then," of what came before, as a way to look at the future of people-of-color queer politics.

Perhaps by looking to our own historical models of resistance—to pre-conquest, pre–slave trade, pre-capitalist-patriarchy worldviews— we may uncover a roadmap to being viably queer in the twenty-first century. I think of the Native concept of "two-spirit," not as it has been appropriated, but as something once known and accepted by many aboriginal peoples of this continent. It was as evident then, as it is now, that there are some of us born this way, possessing pronounced male and female attributes, and that this possession is not a curse, but a blessing with its own integral power, which requires respect from our community.[9]

"Ometéotl," the Mexica (Aztec) Danzantes invoke the name of the divine, the sweet smell of copal smoke rising; the sound of the rattle, the tambor, the call of the conch shell. "Ometéotl." This is no monotheistic god the father, but something else so much more telling of an older world that sought an integral balance within each human being, not defined by opposite sexes. Ometéotl is la fuerza fundamental to creation—both the active principle and passive receptor, capable of conceiving as one entity. And thus, our world is possible.

I remember once, out on Indian land in Tejas, I spotted him/her— a beauty that transgressed all notion of male and female because what was so stunning was the shape-shifting; how with one movement (a toss of hair, a throaty laugh, a wielded hammer) s/he could move from woman to man to boy, to sister, to lover. This is what it means to be "two-spirit," I thought; that literally the male and female spirits, with all their genetic messages and chemical energies, reside within the same body and are made manifest. Freely. What courage it takes to walk in that body when both the dominant culture and our home cultures have forgotten this way.

There is no critique of the "normal" without the queer. The beauty of the queer is that s/he requires society to question itself, its assumptions about desire, about masculinity and femininity, about power. Of course, the majority culture turns away en masse from the real depth of such inquiries; but the inquiry exists, nagging nagging nagging until it one day erupts into revolt.

Am I afraid? Yes. I am afraid that América wants to defrock us of our queer powers.

At the turn of the twenty-first century transgender still remains queer. Today, no amount of surgery or hormones really removes the "queer" from transgender. There is no complete assimilation, no erasing of a person's queer, gender-dissonant history or the fact of the privileges and discriminations she or he experienced inhabiting the body they did as children. Not for now, at least. But what will queer look like, even a generation from now? Will the lover-bodies we assume no longer matter? What will be the site of resistance?

Everything about our consumerist culture looks to a future where technology reigns as savior. In that scenario queers too can become good, law-abiding, tax-paying, and legally married male and female citizens for whom biology lines up perfectly with social gender construction, and "queer liberation" becomes passé. I imagine this is the hope, but is this what the gay, lesbian, feminist, and queer movements struggled for—cultural erasure? As I witness the mainstreaming of what were once sites of political and cultural opposition in U.S. society, I sense a conspiracy is at work here, not to free our queer bodies through technology, but ultimately to have us fall in line with society's mandates about gender and desire.

So, yes, I am afraid. Because I know in my lifetime I will not see the worst. I watch my teenage children's eyes and I know they mirror the fear on my face. I imagine my fear for them scares them and so they reject it, me. Still, I long to convince them (as I want to convince you), queer Xicana mother that I am, that our disappearance is at stake here: as people of color, as queer people, as Indigenous people. First they will theorize you out of existence, as the corporate academy intends. Then they will buy you with comfort. The culture of ownership will devour your work, your play, your children, and your elders; your heart, your spirit, your love, and love-making. And then they've really got you where you live. This is why issues of sexuality and gender and how we shape them—consciously and politically—are so critical to any radical reconstruction of society. Without the defenders of our desire—which is a fundamentally spiritual and sexual site—our liberation strategies remain crippled by patriarchal nationalisms, religious fundamentalism, and fear.

As Linda said, "Not everybody wants to be free." This is the heart of the matter. Choosing freedom. Recognizing the ever-ingenious ways that the dominant culture can begin to shape even our rebellion, so that in a slow bleed of liberalism, it begins to resemble enslavement.

The young transman asks me to really *see* him, to not write him off so easily, to not suspect that he has abandoned me, us, his mothers, sisters. And he opens my eyes to another way to interpret promise in this/his change. In his tattooed, flat-chested, muscled masculinity, I feel him oddly my queer, butch—very butch—daughter. Or is it *son*? I feel him as *my* boy, like I feel my own blood boy. Yes, a "*mama's* boy" and a member of my queer nation.

On these pages I inscribe my questions, my worries, my utter suspicion of this country's neocolonial agenda to have us conform. When I write, "Is there a roadmap to liberation that does not collaborate with our oppressors?" I do so from where I am standing, from the vantage point of thirty-five years of political engagement. I want to warn, guide, urge, implore my daughters and granddaughters of color that indeed even should you choose to transition into man's body, you must still hold on desperately to womanhood in the shaping of that masculinity. You must know that there is something in being born female from a female in a female-hating world that still matters. I honor you—the surgically scarred or merely marred by difference—in whose bodies rebellion continues to live.

Ultimately, my hope is that increasingly there will open avenues of intergenerational support for gender variance within a feminism-of-color framework; that one generation can draw from the knowledge of the previous in shaping that framework; that movement progresses, just like gender . . . in a continuum.[10]

STILL LOVING

Almost twenty-five years ago, in my first play, *Giving Up the Ghost*, a twenty-seven-year-old Chicana pronounced her own queer notion of lesbian love and lovemaking like this: "It makes you feel so good, like your hands are weapons of war."[11]

War. There it is again. Maybe I have just grown comfortable with it. Because war is all I've known, really: from Vietnam to Iraq; from the murders of Harvey Milk to Victoria Mercado; from the aborted radical vision of Malcolm X to Ingrid "Flying Eagle Woman" Washinawatok. From my kitchen to my bedroom, from my neighborhood to my hometown, from my backyard to the backstreet, the threat of "I'm going to kill you!" has been hurled into my queer face more times than I care to remember and always by someone close enough to call me sister or daughter or cousin or lover.

I have also witnessed great acts of love during war times. Once (for there is only one true time that this can occur), I "came out" to my mother, as I packed my 1970 Volkswagen bug for my escape to the anonymity and "freedom" of a family-less (white) lesbianism in Northern California. I came out to her, but not by choice. My emergence from the familial closet was prompted by the fuerza of my mother's words, not mine.

"You're leaving with a secret," she said. And that is all she had to say to let me know that she refused to lose me; that she would withstand anything, even my lesbianism, to keep me from leaving her in the deepest sense. So I came out to her with the truth she had already known. And after tears and threats and gritos and invocations to the gods to remove such a heavy burden off the shoulders of her youngest child, she conceded: "There is nothing you could do that you wouldn't be my daughter."

And that's all she had to say to ensure that I would not leave Los Angeles a queer orphan, that I would start from that day to do the impossible and build a honest-conscienced lesbian life bent on freedom for all of us who ever suffered silence. Because my mother still loved me—in spite of all her most steadfast societal convictions and mores—and she had the courage to tell me so.

In the last years of my mother's life, she forgot this story, as she had forgotten all stories, suffering from Alzheimer's. Still, she remembered me, although at times she referred to me (and my lesbian niece) as "he" instead of "she." I have other butch Latina lesbian friends (my age) who tell me the same: that since the onset of their mother's "amnesia" they have been consistently referred to as males. But some part of me feels that in this great show of intuitive knowing, our "demented" mothers and grandmothers may not be forgetting so much as remembering, reassembling in their now liberated minds a true story of the two-spirit—the way their queer daughters and sons and grandchildren walked in this world before the war.

La Caminante

Epílogo / March 21, 2010

XICANA MIND, BEGINNER MIND

When I was a young woman still living in Los Angeles County, I took a trip north to Monterey Bay, where my boyfriend at the time was stationed at Fort Ord Army base. (It is now the fog-covered campus of a California state university.) The year was 1972 and I was not yet twenty years old.

Thinking of that time, nearly four decades ago, there is the story of a girl who is not me now, but as close to me as compassion can allow. I remember a profound despair, what it was to walk through that sea-salted coastal fog as if heavy gauze were entrapping the heart. I remember speechlessness, talking that had nothing to do with anything that mattered. I imagined such silence as an escape, even as it screamed its disquiet inside of me.

I was a Mexican American girl and a lesbian with no way out of the paradox.

During that trip, my boyfriend took leave from the base and we spent the day in nearby Carmel, in and out of the pseudo-counter-culture shops amid cypress cliffs and English cottage–style houses situated just above the wide plain of a muted slate-blue ocean. I remember a gift shop of sorts, the clatter of insistent wind chimes, having to steer ourselves around the many psychedelic colored candles and leafy plants hanging suspended from their macramé holders. Was it there that I happened upon the small book—its gray paperback cover of black and white design, the red letters? *Zen Mind, Beginner's Mind.* Was it the title that drew me? Its codex-scribe colors? The easy exotic offering of that three-letter word, *Zen*?

I don't quite know why I was attracted to the book, except to say that I was a child of the times. Since the Beat generation of the late 1950s, "Eastern thought," as it were, had infiltrated the popular culture of hippies, flower children, and the "anti-establishment." As a Mexican American daughter, I could not fully inhabit any of those categories. Still, there was a nascent longing in me to find "life's meaning." An existential quest, I thought. But it was more than this. It was the quest to find meaning for suffering. My own, my mother's, my people's. It was a quest that took me onto the long life path of political engagement.

BEGINNER MIND

Thirty years after first opening the pages of that slim gray volume, I finally made my way to the sitting meditation practice described there. I came to it neither as retreat nor respite, but as resignation to the timeless assurance of death. With my mother in the throes of Alzheimer's as my unwitting Zen teacher, I came to understand that memories are stories we tell ourselves, and then we forget the most thoroughly constructed ones, the ones with the greatest conviction, and what remains is only the body's knowing. I came to the sitting practice as the training ground for locating myself in the simple awareness of the present. The fleeting moment, after all, was all we had to offer one another, my mother and I and her companion, Amnesia.

I have put many names to the act of sitting: the sweat lodge (temescal) Inipi ceremony, the medicine of pejuta, the zazen cushion. I sit today as I did intuitively as a child. When the Catholic Church's rituals of confession and penance threatened to drown me in an ocean of torment, I would retreat for solace alone in the church pew. Sitting straight-backed, open palms on my thighs, I returned to the island of my own earnest heart. There the punishing pornography of the blaming mind gave way to the silence of an inner, infinitely compassionate god.

In silence, not prayer, we allow God to talk back.[1]

Now, beyond middle age, I sit in the manner learned from the old ways of this continent: sit up and let what comes come, and always one's pitifulness comes; the confrontation with the mundane thoughts that preoccupy us. But it is truer to say that the thoughts occupy us as in "occupation," as in some exterior force imposing itself upon our natural state. We live in the state of occupation with so many stories to explain away our grief. But I wonder, is it only that we are not our own authors? That we hold others' stories in our minds and try to persuade our hearts that a conquest that occurred more than five hundred years ago is no longer remembered in our DNA? I wonder if we were to grow quiet enough, might we recollect what has been scattered and desecrated by history? Might we re-member ourselves? Might we reconcile a suffering that cannot be rendered in language?

Sitting as in ceremony is about discomfort, the body allowing us this awareness without trying to "fix" it right away, but getting to know oneself inside discomfort and even pain, yes . . . pain on the red road to wellness. And so, during the medicine ceremony when we heave up the poisons of our prisons from a gut wracked with grief, it is referred to as "getting well."

When we sit in mediation it is as one does with the Medicine. This pain, a precursor to the illness that awaits us. This illness, a precursor to death, unless we are taken by surprise. I sit because we *are* taken by surprise daily, moment by moment. The earth's upheaval in Haiti, followed by Chile's devastation, provides irrefutable testimony to this. We imagine we have control when we don't; and suffer in the effort to have some elusive, deluded sense of control when our beloveds become old and die anyway or are blasted down by execution fire (not hyperbole) or are bludgeoned to death by their only son. The surprise deaths of Ingrid Washinawatok and Marsha Gómez within a year of each other at the close of the twentieth century changed my life forever.[2] Their deaths were what I knew and feared as a child; that prayers do not ward off death; prayers simply bear witness. And death happens.

The United States as a collective body confronted its lack of control when those twin towers crumbled like toast at the dawn of this century. Even as a nation-state, we could not keep death at abeyance. Ashamedly, we send our children to do that futile job for us; call it by many names, but probably the "War on Terror" is the most apt, as terror is nothing more than organized fear—our own, as a country.

We fight "terror" like we are fighting windmills.

More than a generation ago, I landed upon a small and first book that spoke of the practice of sitting meditation. The profoundly simple meaning of the book, which lay occulted in the white space surrounding the black glyphs of letters on its pages, surely escaped me as a twenty-year-old. Now, returning to the book a lifetime later, its deepest meanings may escape me still. However, what I do retain of the essence of the slim book's meaning, even from my first partial read of it, is this: that if we are filled up, that if we believe that we already know, we will learn nothing because there is no empty space, no not-knowing space in which to learn, in which to change.

Has my education then been nothing more than the process of unlearning, acquiring knowledges (ancient and prophetic) that do not cling to us, that do not become armor in the battle against ignorance, but pass through the body, altering cells of memory with the lightness, clarity, and evanescence of meaning?

XICANA MIND

Speaking for the ancestors . . .

Recently, my sixteen-year-old son began to take on the body of a man. I cannot say that our years together have gone quickly. I can say that looking back, whole years take only a moment to remember. They accumulate in this way, in the way in which we say my how time flies, but it does not fly, it labors. There are moments of flight, yes, when we glimpse change already complete, when we forget to knock and catch the naked length of our teenage daughter with a woman's full pubes. She, still with a girl's mind, still a whirlwind of fantasía and delight. The disconnect unsettles; a fragile equilibrium disturbed. As it is so in the changing countenance of my son.

Time does not fly. It labors to understand what just got left behind.

Yesterday, I was happy. Yesterday, I played a board game with my son after making him some quesadillas for dinner, and the bright sun set with an encroaching chill through the bay view of our window. Neither of us wished we were somewhere else. That is so much to say; knowing that on the other side is death, on the other side of the ocean, the other side of the city block, the other side of the kitchen table. We were happy, as we will be and have been sad, as sad and happy slip away, as childhood slips into the old age of my son that I will never witness.

Still, we remember and mark the time.

I remember, it was a few months after my mother's passing—I come into the house after walking the dog. I wash my hands, remove my jacket and go straight away to finishing the few leftover dishes in the sink. Rafael comes in. I feel him at my back, standing some distance from me in the doorway. I don't remember if he says anything to me. It feels like he just came into the kitchen to know, to acknowledge, I had returned. And I stand at the sink in the full weight of motherhood. I am someone's only mother, as my mother was to me. And at that moment I know the space that my body occupies, that physicality, is what most matters, that I am *not* gone, that I have returned, that I will most likely return again after long walks with the dog in the rain. And this is what I miss most about my own mother; that she will not return to me, embodied in this way.

I conclude this book as my boy assumes the body of a man. On this day, I sit at my altar and ask for the courage to release him. These are the words that come to me—simple, direct: "Help me let him go." And I whisper them aloud so that my body hears the sound of the same exact language I had used throughout my mother's dying years and those first hardest months of mourning. It feels the same. I know this viscerally, a DNA knowing.

If my mother's last years in the awe of Alzheimer's taught me anything, it was the necessity to love without holding on. It is a lesson that the body refuses; that requires soul to enact; that must be practiced daily and relearned in ruthless confrontation with those most pivotal moments of change in our lives.

Today as I witness the final waning of my son's boyhood, I remember how in the first month of his life, as his two pounds of skin and bone and organ lay under the surgeon's blade, I prayed in the effort to release him, should he or the universe decide this.[3] It countered every instinct in me and drew from a place of soul, to believe that there are greater rhymes and reasons for our existences—short and long—than mere survival.

Linda Hogan writes: "We Indian people who had inhabited the land . . . had not been meant to survive and yet we did, some of us, carrying the souls of our ancestors, and now they speak through us. It was this that saved my life . . ."[4]

This is what the elders teach; this is what I have learned in ceremony; what I have looked at in the white space of meditation that is the mirror of death. That our actions in this life can heal our ancestors on the other side, that this corporeal knowing does not hold us, that we can remember histories and futures through and in spite of the body we wear. And my relatives are with me before and after my coming; and the son I raise is my blood ancestor returned; and my beloved is someone I knew like this before.

These are knowings, not imaginings, not stories we tell ourselves to bring comfort to the grieving. Because they do not comfort, they provide energy for hard change and transformation. In them resides the meaning of the loss—from my mother's demented and illuminated passing to the horror of Haiti's quaking devastation—that we might become well again—she and I, Haiti, and . . .

All our relations.

POSTSCRIPT

In this relative reality called my identity, I carve out a new way of seeing that holds nothing in the face of death. This is all I can offer of what
I know of conciencia, that it occurs from a mind outside of conviction,
that true consciousness responds to the intuitive, the less than visible,
the hidden impulse, the viscerality of the discontent.

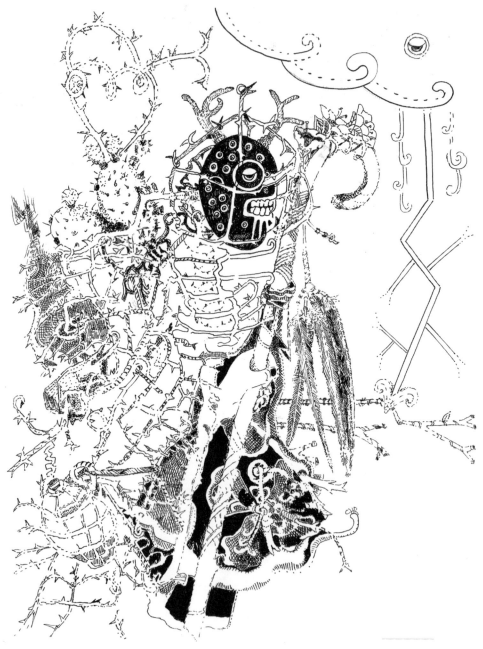

Relámpago

Appendix: Sola, Pero Bien Acompañada / 2006

THE ART OF CELIA HERRERA RODRÍGUEZ

> As Chicana/os, we are a displaced people of many nations of
> origin, living in diaspora in the United States. Our mestizaje—
> perhaps more a political idea rather than a fact of biology—
> was forced upon us. How do we recover from the shock of
> displacement, the loss of Indigenous memory? How do we
> rekindle the home-fire? The painting is the record along the
> road. It allows me to think, meditate, to assume the posture
> of ceremony, to pay attention in that deep way. The door
> opens to us, just by spending time looking at the images, the
> symbols. And we begin to understand. These paintings and
> installations are a conceptual language, a suggestion of how
> to find our way back to home.
>
> Celia Herrera Rodríguez

Celia Herrera's[1] work, based in the language of the symbol, is a directed gesture toward the recuperation of a history, a way of knowing,
lost to Xicanos and Xicanas. It is epitomized in *Un rezo en cuatro cami-
nos* (A prayer on four roads), the centerpiece of "Sola, Pero Bien Acompañada," her solo exhibition at the C. N. Gorman Museum in 2006.[2] Its
title invokes the four directions, the four paths to knowing. In many
ways the work, which was originally presented at the third Bienal Inter-

nacional de Estandartes Tijuana in 2004, represents the center-stone of Herrera's own viewpoint as a transplanted MeXicana artist of Tepehuan (Odami) origins. It speaks to the artist's complete confidence in the history of our interconnectedness and interdependence as Native peoples throughout the continent.

She states:

> Looking at indigenous cultures, before all of the claiming of territory and borders, certain elements recur. There is consistency underneath all the variations in our nations that are older than contemporary formations of tribal affiliations. The simple fact is that knowledge was passed down and shared among Indigenous peoples of this land. Acknowledging this can give us an idea of the development of thought on this continent. By looking at symbols and responding intuitively to them (and this can be deceptive because of colonization, with its patriarchal and Christian overlays), we can base our interpretation on something more reliable than the politics of the day. This requires that we "get out of the way to know." Sometimes we're wrong. But if we don't take the chance we are left with the uninspired, perverse version of ourselves that the U.S. and México have handed to us.[3]

Going to several pueblos of the Southwest and northern México, including those of the Paquimé culture of Casa Grandes, Chihuahua, Herrera began to investigate the way spiritual knowledges had traveled in América, along the same trade routes where sacred objects—such as parrot feathers, seeds pods, and clay vessels, along with other "trade commodities"—had been exchanged. Such ruminations brought her to reconsider the peyote medicine ceremony, part of her own traditional practice. Following the "routes" that the symbols of the ceremony took, she returned to the four elements—fire, water, wind, and earth—and uncovered the ánima contained within the major symbols explored in this exhibition.

As Herrera describes it, "The symbols in my work are not words but they act as words, as they did in the earliest forms of writing." The act of painting is the effort to re-animinate the *alchemy of the word*. She explains, "The word is magic. It is sacred. Visual language is not limited

by culture and verbal vocabulary. It isn't even limited by my own interpretation. It is the opposite of rhetoric." She describes her process as a
painter as one in which what she does with her hands creates an opening, an allowance for this animation to occur. "It may not make a whole
sentence," she says, "but it attempts to put life into something, to say
something that causes change in thought and action." Herrera views
the use of watercolor as integral to this animation process. "Watercolor
is alchemy." She continues:

> The pigment and binder are made from minerals or extracted from
> a plant or animal source. That is to say that the paint is derived from
> a substance of the earth that then rides on the element of water. The
> pigment adheres to the fiber of the paper by the elements of air and
> heat (fire). The paper itself is shaped by water and bound together
> by the relocation of its fibers. All this is accomplished by the actions
> of the human hand. When I am putting the color down, drawing
> out the shapes, the colors radiate in the light. When the paint is wet,
> the shapes talk to me, as if I were full of medicine. I am outside of
> time, like meditation. I am not exactly praying, but I am in a differ-
> ent higher place, without worry . . . just moving the paint across the
> paper. I am aware of how the different colors stimulate my psyche.
> It transforms the way I am thinking. Once dry, the paper changes
> texture, the color changes.
>
> I feel a spiritual connection with the pigment. I wait for a long
> time for the symbols to emerge. I put one symbol down and wait to
> see what next emerges—something like how a dream unfolds. If I
> focus too soon, I change the story. If I am not conscious, I lose the
> thread of the dream. If I move before I am certain, I end up with
> murky spots, places that require resolution to keep the "whole" of
> the painting. What at first may have seemed simple, in the act of
> trying to render a certain symbol I discover how complicated it is. I
> have to keep following it through until it reaches the point of satis-
> faction. Sometimes it is a good painting—it does what I had hoped.
> Sometimes it's just a step in the path.

The history and living practice of ceremony as understood through
the elemental is what Herrera's work considers. The water bird, the

female-figured gourd-vessels, the lighting rod of male fire, the huichol deer, and the night moth appear as apertures in her paintings, invitations to a return to the elemental, that deepest site of knowing.

In her installations, the "sacred" is similarly expressed. The painted symbol becomes object; two dimensions emerge into three. What we can hold and touch in our hands, what we can smell and taste—corn husk, pottery shard, metal nail, and cotton cloth—these are the elements of ceremony, of a prayerful awareness. Objects are regarded as sacred items because the objects hold memory, meaning. They are carriers of knowledge. Although they may at first appear ordinary and mundane, within the displaced MeXicana household, the metal pot and cup and the bag of beans represent ways of making home that have survived migration.

Some of the installation objects bring with them a history of other installations and performance works by the artist. The broken dishes are the actual remnants of her performance piece *Las Cositas Quebradas*, which Herrera took to Málaga, Spain, and Boston. In protest against the centuries-old theft and destruction of the sacred items of Indigenous América by Europe and Euroamerica, Herrera publicly "returns the favor" to the colonizer by ceremoniously destroying some of his own revered objects. The tobacco ties used in her installations come from many people, many places, including a memorial for the Xicana poet and philosopher Gloria Anzaldúa. Mainly associated with Lakota tradition, here the tobacco ties are made of paper, acknowledging the traditional sacred use of paper as a medium of prayer throughout the continent—from the pre-Columbian Mexica culture to the contemporary spiritual practices of the Huichol and Otomí. The ties in this exhibition link a continent through shared prayer. In the act, the divisions among us imposed by a Spanish- and Anglo-America dissolve.

In *Prayer for the Mother Waters*, Herrera uses hundreds of draping prayer ties in an installation to honor "Grandma Flora" (Florence Curl Jones), the leader of the Winnemem Wintu and a traditional California healer, who passed away in 2003. Herrera counts the elder healer as critical to her very survival—a claim, no doubt, which could be made by the thousands of others whom Flora Jones touched. Reflecting on the installation and the elder who inspired it, the artist states: "It symbolizes the meaning and energy of female water that emerges from the earth, because that was one of [Grandma Flora's] strongest prayers in the latter part of her life. Part of her teaching was to foresee that the waters were coming; that we needed to keep the sacred fires burning to keep waters in balance. Everything the California elders had predicted has come to pass: AIDS, the eruption of Mount St. Helens, the culture of chaos that has so deeply affected our communities, the tsunamis . . . Katrina."

Herrera goes on to discuss "development" plans to exploit water reserves in the Shasta area, which will have a devastating effect on the Winnemem Wintu and the environment. "Now the Water District wants to flood sacred lands where the Winnemem bless their newborns and young women. How then do they direct their children without these ceremonies? How are we all affected without the grounding of the sacred? Stick a tube down into the sacred waters and draw it out for bottled water? It's rape."[4]

Growing up in the great shadow of Mt. Shasta in Sacramento in the late sixties and early seventies, Herrera found resonance for her impulses as an artist through the Northern California Native communities and the Chicano movement, which first opened the door to her understanding of the intercultural and spiritual connections among indigenous traditions. Angelbertha Cobb, an early cultural activist in the Sacramento Valley, stands out as a significant influence in this regard. Herrera's undergraduate work in ethnic studies at California State University, Sacramento, introduced her to several Northern California Native artists and teachers, as well as to the contagious energy and political vision of the Royal Chicano Air Force, a Sacramento-based Chicano arts collective. These early influences are what forged in Herrera's political vision and art practice the necessary link between the struggle of Northern Native peoples to regain and retain cultural and legal sovereignty, and the mandate of Xicanos to refuse to relinquish our Native identities to U.S. citizenship. As the artist puts it, "This is the truth of this continent: that our many cultures have developed side by side, sometimes in conflict, but always in communication. There is no denying one another's existence."

Among those who impacted Herrera's life, her cannery-worker grandmother who raised her continues to affect the artist in the spirit and in the forms of her art practice. Herrera attributes her earliest desire to draw to the embroidery work she did as a young girl during her visits to her grandmother's homeland of Sandías Tepehuanes, Durango, in México. She states, "My first impulse was to use line." She goes on to describe how this was discouraged in her art school, where to draw the illusion of three-dimension, "to see as you would look through a window," was privileged over the two-dimensional forms one might see on an embroidered tablecloth or a Mesoamerican manuscript.[5] She explains: "Art school has a way of belittling women's work. Anything involving textiles or originating from the home is considered less serious, more 'craft' than art. Much later I started to look at what was left in the domestic sphere of our culture that had not been stolen from us: sweeping, cooking, mundane objects like wash bins or the molcajete. This all came directly from my grandmother. I had to free myself to be able to draw symbols the way I had seen them used in cloth." For Herrera, the symbols became a way to return to her origins. And learning to value those seemingly ordinary household objects regenerated the home ethos that had originated from her grandmother, Domitila García, and their Tepehuan past.

Domitila's teachings would take a generation for the artist to begin to comprehend, in the same way Grandma Flora's instruction "to see spirit as clearly as one sees every day mundane objects" remains a life work. In this light, the title of this exhibition has resonant meaning, that this *solo* show is the result of *many* hands, *many* prayers, and much "good company."

The impetus for Herrera's vision as a conceptual artist can also be attributed to profoundly intuitive research. "The books fall open in front of me," she says of the intensive study that runs concurrent with her visual and performative explorations. Research, then, for Herrera is the road traveled, the image on a wall painting, the impromptu conversation with an elder about an herb that soothes a sore throat. It is reading between the lines of the anthropologist's interpretation. The impetus for an art piece can be drawn as much from a moment's illumination during a ceremony as from the ordinary function of a chipped teacup once used by her grandmother. For Herrera, research is simply "making the connections between things."

The result of this research is to teach through art practice, possibly even to teach what is unknown—what the artist, herself, cannot wholly articulate. Celia Herrera's art is a single movement, performed within the good company of many others of similar thought and practice. It signifies a return to the earliest mandate of Chicano art—protest; but here it is protest against amnesia. "When the Spanish arrived," the artist reminds us, "they burned our books. Colonized people are not supposed to practice our writing, our language." For Herrera, language resides in the symbol—placed on the page, the wall, the floor, the home, the body. When the body enters the living painting, as it does in her performance work (which may be yet the most integral expression of Herrera's vision), we are invited to perform the actions that the objects (symbols) require. Grinding stone against metate, we sit on the ground, we eat the sacreds (corn, meat, fruit, water). We "perform" memory. We remember. We are not so lost after all.

Notes

PRÓLOGO: A LIVING CODEX

1 *Tlacuilo* is the Nahuatl word to designate the scribe; i.e., the painter and interpreter of the Mesoamerican codices.

2 Each essay in this collection is listed with the date of its original version,
though all reflect the re-visioning process that occurs over time.

3 "Art in América con Acento" is an essay published in my book *The Last Generation*, which critiques the United States for its Anglo-American ethnocentrism,
describing it as an America "without the accent."

4 I refer to Arizona Senate Bill 1070, which, among other provisions, criminalizes undocumented immigrants, encourages racial profiling, and promotes
the unlawful detention of mestizo and other Indigenous people regardless of
their legal status until they can prove their legal residency or citizenship. On
July 28, 2010, just before the bill went into effect, Susan Bolt, a federal judge
in Phoenix, issued a temporary injunction blocking implementation of key
portions of the law.

A XICANADYKE CODEX OF CHANGING CONSCIOUSNESS

This essay originated as the Kessler Award lecture sponsored by the Center for
Lesbian and Gay Studies (CLAGS) of the City University of New York, presented on December 8, 2000.

1 Alexie, *One Stick Song*, 17.
2 Rich, "An Old House in America," 130.
3 Arteaga, *Frozen Accident*, 42.
4 The audience that attended the CLAGS lecture, the original forum for this essay, was mostly white.
5 Moraga, *Loving in the War Years*, 117.
6 I refer to the period just before the wave of Mexican immigration that New York witnessed in the late 1980s and thereafter.
7 Allison, *The Women Who Hate Me*.
8 Born in 1930, Dolores Huerta was the co-founder, with César Chávez, of the United Farm Workers and was inducted into the National Women's Hall of Fame in 1993 as one the most respected and powerful labor movement leaders of the twentieth century.
9 From an untitled work in progress.

FROM INSIDE THE FIRST WORLD

1 An earlier version of this essay originally appeared as my foreword to the twentieth-anniversary edition of *This Bridge Called My Back: Writings by Radical Women of Color*, a book I co-edited with Gloria Anzaldúa (Berkeley, Calif.: Third Woman Press, 2002). Initially published in 1981, *This Bridge Called My Back* was a landmark text which introduced to the national political landscape a woman-of-color feminism developed by U.S. Third World women of diverse ethnicities, races, and class backgrounds, including both heterosexual and lesbian activists.
2 Gloria Yamato drew this poignant phrase by Amanda White from a People of Colour as Allies Workshop, which Gloria facilitated, in Vancouver, B.C., during the late eighties. Here is Amanda White's full statement: "My mom took me to a park and, pointing to a statue of a Black man of note, said, 'We are the first Americans, they are the forced Americans . . . the first Americans and the forced Americans are going to have to work together to help get things right.'"
3 "Refugees of a World on Fire" is the title of the foreword to the second edition of *This Bridge Called My Back*.
4 Such cultural specificity has been critical to the work of feminisms of color and counters first-world definitions of a monolithic global feminism.
5 I first heard this term in a discussion with a South Asian transnational feminist that was broadcast in the days after 9/11 on KPFA radio, based in Berkeley, California.
6 The following are a few examples of U.S. foreign policy decisions that defended corporate interests to the detriment of the global environment, and the economic self-sustainability or the political autonomy of developing countries. Within George W. Bush's first year in office, he announced his refusal to

abide by the Kyoto Protocol to reduce global warming, signed by President Bill Clinton in 1997. Earlier, in 1992, five hundred years after the arrival of Columbus, in a gesture of unrelenting conquistador bravado, the elder George Bush refused to sign the agreement from the Earth Summit in Rio de Janeiro. And as recently as one week before the tragedy of September 11, the United States withdrew from the United Nations World Conference against Racism in Durban, South Africa, in protest over the conference's working declaration, which equated Zionism with racism.

7 Peter Jennings, ABC live broadcast, September 11, 2001.

8 "Selected" refers to the controversial manner in which the very close competition for the U.S. presidency between George W. Bush and Al Gore in 2000 was decided in favor of Bush after an unreliable count of the Florida vote.

9 As heard on a radio broadcast of KPFA, Berkeley, Calif., in the days after 9/11.

10 Red, white, and blue "loyalty ribbons" first appeared a few days after the 9/11 attacks. They were used to express grief over the tragedy, and to show solidarity and support for the United States.

11 See her foreword to the original edition of *This Bridge Called My Back*.

12 Bambara, *These Bones Are Not My Child*, 8. The novel, published posthumously and edited by Toni Morrison, explores the brutal murders of more than forty African American children over a period of two years (1979–81) in Atlanta, Georgia.

13 Davis, "The Color of Violence against Women" (originally the keynote address at the "Color of Violence" conference at the University of California, Santa Cruz, April 28–29, 2000), 4–8.

14 For further discussion complicating the use of the word *tribe* within the framework of progressive politics, see "Indígena as Scribe: The (W)rite to Remember" and "The 'Impossible' Gloria Anzaldúa" in this collection.

15 The Northern Native concept of "two-spirit" for gay, lesbian, or transgender folk is distinct from the U.S. queer movement, but has yet to be foundationally integrated into U.S. people-of-color political strategies. In recent years, two-spirit gatherings have emerged throughout the country, where Northern Natives, Xicanas and Xicanos, and African American Indians are finding political and cultural correspondence with one another.

16 Bambara, foreword to *This Bridge Called My Back*, vi.

17 Ibid.

18 Up through my college years, I carried the adopted surname of my father, "Lawrence." "Moraga" is my mother's family name.

19 Bambara, *The Salt Eaters*, 106.

AN IRREVOCABLE PROMISE

This essay was first presented at the third Congreso Internacional de Literature Chicana on May 21, 2002, in Málaga, Spain. On July 25 of the same year, it was presented in an expanded version as the keynote address for the American Theater in Higher Education conference in San Diego, California.

1   I refer to the character of Corky in *Giving Up the Ghost*. The play was first presented at Foot of the Mountain Theater in Minneapolis in 1984. It was directed by Kim Hines.

2   "Strange Fruit" was written first as a poem, by Abel Meeropol, a Jewish high-school teacher and union activist from the Bronx. He put it to music and published it under the pseudonym Lewis Allan. In 1939, fearing a public backlash, Columbia Records refused Billie Holiday's request to record it. Instead, they allowed Holiday a one-session release from her contract in order to record the song with Vocalion Records.

3   *Shadow of a Man* had its world premiere in San Francisco on November 10, 1990. It was produced by the Eureka Theater Company and Brava! for Women in the Arts. Lupe was played by Jade Power Sotomayor.

4   "Warrior Words / Word Warriors" was the theme of the tenth annual Border Books Festival, which took place in Las Cruces, New Mexico, in 2004. The phrase was coined by Chávez, a fiction writer and director of the festival.

5   From a public address given at the conference "Crossing Borders '99: Latino/a and Latin American Lesbian and Gay Testimony, Autobiography, and Self-Figuration," at the Center for Lesbian and Gay Studies at the City University of New York in March 1999. For a further discussion of abjection, see Julia Kristeva's *Powers of Horror: An Essay on Abjection*.

6   La Malinche or Malintzín Tenepal was a young woman of the Aztec ruling class who was sold into slavery and presented as a gift to the Spaniard Hernán Cortés upon his arrival in Veracruz in 1519. As enslaved translator, tactical advisor, and courtesan to Cortés, she served him in his efforts to conquer Indigenous México. She is a controversial figure in MeXicano and MeXicana history, considered by some to be a kind of Mexican Eve for what is seen as her complicity in the conquest. By others, especially Xicana feminists, she has been characterized as a woman who rose beyond her slave status to become a political leader in her own right, and whose actions were prompted by a deep spiritual mandate. See my essay "A Long Line of Vendidas" in *Loving in the War Years*; Norma Alarcón's "Chicana's Feminist Literature"; and Aleida del Castillos's "Malintzín Tenepal."

7   I was reminded of how dangerous Xicana-identified writing can be within the framework of male-identified Chicano teatro when not one woman's play was selected to be part of a Chicano classics theater festival held at the University of California, Los Angeles, from June 25–30, 2002. The festival was organized

by a Consortium of Theater Educators and Artists and was hosted by UCLA's School of Theater, Film, and Television. I decided to boycott the conference in protest against its decision to feature only plays that were written or developed by men or male-directed teatros. In an open letter to the conference organizers I wrote: "There are reasons so few of us [Xicanas] were writing this kind of work . . . during El Movimiento. Many women of my generation could speak to this, this history of real self-censorship imposed from male leadership and by 'collective' agreement. Ask the women of El Teatro Campesino during its 'classic' period. . . . What remains taboo in Chicano Teatro [is] complex female desire portrayed by us women—gay and straight." The unpublished letter was distributed to participants at the conference. For a description of the conference, visit: http://www.tft.ucla.edu/news/event/30-festival_chicano-classics (accessed October 20, 2010).

8 In the mid-seventies, just a few years after I had first begun to enact my lesbian sexuality, I landed on an essay, "What We Mean to Say: Notes Toward Defining the Nature of Lesbian Literature," by a white lesbian novelist, Bertha Harris. It was published in the New York–based feminist magazine *Heresies*, and described the lesbian as the prototype of the monster in the Western literary imagination. This was 1977 and resonated with my own *living* experience of the danger of lesbianism to the status quo.

9 *Digging Up the Dirt* premiered at Breath of Fire Latina Theater, in a coproduction with See-what (Cihuatl) Productions, in Santa Ana, California, on July 30, 2010. I co-directed this production with Adelina Anthony.

10 Sandoval Sánchez, public address given at the conference "Crossing Borders '99: Latino/a and Latin American Lesbian and Gay Testimony, Autobiography, and Self-Figuration," at the Center for Lesbian and Gay Studies at the City University of New York in March 1999.

11 Julia Pastrana, who had hypertrichosis terminalis (her face and body were covered in black hair), was an Indigenous Mexican woman of the midnineteenth century. She was bought for exhibition by a man who would later become her husband. After her death and the death of her three-day-old baby, also suffering the same condition, the two were mummified and continued to be exhibited by the husband.

12 Excerpt from *Digging Up the Dirt* (Albuquerque: West End Press, 2012). The play tells the parallel stories of two murders and their perpetrators. In one, Amada, who has been killed by her son, returns to reconcile this violent passing through the Poet's own scripting of it.

13 Sanjinés, "Indianizing the Q'ara," 165.

14 Celia Herrera Rodríguez is a painter and installation and performance artist based in the Bay Area who teaches in the Chicano Studies program at the University of California, Berkeley.

15 Manzor, "From Minimalism to Performative Excess," 382. In her mid-thirties,

Mendieta fell or was thrown from the thirty-fourth-floor window of a New York apartment belonging to Carle Andre, "a well-known minimalist sculptor." Manzor states: "Carl Andre was indicted three times and finally acquitted of charges of having killed Mendieta" (373).

WEAPONS OF THE WEAK

An earlier version of this essay was presented at the "Women and Power Conference: Reclaiming Faith—Socially, Spiritually, Artistically," on February 28, 2003, at Middle Tennessee State University, Murfreesboro. Part of this essay (see section, "The Warring Inside," 59), was also presented at the INCITE! "Color of Violence" conference in Chicago in 2002, until my speech was interrupted by conference organizers, citing time restraints. I was barely ten minutes into my keynote. In part, I attribute the interruption to the controversy that emerged at the conference when many indígena-identified Xicanas (including myself) refused to disavow our Native identities or to exclusively frame our discussion of "Latinas" within the context of immigration.

1 Rich, "An Old House in America," 130. I also reference this poem in the first essay of this collection.

2 On February 20, 2003, a fire ignited by a rock band's pyrotechnics display left one hundred people dead and nearly two hundred injured at a Rhode Island nightclub. "5 Years After a Nightclub Fire, Survivors Struggle to Remake Their Lives," *New York Times*, February 17, 2008, http://www.nytimes.com (accessed October 20, 2010).

3 In the aftermath of 9/11 and the anthrax scare, officials from Bush's Homeland Security team recommended sealing home windows with duct tape and plastic sheets as a viable defense in the event of terrorist attacks.

4 Cervantes, "Poem for the Young White Man Who Asked Me How I, an Intelligent Well-Read Person Could Believe in the War Between Races," in *Emplumada*, 35–37.

5 Formed by both consciousness and conscience.

6 The actor Ronald Reagan, who would later be elected U.S. president, served as the governor of California from 1967 to 1975.

7 Two years earlier, Arnie was already being groomed for the governor's job in a hotel room in Los Angeles. In an "invitation-only meeting" with the Enron boss Kenneth Lay and others, plans were being drawn to circumvent a lawsuit spearheaded by Lieutenant Governor Cruz Bustamante, which would require power companies to return the $9 billion they robbed from California customers during our state's so-called energy crisis. At the same time, George W. Bush's Federal Energy Regulatory Commission was trying to work out a sweetheart deal which would only require power companies to pay about 2 percent of what they owed. The trouble for Bush is that Governor Gray

Davis won't go for the deal because he badly needs the $9 billion to salvage the state's enormous deficit. The Republican solution: recall the governor and replace him with Arnie. And since Arnie has no problem paying millions of dollars of his own money to get elected, he's the man for the job. This is *not* a democracy. This is a government that is being bought and sold in private meetings with CEOs in hotel rooms across the United States.

8 Nhat Hanh, *No Death, No Fear*, 150.

9 Said, "A Monument to Hypocrisy," *Al-Ahram*, February 13–19, 2003, http://weekly.ahram.org (accessed October 20, 2010).

INDÍGENA AS SCRIBE

This essay was originally presented at the eighteenth annual MELUS (Multi-Ethnic Literature of the United States) conference, March 11, 2004, University of Texas, San Antonio. It was revised occasionally up through 2006 and presented at various speaking engagements at universities throughout the country. A version also appears in *Companion to Latino Studies*, edited by Juan Flores and Renato Rosaldo (Oxford: Blackwell, 2007), 376–92.

1 Coyolxauhqui is the moon goddess and Huitzilopochtli, the sun god, in the Aztec pantheon.

2 León-Portilla, *Fifteen Poets of the Aztec World*, 80. This excerpt of the Nezahual-coyotl verse originally appeared in *Cantares mexicanos*, fol. 17v, a sixteenth-century manuscript in Nahuatl, preserved in the Biblioteca Nacional de México in Mexico City.

3 From the film *Fuego de Tierra*, on the life and work of Ana Mendieta, by Nereyda García Ferraz, Kate Horsfield, and Branda Miller, 1987. Kate Horsfield, producer, New York. Distributed by Women Make Movies, http://wmm.com/filmcatalog/pages/c323.shtml (accessed October 20, 2010).

4 See Tsinhnahjinnie's artist website, http://www.hulleah.com (accessed August 9, 2010). Specifically, see "Aboriginal World View" under "Videos" and "Slide Show."

5 L. Frank Manríquez is a Tongva and Ajachmem painter and tribal activist. She is quoted from a guest artist lecture she gave in Celia Herrera Rodríguez's Chicano studies class "Memory and Recollection in MeXicana/o Art Practice," held during the spring 2006 semester at the University of California, Berkeley.

6 The student, Linda Chávez, is now an independent filmmaker living in Los Angeles. Her film, *The ONE WAYz*, inspired by Linda's hometown of Norwalk, Califas, was produced in 2008 by La Guerrera Films.

7 Ironically, the Chicano movement's use of the term *mestizo*, as coined in the late 1960s, was intended to *reaffirm* the Indigenous identities of Mexicans in the United States. We identified as part of "La Raza Cósmica," but with the emphasis on our Indian origins (not the European), in a radical departure

from José Vasconcelos's modernist tract by the same name from 1925. As citizens of "Aztlán," "mestizos" held native entitlement to the Southwest, which had been ceded to the United States in the Mexican-American War. (Unfortunately, the contradiction of invoking *Spanish*-granted land titles as justification for Chicano land rights was never adequately addressed by activists of the period.) Fifteen years later, Gloria Anzaldúa introduced in *Borderlands / La Frontera* the concept of "La Nueva Mestiza," expanding the definition of *mestiza* to include mixings of gender and sexual identities that resided outside the rigid borders of mainstream America. Used in the ways described above, *mestizo* broke rules, broke convention. It transgressed in some way against the social order and, most importantly, grew out of viable movements of social protest, including the Chicano movement, the gay and lesbian movement, and women-of-color feminism.

8 The institutional privileging of biraciality (partially white) over non-mixed people of color and those of diverse non-white racial backgrounds is evident in everything from school admissions to the presidency. African Americans can cite a history of such preferential treatment since the days of slavery, when the lighter-skinned Black person was more often found working inside the landowner's home (as the "house Negro") than in the fields. Ideologically, Latinos and Latinas are encouraged to claim and identify themselves as "Hispanic," emphasizing their European origins instead of their African or Native American roots, regardless of blood quantum. Such "preferencing" has also been my lived experience as a Xicana with a light-skinned European complexion.

9 *Tu Ciudad*, February 2007 issue. By 2009, the magazine had ceased publication.

10 The declaration was adopted by the General Assembly on September 13, 2007, by a majority of 144 states. The United States and Canada were two of the four states who opposed the passage of the forty-six articles in the resolution, which took over twenty years to fully formulate. See the UN's page on the declaration: http://www.un.org/esa/socdev/unpfii/en/declaration.html (accessed July 28, 2010).

11 See Moraga, "Queer Aztlán: The Re-formation of Chicano Tribe."

12 See *The Hungry Woman*, a two-play volume that includes a Xicana reinterpretation of *Medea* and the *Popol Vuh*. The preceding several paragraphs were adapted from the introduction to the volume.

13 Celia Herrera Rodríguez has performed *Las Cositas Quebradas* in a variety of settings, most notably at the third Congreso Internacional de Literatura Chicana in Málaga, Spain, in 2002.

14 León-Portilla, *Fifteen Poets of the Aztec World*, 81. See note 2 for further information.

AND IT IS ALL THESE THINGS THAT ARE OUR GRIEF

This piece was originally penned for Marsha's memorial service at Alma de Mujer outside Austin, Texas, on October 4, 1998. Although outside the "decade" framework of this collection, I included it because the suddenness of her death, along with its tragic circumstances, changed the very foundation of how I and so many others close to Marsha were to enter the twenty-first century.

1   Alma de Mujer Center for Social Change is a retreat center and home to the Indigenous Women's Network. Marsha Gómez had served as the center's director for many years. In 1996, through Marsha's support, the property was donated to IWN.

2   Meyaka Gómez, Marsha's only son, was a diagnosed schizophrenic. He suffered for years, along with his mother, looking unsuccessfully for a way to manage the illness. Meyaka was also a fine artist in his own right.

POETRY OF HEROISM

Presented at "Sister Comrade: Celebrating the Lives of Audre Lorde and Pat Parker" on November 3, 2007, at the First Congregational Church in Oakland, California. Angela Davis, Judy Grahn, Jewelle Gomez, Holly Near, Linda Tillery, and Mary Watkins were among the presenters who gave memorial tribute to these foremothers of the lesbian-of-color movement.

1   Lorde, "Litany for Survival," 31–32.

2   Judy Grahn, who presented poems at this tribute for Lorde and Parker, is the author of many books of poetry, including *A Woman Is Talking to Death*. As a working class–identified and out-lesbian writer with an eloquent and hard-hitting original voice, her work had an enormous impact on me, especially in the late 1970s, as I emerged as a lesbian poet.

3   Lorde, "The Brown Menace," 48.

4   Lorde, "The Uses of the Erotic," 53.

5   After her surgery for breast cancer, Audre refused a prosthesis. Instead, she always hung an amulet where her breast had been.

6   *Movement in Black* is the title of Pat Parker's 1978 collection of poems.

7   Lorde, "Power," 108–9.

THE SALT THAT CURES

The earliest version of this essay began as a memorial tribute for Gloria Anzaldúa after her death in 2004. It was presented first at a gathering at the Women's Building in San Francisco in June of that year and then later, at another memorial service, organized by Randy Conner and David Sparks at the San Francisco Public Library. Luisah Teish and Sally Gearhart, among others, spoke and Celia Herrera Rodríguez created an altar for the honoring. The short tribute was also presented at a Día de los Muertos gathering and ceremony, in which Celia and I participated in Austin, Texas, that same year. AnaLouise Keating was among the other speakers. In 2009, when I decided to include the tribute in this collection, I was encouraged to develop the essay much further. One pre-publication report from a Duke reader suggested that I "allow [my] private, personal life with Gloria to intrude upon [my] public persona" and recommended "a deeper more profound interrogation" of Gloria "as a writer and intellectual." I felt terrified, challenged, and compelled by the call to do just that, since so many others, over the years, had asked the same of me, believing it was important, especially to Xicana and other women-of-color readers. I am also grateful to Randy Conner, Cathy Arellano, and Celia Herrera Rodríguez for their consejo along the way of this writing.

1   My collection *Loving in the War Years*, and *Cuentos: Stories by Latinas*, which I co-edited with Alma Gómez and Mariana Romo Carmona, had just come out in 1983. I often wondered if the timing of these publications, especially *Loving in the War Years*, which came in advance of Gloria's own single-authored work (*Borderlands/La Frontera*, 1987), could have disturbed what Gloria might have perceived as her entitlement to the *origins* of certain ideas. (I will never know.) *Borderlands*, of course, is completely distinct from those writings.

2   One such mentor who would appear on my writer's landscape several years later was the Mexican conceptual and performance artist Guadalupe García. My collaboration as playscript writer and director in García's *Coatlicue's Call* introduced me to the feminist components of many female icons in the Mexica pantheon. *Coatlicue's Call* was performed at Theater Artaud in San Francisco on October 25, 1990.

3   Anzaldúa, *Borderlands/La Frontera*, 45.

4   Unbound Feet was a performance group which included the poets Nellie Wong and Merle Woo (who were also members of Radical Women), along with Canyon Sam, the author of the memoir *Sky Train: Tibetan Women on the Edge of History*.

5   Anzaldúa, "La vulva es una herida abierta / The vulva is an open wound," in Keating, *The Gloria Anzaldúa Reader*, 198–202.

6   Ibid., 200.

7   When it was our "time of the month," my sister or I would take a trip to the grocery store, heading first to the produce section to grab a large paper bag. Then we would make our way to the female hygiene aisle (not marked as such in the 1960s) and would slip the "napkins" discreetly into the paper sack. It was a matter of showing "vergüenza" in public, watching the sack make its way along the rolling belt of the check-out stand. The Anglo male or female cashier would look at us suspiciously as they checked for the price on the box inside

the bag, which they then placed in a larger shopping bag for our trek home. Double-cover.

8 Anzaldúa, *Borderlands / La Frontera*, 50.

9 Ibid., 48.

10 Persephone Press was an important and successful white, lesbian, radical feminist press, founded in 1976 in Watertown, Massachusetts. The publication of *This Bridge Called My Back* with Persephone was made possible by the support of two key white lesbian feminist writers. Sally Gearhart, the lesbian activist and educator, had published *Wanderground* with Persephone Press in 1978 and brought *This Bridge Called My Back* (under a different title at the time) to the press's attention. Sally had been my mentor, teacher, and advisor at San Francisco State when I was in graduate school there. Around the same time, Adrienne Rich had read my essay "La Güera," which I had sent to her as the first essay written for our women-of-color collection. At this time, Rich had just written the foreword to *The Coming Out Stories*, to be published by Persephone in 1980 and edited by Julia Penelope and Sudan Wolfe. She recommended "La Güera" for inclusion in the anthology, and also encouraged *Bridge*'s publication with Persephone. With the support of these two writers, *Bridge* found a viable publisher with national distribution, and the book was published in 1981. By 1983, however, Persephone abruptly disbanded and was sold to Beacon Press. Kitchen Table: Women of Color Press (which I co-founded with Barbara Smith, Audre Lorde, Hattie Gossett, and others) was established, in part, to reissue the collection through an autonomous women-of-color enterprise. Since that time and with the closure of Kitchen Table Press, *Bridge* has gone in and out of print. Its last publication was a limited-run of a twentieth-anniversary edition, published by Third Woman Press of Berkeley in 2002. Third Woman Press is no longer in operation. At the time of this writing, *This Bridge Called My Back* is scheduled to be re-issued in a thirtieth-anniversary edition by the State University of New York Press in 2011.

11 "Most people self-define by what they exclude." Anzaldúa, "(Un)natural bridges, (Un)safe spaces," 245 (this essay originally appeared as the introduction to *This Bridge We Called Home*).

12 *Colonize This! Young Women of Color on Today's Feminism*, edited by Daisy Hernandez and S. Bushra Rehman, was released in the same year and I began to think a new generation of women of color might better serve the mandate of defining a new feminism of color in this country.

13 Anzaldúa, "(Un)natural bridges, (Un)safe spaces."

14 Anzaldúa, "now let us shift . . . ," in Anzaldúa and Keating, *This Bridge We Call Home*, 574.

15 Randy Connor, personal email correspondence, November 10, 2009.

16 Carrasco and Lint Sagarena, "The Religious Vision of Gloria Anzaldúa," 227. Speaking of those passageways, called *malinalli*, in relation to Anzaldúa's spiri-

tual communications, Carrasco and Lint Sagarena write: "Located in caves, near ponds, or inside of trees, they (*malinalli*) served as conduits of ancestral and sacred powers streaming through the natural and human world. They were the *dynamic passageways between the human and spirit world* and in our view, Anzaldúa's religious imagination functions more like a malinalli then as 'reason' or 'story'" (my emphasis; 224).

17 See my discussion of hybridity and mestizaje in the essay "Indígena as Scribe: The (W)rite to Remember" in the present volume.

18 Anzaldúa, "(Un)natural bridges, (Un)safe spaces," 245; Anzaldúa, *Borderlands / La Frontera*, 3.

19 Anzaldúa, "Speaking across the Divide," in Keating, *The Gloria Anzaldúa Reader*, 287.

20 Although the term *tribe* is used by many Indigenous peoples (e.g., the White Mountain Apache Tribe), it should be noted that the word is not uniformly accepted and remains problematic for some sectors of Indigenous communities, due to its colonial origins.

21 Anzaldúa, "Memoir—My Calling; or, Notes for 'How Prieta Came to Write,'" in Keating, *The Gloria Anzaldúa Reader*, 236.

22 Ironically, she was already detribalized as an Indigenous person by being disappeared as an "Indian" through México's nationalized de-Indianization policies, as well as the U.S. government's tribal enrollment requirements.

23 See Moraga, "Queer Aztlán."

24 Anzaldúa, "now let us shift . . . ," in Anzaldúa and Keating, *This Bridge We Call Home*, 545.

25 Anzaldúa, "Foreword to *Cassells Encyclopedia of Queer Myth, Symbol and Spirit*," in Keating, *The Gloria Anzaldúa Reader*, 230.

26 "La Prieta" and "La Güera," respectively, are the titles of the first essays Gloria Anzaldúa and I wrote for *This Bridge Called My Back*.

27 This is a fundamental tenet of Buddhist thought, and I thank Sensei Ryumon Gutiérrez Baldoquín for her informed discussion of it in Dharma talk exchanges.

28 From an essay by same title in Lorde's *Sister Outsider*, 36–39.

29 Anzaldúa, *Borderlands / La Frontera*, 23.

30 As one of the executors of Gloria Anzaldúa's literary trust, AnaLouise Keating has made an important contribution with her edited collection *The Gloria Anzaldúa Reader*, which contains some of Gloria's previously published and formerly unpublished writings.

31 Anzaldúa, "Let us be the healing of the wound: The Coyolxauhqui imperative—la sombra y el sueño," in Keating, *The Gloria Anzaldúa Reader*, 303.

THE OTHER FACE OF (IM)MIGRATION

An earlier version of this essay was presented at the nineteenth International Iranian Women's Studies Foundation Conference, held at the University of California, Berkeley, on July 4, 2008.

1 See "From Inside the First World: On 9/11 and Women-of-Color Feminism" in the present volume.

2 The nation of the Tohono O'odham resides on both sides of the U.S.-México border in the Sonora Desert. Immigration laws prevent the Tohono O'odham from crossing through their own territories freely. The intrusion of additional border patrols in the area, along with the construction of new barriers, has translated into the increased harassment, illegal incarceration, and disruption of ceremonial practices of a sovereign people in their own land.

3 A later and more popular (and I would add, patriarchal) version of the story goes something like this: a woman murders her two children by drowning them in a river as an act of revenge against her unfaithful husband. Her punishment for the crime is to wander the world in search of her lost children, for she is unable enter "heaven" without them. (The husband's transgressions go unpunished in afterlife, I imagine.) The story is often told to campesino children to keep them away from waterways like irrigation canals, where La Llorona is said to be lurking, ready to abduct any child to replace her missing ones. It is also said that when the wind blows in the countryside, one can hear her crying in deep lament, calling in search of her lost children. "Ay! Mis hijos!"

4 La Red Xicana Indígena's origins date back to 1997 with the Cihuatlatokan gatherings of 1998 and 2000 in Southern California. The organization has evolved into a network of Xicanas Indígenas who are actively involved in political, educational, and cultural work that serves to raise Indigenous consciousness among our communities and supports the social justice struggles of Indigenous peoples throughout the Western Hemisphere. Celia Herrera Rodríguez was one of the founding members.

5 On August 19, 2007, Elvira Arellano was arrested outside of Our Lady Queen of Angeles Church in Los Angeles during a political rally and deported to México. She, along with her son, remains in México where Arellano continues her political activism.

6 "In My Country" is also the title of a poem by Ana Castillo in *My Father Was A Toltec*.

7 The deaths of these women are also believed to be tied to Mexican drug cartels. See Diana Washington Valdez's *The Killing Fields*. See also Lourdes Portillo's moving and poetic documentary *La Señorita Extraviada* (San Francisco: Xochitl Films Production; produced in collaboration with the Center for Independent Documentary, 2001).

8 In 2009 news of similar murders of women, who were dismissed as prostitutes and drug addicts, appeared in the New Mexico papers. Reports counted the bodies of eleven women buried in the West Mesa area of Albuquerque.

MODERN-DAY MALINCHES

This reflection piece draws, in part, from remarks I made at the "Future of Minority Studies" symposium at Spelman College on September 19, 2008. I presented with M. Jacqui Alexander on the subject of women-of-color feminism in the academy and its current distance from activist engagement.

1 These "knowings," of course, often have to do with sacred knowledges. M. Jacqui Alexander writes: "Yet, it is not only that (post)modernity's secularism renders the Sacred as tradition, but it is also that tradition, understood as an extreme alterity, is always made to reside elsewhere and denied entry into the modern" ("Pedagogies of the Sacred," 296).

2 Ibid., 289.

3 "Minority" in the context of academia.

4 Gloria Anzaldúa's works serves as an effective counterpoint in this regard. In discussing her writing process for *Borderlands*, she mentions that her ideas were often considered derivative of theorists such as Michel Foucault, Jacques Derrida, and the French feminists when they were simply drawn from "our fractured lives." Gloria retorts, "I hadn't read them." Anzaldúa, "On the Process of Writing Borderlands / La Frontera," in Keating, *The Gloria Anzaldúa Reader*, 192–93.

5 Alexander, "Pedagogies of the Sacred," 315.

6 Malinalli is one of the twenty day signs of the Aztec calendar and, given its phonetic proximity to the name Malinche, it is believed by some to be her original Nahuatl name. In *Pocahontas*, Paula Gunn Allen writes of Malinalli: "[Her] mission was defined, ignited, and energized by those forces or powers that lie behind, beyond, and beneath the mundane" (120–21). For more on Malinche, see note 6 in "An Irrevocable Promise" in the present volume. For a dramatized Xicana feminist exploration of the complex figure, see my play, *The Mathematics of Love*. For more information on the play, visit http://www .cherriemoraga.com.

7 The expression "sleeping with the enemy" is used figuratively here, since as Cortés's slave, Malinalli could not have had a choice regarding her sexual liaison with the conquistador. Martín Cortés was in fact Malinalli's first born, who at the age of six was separated from his mother and sent to Spain in the company of Cortés. Martín would grow up to become a soldier and would eventually die in the War of Granada. Her son lost his claim to his father's herencia upon the birth of Cortés's full-blood Spanish son, also named Martín. In the way of analogy, I couldn't miss the contemporary parallels of women

of color sending their children off to die in imperialist wars against the Moors'
cultural descendants in Iraq and Afghanistan. See Karttunen, "Rethinking
Malinche," 308.

WHAT'S RACE GOTTA DO WITH IT?

This essay was first presented in its entirety at Wellesley College, in a talk sponsored by the women's studies department on November 20, 2008.

1 "Fast for Our Future" was a hunger-protest campaign that took place in the
central downtown plaza (La Placita) of Los Angeles. It occurred twenty-one
days before the national election in the effort to urge Latinos to vote and to
bring attention to issues related to immigrant rights.

2 I have yet to encounter any formal acknowledgment from the Obama campaign that Dolores Huerta first conceived the phrase in Spanish as a rallying
cry for the United Farm Workers.

3 Combahee River Collective, "A Black Feminist Statement," 215.

4 "The Toll of War in Iraq: U.S. Casualties and Civilian Deaths," month-by-
month chart of statistics since March 2003, NPR.org, August 4, 2009, http://
www.npr.org/news/specials/tollofwar/tollofwarmain.html (accessed October 20, 2010).

THIS BENIGHTED NATION WE NAME HOME

This essay was originally presented at the ethnic studies department's com-
mencement on May 15, 2009, at the Zellerbach Playhouse at the University of
California, Berkeley. A revised and abbreviated version of it was presented on
February 26, 2010, at "Decolonizing the University: Fulfilling the Dream of a
Third World College," a conference held at the same university.

1 Born in 1938, Richard Aoki was an Oakland-based Japanese American who
served as a key leader in the Third World Liberation Front strike to form
a "Third World College" at the University of California, Berkeley. During
World War II he and his family had been interned in a camp in Topaz, Utah.
Aoki died on March 15, 2009, three months before I delivered the speech from
which this essay is derived.

2 Luis Valdez spoke at an honoring for the Chicano theater historian Professor
Jorge Huerta on the occasion of his retirement, at the Potiker Theater at the
University of California, San Diego on May 9, 2009.

3 I refer to the H1N1 virus, popularly referred to as the "swine flu." The out-
break of this influenza in 2009 was believed to have originated in pig farms in
México, and further aggravated anti-Mexican immigrant sentiment with fears
of contagion in the United States.

4 COINTELPRO is an acronym for the FBI's counterintelligence programs

which operated from 1956 to 1971. COINTELPRO infiltrated politically dissident organizations in the effort to discredit, subvert, and ultimately dismantle
them. These included socialist, communist, civil rights, Black Power, Chicano,
Puerto Rican, Native, and women's movement groups.

5 An important exception: during the 1980s, Central American solidarity movements, composed of leftist émigrés from Nicaragua, El Salvador, and Guatemala, as well as predominantly (but not exclusively) white North Americans,
were extensive and well organized throughout many major U.S. cities. Political dissidents who had emigrated from Argentina and Chile during those
countries' repressive military regimes of the 1970s also worked in coalition
with such groups.

6 One example of such reactionary legislation is Proposition 187 from 1994,
which intended to prohibit undocumented immigrants from using health
care, public education, and other social services. It was deemed unconstitu-
tional by the federal court and was, therefore, never fully executed by law.

7 From the title of Rodolfo F. Acuña's book, *Occupied America: A History of Chicanos*.

8 I am reminded of a conversation I had with David Carrasco, a Mesoameri-
canist scholar and professor at the Harvard Divinity School. We met for the
first time in 2009, while David was serving as a visiting professor at Stanford
University. In that meeting, he described how as a young man he had imagined that the studies he had begun in the area of Mesoamerican philosophy
and religion were so significant to Americanism itself that they would by now
have been fully integrated into the canon of academic inquiry. But, of course,
this would have required a dramatic shift of the privileged position Western
thought retains in academia.

9 Interview with Amy Goodman, "Democracy Now," Pacifica Radio (KPFA),
May 13, 2009.

10 The bad news and the good news: as a result of the dire financial crisis in which
the state of California finds itself (in its refusal to raise corporate taxes), the
University of California system has instituted major budget cuts including the
layoff of hundreds of workers, the imposition of unpaid furloughs on non-
union employees, and reductions in course offerings. The board of regents has
also proposed a 45 percent increase (of more than three thousand dollars) over
last year's tuition, which would prevent many lower- and middle-income students from continuing their education. On September 24, 2009, a state-wide
organized protest took place on University of California campuses, during
which thousands of students and workers walked out. At UC Berkeley, a two-
hour rally on Sproul Plaza, attended by an estimated five thousand students,
spontaneously took to the streets. As a result of the cutbacks, a new student
activism is beginning to reemerge throughout the state.

11 The title of Celia Herrera Rodríguez's installation piece, which was first shown

as part of the group exhibition "Chicana/o Identities" at the Richard Reynolds Gallery at the University of the Pacific in Stockton, California, in 2000.

STILL LOVING IN THE (STILL) WAR YEARS

This essay was presented at the "Empowering Women of Color" conference at the University of California, Berkeley, on Valentine's Day in 2009. Earlier versions of this essay were presented at the National Association of Chicana and Chicano Studies Joto Caucus conference at California State University, Los Angeles, on October 11, 2008; and at the University of Illinois, Urbana-Champaign, as the Rolando Hinojosa Smith Lecture, sponsored by the Latino and Latina studies program on October 15, 2008.

1 Early in his second year as president, George W. Bush presented a welfare reform plan that included allocating $300 million for programs that promoted marriage between low-income heterosexual couples. He promised that his administration would give "unprecedented support to strengthening marriages" and asserted that "stable families should be the central goal of American welfare policy." "Bush Welfare Plan Promotes Marriage, Work," CNN.com, February 27, 2002, http://edition.cnn.com (accessed October 20, 2010).

2 Quotations appeared on a variety of blogs during the height of the 2008 campaign (throughout the month of October until Election Day on November 5).

3 Of course, the issue of sexism endemic to the institution of marriage and prevalent in many religious traditions is one against which progressive practitioners—Muslim, Jewish, and Catholic alike—have been struggling for decades.

4 The following are excerpts from a letter sent from the First Presidency of the Church of Jesus Christ of Latter-day Saints to Church leaders in California to be read to all congregations on June 29, 2008: "The Church's teachings and position on this moral issue are unequivocal. Marriage between a man and a woman is ordained of God, and the formation of families is central to the Creator's plan for His children. Children are entitled to be born within this bond of marriage. . . . We ask that you do all you can to support the proposed constitutional amendment by donating of your means and time to assure that marriage in California is legally defined as being between a man and a woman. Our best efforts are required to preserve the sacred institution of marriage." From the "Newsroom" of the Church of Jesus Christ of the Latter Day Saints, http://www.newsroom.lds.org, posted on June 30, 2008. A copy of the official LDS Proposition 8 Letter can also be found on a link through http://lds501c3 .wordpress.com (accessed October 20, 2010).

5 The first Mormon missionaries arrived in Tonga in 1891. Today Tonga has the largest number of Mormons per capita of any nation in the world.

6 The murder of Gwen Amber Rose Araujo was not tried as a hate crime, al-

though ironically the perpetrators tried to justify their actions through a "gay panic" defense.

7 Allen Andrade, a Latino, certainly did not see the transgendered teen Angie Zapata as one of us (Raza). While on a date with her, he brutally murdered her upon discovering her born-gender. In April 2009, the Colorado man was convicted of first-degree murder for the "bias-motivated" crime and was sentence to life imprisonment without parole. It is interesting to consider, however, the racial biases that may have been at work here, when after only two hours of deliberation, the jury arrived at the verdict. According to the Gay and Lesbian Alliance Against Defamation, this "was the first time in the nation that a state hate crime statute resulted in a conviction in a transgender person's murder." "Transgender Murder, Hate Crime Conviction a First," CNN.com, April 23, 2009, http://edition.cnn.com (accessed October 20, 2010). I applaud the state's recognition of the heinous character of the crime. But I wonder why it is that some of Gwen Araujo's *white* assailants were charged with only second-degree murder, and others just got away.

8 I refer to a conversation I had with a group of LGBT people who attended my presentation of an earlier version of this essay at the University of Massachusetts, Amherst, on October 5, 2010, sponsored by the Stonewall Center. I am grateful to their critique, which aided me in my own revisions of this essay. I am also grateful for the open-hearted quality of their response.

9 I do not mean to suggest that all pre-conquest and pre-Christian Indigenous nations were non-patriarchal and free of homophobia, only that many indigenous traditions afforded women, homosexuals, and transpeople greater social power through matrilineal and matrifocal communities, or through gender flexible roles (e.g., two-spirit curanderos, female warriors, and homosexual "marriages").

10 Some LGBT organizations that work to support self-determined gender identity and expression, especially serving young people of color, include the Sylvia Rivera Law Project of New York City (http://srlp.org/about); the Brown Boi Project of Oakland, California (http://brownboiproject.org/mission_core_values.html); and the Audre Lorde Project, with offices in Brooklyn and New York (http://alp.org/about).

11 Moraga, *Giving Up the Ghost*, 57.

EPÍLOGO

1 As told to me during a dharma talk with Sensei Ryumon Baldoquín Gutiérrez.

2 Ingrid "Flying Eagle Woman" Washinawatok El-Issa (Menominee) was kidnapped and murdered by FARC guerrillas along the Colombia border in 1999. She and two other activists, Lahe'ena'e Gay and Terence Freitas, who were also murdered, had been invited by the U'wa people to help set up a culturally

sovereign school. Ingrid was a friend with whom I had done some women-of-color organizing in the early 1980s. On Marsha Gómez's death, see "And It Is All These Things That Are Our Grief" in this volume.

3 My son was born three months premature, weighing two and a half pounds. He endured two major surgeries in the first months of his life and survived it all in good health. For a full account of the experience, see my *Waiting in the Wings*.

4 Hogan, *The Woman Who Watches Over the World*, 49.

APPENDIX

1 Per the artist's preference. In subsequent references to the artist, I will use her maternal last name, Herrera.

2 Herrera's solo show of paintings and installations was displayed at the C. N. Gorman Museum (University of California, Davis), from January 5 through March 31, 2006. I wrote this essay, under the English title "Alone, But in Good Company," for that exhibition. To view images from "Sola, Pero Bien Acompañada," visit Herrera's "Artist Page" on Facebook: "Celia Herrera Rodríguez, Visual and Performance Artist, Designer."

3 All quotations by Herrera are taken from an interview I conducted with her on December 28, 2005, at her studio in Oakland, California.

4 See the Winnemem Wintu Tribe's website, http://winnememwintu.us, especially the words by the principal chief and spiritual leader, Caleen Sisk-Franco ("Hu'p Chonas—dance in the old way—war dance"; accessed August 2, 2010).

5 The artist's drawings reproduced in the present volume reflect this two-dimensionality.

Bibliography

Acuña, Rodolfo F. *Occupied America: A History of Chicanos*. 6th ed. New York: Longman, 2006.

Ahmed, Leila. *A Border Passage: From Cairo to America—A Woman's Journey*. New York: Penguin, 2000.

Alarcón, Norma. "Chicana's Feminist Literature: A Re-Vision through Malintzín or Malintzin; Putting Flesh Back on the Object." *This Bridge Called My Back: Writings by Radical Women of Color*. 2nd ed., edited by Cherríe Moraga and Gloria Anzaldúa, 182–90. New York: Kitchen Table: Women of Color Press, 1983.

Alexander, M. Jacqui. "Pedagogies of the Sacred: Making the Invisible Tangible." *Pedagogies of Crossing: Meditations on Feminism, Sexual Politics, Memory, and the Sacred*, 287–332. Durham, N.C.: Duke University Press, 2005.

Alexander, M. Jacqui, and Chandra Talpade Mohanty, eds. *Feminist Genealogies, Colonial Legacies, Democratic Futures*. New York: Routledge, 1996.

Alexie, Sherman. *One Stick Song*. Brooklyn: Hanging Loose, 2000.

Allison, Dorothy. *The Women Who Hate Me*. Ithaca, N.Y.: Firebrand, 1991.

Anzaldúa, Gloria. *Borderlands / La Frontera: The New Mestiza*. San Francisco: Aunt Lute, 1987.

———. "Haciendo caras, una entrada." *Making Face, Making Soul / Haciendo*

Caras: Creative and Critical Perspectives by Feminists of Color, xv–xxviii. San Francisco: Aunt Lute, 1990.

———. "Let us be the healing of the wound: The Coyolxauhqui imperative—la sombra y el sueño." *The Gloria Anzaldúa Reader*, edited by AnaLouise Keating, 303–17. Durham, N.C.: Duke University Press, 2010.

———. "now let us shift . . . the path of conocimiento . . . inner work, public acts." *this bridge we call home: radical visions for transformation*, edited by Gloria Anzaldúa and AnaLouise Keating, 540–76. New York: Routledge, 2002.

———. "On the Process of Writing *Borderlands / La Frontera*." *The Gloria Anzaldúa Reader*, edited by AnaLouise Keating, 192–93. Durham, N.C.: Duke University Press, 2010.

———. "(Un)natural bridges, (Un)safe spaces." *The Gloria Anzaldúa Reader*, edited by AnaLouise Keating, 243–48. Durham, N.C.: Duke University Press, 2010.

Arrizón, Alicia. *Queering Mestizaje: Transculturation and Performance*. Ann Arbor: University of Michigan Press, 2006.

Arrizón, Alicia, and Lillian Manzor, eds. *Latinas on Stage*. Berkeley, Calif.: Third Woman, 2000.

Arteaga, Alfred. *Chicano Poetics: Heterotexts and Hybridities*. Cambridge: Cambridge University Press, 1997.

———. *Frozen Accident: Philosophy of Spatial Act*. Sylmar, Calif.: Tia Chucha, 2007.

Bacon, David. *Illegal People: How Globalization Creates Migration and Criminalizes Immigrants*. Boston: Beacon, 2008.

Bambara, Toni Cade. Foreword to *This Bridge Called My Back: Writings by Radical Women of Color*. 2nd ed., edited by Cherríe Moraga and Gloria Anzaldúa, vi–viii. New York: Kitchen Table: Women of Color Press, 1983.

———. *The Salt Eaters*. New York: Random House, 1981.

———. *These Bones Are Not My Child*. New York: Pantheon, 1999.

Bhabha, Homi K. "DissemiNation: Time, Narrative, and the Margins of the Modern Nation." *Nation and Narration*, edited by Homi K. Bhabha, 291–322. New York: Routledge, 1990.

———. "Introduction: Narrating the Nation." *Nation and Narration*, edited by Homi K. Bhabha, 1–7. New York: Routledge, 1990.

Blocker, Jane. *Where Is Ana Mendieta? Identity, Performativity, and Exile*. Durham, N.C.: Duke University Press, 1999.

Boal, Augusto. *Theatre of the Oppressed*. Translated by Charles A. McBride and Maria-Odilia Leal McBride. London: Pluto, 1979.

Bonfil Batalla, Guillermo. *México Profundo: Reclaiming a Civilization*. Austin: University of Texas Press, 1996.

Brady, Mary Pat. *Extinct Lands, Temporal Geographies: Chicano Literature and the Urgency of Space*. Durham, N.C.: Duke University Press, 2002.

Carrasco, David, ed. *The History of the Conquest of New Spain by Bernal Díaz del Castillo*. Albuquerque: University of New Mexico Press, 2008.

Carrasco, David, and Roberto Lint Sagarena. "The Religious Vision of Gloria Anzaldúa: Borderlands / La Frontera as Shamanistic Space." *Mexican American Religions: Spirituality, Activism, and Culture*, edited by Gastón Espinosa and Mario T. García, 223–41. Durham, N.C.: Duke University Press, 2008.

Carrasco, David, and Scott Sessions, eds. *Cave, City, and Eagle's Nest: An Interpretive Journey through the Mapa de Cuauhtinchan No. 2*. Albuquerque: University of New Mexico Press, 2007.

Carrera, Magali Marie. *Imagining Identity in New Spain: Race, Lineage, and the Colonial Body in Portraiture and Casta Paintings*. Austin: University of Texas Press, 2003.

Castillo, Ana. "In My County." *My Father Was a Toltec*, 73–75. Albuquerque, N.M.: West End, 1988.

Castillo, Aleida del. "Malintzín Tenepal: A Preliminary Look into a New Perspective." *Essays on La Mujer*, edited by Rosaura Sánchez and Rosa Martínez Cruz, 131–41. Los Angeles: University of California, Los Angeles, Chicano Studies Center Publications, 1977.

Cervantes, Lorna Dee. *Emplumada*. Pittsburgh: University of Pittsburgh Press, 1981.

Chodron, Pema. *No Time Left to Lose: A Timely Guide to the Way of the Bodhisattva*. Boston: Shambala, 2005.

Chomsky, Noam. *Hegemony or Survival: America's Quest for Global Dominance*. New York: Henry Holt, 2003.

Churchill, Ward. *From a Native Son: Selected Essays in Indigenism, 1985–1995*. Boston: South End, 1996.

Clendinnen, Inga. *Ambivalent Conquests: Maya and Spaniard in Yucatan, 1517–1570*. Cambridge: Cambridge University Press, 1987.

Combahee River Collective. "A Black Feminist Statement." *This Bridge Called My Back: Writings by Radical Women of Color*. 2nd ed., edited by Cherríe Moraga and Gloria Anzaldúa, 210–18. New York: Kitchen Table: Women of Color Press, 1983.

Davis, Angela. "The Color of Violence against Women." *Colorlines* 3, no. 3 (2000): 4–8.

Florescano, Enrique. *Memory, Myth, and Time in Mexico: From Aztecs to Independence*. Austin: University of Texas Press, 1994.

Freire, Paulo. *Pedagogy of the Oppressed*. New York: Seabury, 1970.

Gaspar de Alba, Alicia. "Los Derechos de Malinche." *Mystery of Survival and Other Stories*, 47–52. Tempe, Ariz.: Bilingual Review, 1993.

Gómez-Peña, Guillermo. *The New World Border: Prophecies, Poems, and Loqueras for the End of the Century*. San Francisco: City Lights, 1996.

Grahn, Judy. "The Common Woman." *The Work of a Common Woman: The Collected Poetry of Judy Grahn, 1964–1977*, 59–73. Oakland, Calif.: Diana, 1978.

———. "A Woman Is Talking to Death." *The Work of a Common Woman: The Collected Poetry of Judy Grahn, 1964–1977*, 111–31. Oakland, Calif.: Diana, 1978.

Gunn Allen, Paula. *Pocahontas: Medicine Woman, Spy, Entrepreneur, Diplomat*. San Francisco: HarperSanFrancisco, 2004.

Gutiérrez, Ramón. *When Jesus Came, the Corn Mothers Went Away: Marriage, Sexuality, and Power in New Mexico, 1500–1846*. Stanford, Calif.: Stanford University Press, 1991.

Gutiérrez Baldoquín, Hilda, ed. *Dharma, Color, and Culture: New Voices in Western Buddhism*. Berkeley, Calif.: Parallax, 2004.

Harjo, Joy. *How We Became Human: New and Selected Poems*. New York: Norton, 2002.

Harris, Bertha. "What We Mean to Say: Notes Toward Defining the Nature of Lesbian Literature." *Heresies: A Feminist Publication on Arts and Politics* 1, no. 3 (1977): 5–8.

Hogan, Linda. *Dwellings: A Spiritual History of the Living World*. New York: Norton, 1995.

———. *The Woman Who Watches Over the World*. New York: Norton, 2001.

Hollibaugh, Amber. *My Dangerous Desires: A Queer Girl Dreaming Her Way Home*. Durham, N.C.: Duke University Press, 2000.

Incite! Women of Color Against Violence. *The Color of Violence: The Incite! Anthology*. Cambridge, Mass.: South End Press, 2006.

Joseph, May, and Jennifer Natalya Fink, eds. *Performing Hybridity*. Minneapolis: University of Minnesota Press, 1999.

Karttunen, Frances. "Rethinking Malinche." *Indian Woman of Early Mexico*, edited by Susan Schroeder, Stephanie Wood, and Robert Haskett, 291–312. Norman: University of Oklahoma Press, 1997.

Katzew, Ilona. *Casta Painting: Images of Race in Eighteenth-Century Mexico*. New Haven, Conn.: Yale University Press, 2004.

Keating, AnaLouise, ed. *The Gloria Anzaldúa Reader*. Durham, N.C.: Duke University Press, 2010.

Kristeva, Julia. *Powers of Horror: An Essay on Abjection*. Translated by Leon S. Roudiez. New York: Columbia University Press, 1982.

León-Portilla, Miguel. *Fifteen Poets of the Aztec World*. Norman: University of Oklahoma Press, 1992. First published as *Trece poetas del mundo azteca*, 1967.

———. *Time and Reality in the Thought of the Maya*. 2nd ed. Norman: University of Oklahoma Press, 1988. First published as *Tiempo y realidad en el pensamiento Maya: Ensayos de acercamiento*, 1968.

Lorde, Audre. "The Brown Menace or Poem to the Survival of Roaches." *The New York Head Shop and Museum*, 48–49. Detroit: Broadside, 1974.

———. "Litany for Survival." *The Black Unicorn*, 31–32. New York: Norton, 1978.

———. "The Master's Tools Will Never Dismantle the Master's House." *This Bridge Called My Back: Writings by Radical Women of Color*. 2nd ed., edited by Cherríe Moraga and Gloria Anzaldúa, 98–101. New York: Kitchen Table: Women of Color Press, 1983.

———. "Power." *The Black Unicorn*, 108–9. New York: Norton, 1978.

———. "The Uses of the Erotic: The Erotic as Power." *Sister Outsider: Essays and Speeches*, 53–59. Trumansburg, N.Y.: Crossing, 1984.

Lugones, María. *Pilgrimages/Peregrinajes: Theorizing Coalition against Multiple Opressions*. Lanham, Md.: Rowman and Littlefield, 2003.

Mani, Lata. *Interleaves: Ruminations on Illness and Spiritual Life*. Oakland, Calif.: self-published, 2001.

———. *SacredSecular: Contemplative Cultural Critique*. New Delhi: Routledge India, 2009.

Manzor, Lillian. "From Minimalism to Performative Excess: The Two Tropicanas." *Latinas on Stage*, edited by Alicia Arrizón and Lillian Manzor, 370–96. Berkeley, Calif.: Third Woman, 2000.

Mignolo, Walter D. *Local Histories / Global Designs: Coloniality, Subaltern Knowledges, and Border Thinking*. Princeton, N.J.: Princeton University Press, 2000.

Momaday, N. Scott. *The Man Made of Words: Essays, Stories, Passages*. New York: St. Martin's Griffin, 1997.

Moraga, Cherríe. *Giving Up the Ghost*. Albuquerque, N.M.: West End, 1986.

———. *Heroes and Saints and Other Plays*. Albuquerque, N.M.: West End, 1994.

———. *The Hungry Woman*. Albuquerque, N.M.: West End, 2001.

———. "A Long Line of Vendidas." *Loving in the War Years: Lo que nunca pasó por sus labios*, 90–144. Boston: South End Press, 1983.

———. *Loving in the War Years: Lo que nunca pasó por sus labios*. 2nd ed. Cambridge, Mass.: South End, 2000.

———. "Queer Aztlán: The Re-formation of Chicano Tribe." *The Last Generation*, 145–74. Boston: South End, 1993.

———. *Sola, Pero Bien Acompañada: Celia Herrera-Rodríguez*. Davis, Calif.: Gorman Museum, University of California, Davis, 2006.

———. *Waiting in the Wings: Portrait of a Queer Motherhood*. Ithaca, N.Y.: Firebrand, 1997.

Moraga, Cherríe, and Gloria Anzaldúa, eds. *This Bridge Called My Back: Writings by Radical Women of Color*. 2nd ed. New York: Kitchen Table: Women of Color Press, 1983.

Moya, Paula. *Learning from Experience: Minority Identities, Multicultural Struggles*. Berkeley: University of California Press, 2002.

Muñoz, José Esteban. *Disidentifications: Queers of Color and the Performance of Politics*. Minneapolis: University of Minnesota Press, 1999.

Nabhan, Gary Paul. *The Desert Smells Like Rain: A Naturalist in O'odham Country*. San Francisco: North Point, 1982.

Narby, Jeremy. *The Cosmic Serpent: DNA and the Origins of Knowledge*. New York: Penguin Putnam, 1998.

Nhat Hanh, Thich. *Anger: Wisdom for Cooling the Flames*. New York: Riverhead, 2001.

———. *No Death, No Fear: Comforting Wisdom for Life*. New York: Riverhead, 2002.

Obama, Barack. *Dreams from My Father*. New York: Three Rivers, 1995.

Ortiz, Simon, ed. *Speaking for the Generations: Native Writers on Writing*. Tucson: University of Arizona Press, 1998.

Parker, Pat. *Movement in Black*. Trumansburg, N.Y.: Crossing, 1978.

Perez, Laura E. *Chicana Art: The Politics of Spiritual and Aesthetic Altarities*. Durham, N.C.: Duke University Press, 2007.

Phelan, Peggy, and Jill Lane, eds. *The Ends of Performance*. New York: New York University Press, 1998.

Rich, Adrienne. "An Old House in America." *The Fact of a Doorframe: Selected Poems, 1950–2001*, 119–30. New York: Norton, 2002.

Rodríguez, Richard. *Brown: The Last Discovery of America*. New York: Viking, 2002.

———. *Days of Obligation: An Argument with My Mexican Father*. New York: Viking Penquin, 1992

Rodríguez, Roberto. *The X in La Raza*. Albuquerque, N.M.: self-published, 1996.

Said, Edward W. *Out of Place: A Memoir*. New York: Vintage, 1999.

Sam, Canyon. *Sky Train: Tibetan Women on the Edge of History*. Seattle: University of Washington Press, 2009.

Sandoval, Chela. *Methodology of the Oppressed*. Minneapolis: University of Minnesota Press, 2002.

Sandoval-Sánchez, Alberto. "Politicizing Abjection: In the Manner of a Prologue for the Articulation of AIDS Latino Queer Identities." *American Literary History* 17, no. 3 (2005): 542–49.

Sanjinés C., Javier. "Indianizaing the Q'ara." *Mestizaje Upside Down: Aesthetic Politics in Modern Bolivia*, 149–89. Pittsburgh, Pa.: University of Pittsburgh Press, 2004.

Schechner, Richard. *Between Theater and Anthropology*. Philadelphia: University of Pennsylvania Press, 1985.

Shenk, David. *The Forgetting: Alzheimer's; Portrait of an Epidemic*. New York: Doubleday, 2001.

Shohat, Ella. "Taboo Memories, Diasporic Visions: Columbus, Palestine, and Arab Jews." *Taboo Memories, Diasporic Visions*, 201–31. Durham, N.C.: Duke University Press, 2006.

Somé, Malidoma Patrice. *Ritual: Power, Healing, and Community*. New York: Penguin, 1993.

St. Pierre, Mark, and Tilda Long Soldier. *Walking in the Sacred Manner: Healers, Dreamers, and Pipe Carriers—Medicine Women of the Plains Indians*. New York: Simon and Schuster, 1995.

Talpade Mohanty, Chandra. *Feminism without Borders: Decolonizing Theory, Practicing Solidarity*. Durham, N.C.: Duke University Press, 2003.

Taylor, Diana. *The Archive and the Repertoire: Performing Cultural Memory in the Americas*. Durham, N.C.: Duke University Press, 2003.

Taylor, Diana, and Roselyn Costantino, eds. *Holy Terrors: Latin American Women Perform*. Durham, N.C.: Duke University Press, 2003.

Vasconcelos, José. *The Cosmic Race / La Raza Cósmica*. Baltimore: John Hopkins University Press, 1997. Original Spanish edition published in 1925.

Washington Valdez, Diana. *The Killing Fields: Harvest of Women*. Burbank, Calif.: Peace at the Border, 2006.

Weaver, Jace, and Laura Adams Weaver. "Indigenous Migrations, Pilgrimage Trails, and Sacred Geography." *Cave, City, and Eagle's Nest: An Interpretive Journey through the Mapa de Cuauhtinchan No. 2*, edited by David Carrasco and Scott Sessions, 335–55. Albuquerque: University of New Mexico Press, 2007.

Zepeda, Ofelia. *Ocean Power: Poems from the Desert*. Tucson: University of Arizona Press, 1995.

Index

abjection, 41–42

activists, 8, 15–16, 20, 28, 64, 67, 107, 112, 141, 163–64, 172, 205, 216 n. 7, 222, 226 n. 2; tribal, 215 n. 5; union, 212 n. 2; writers as, 149

Acuña, Rodolfo, 170, 224 n. 7

adoption, 178

Afghanistan, 28, 30, 138, 222–23 n. 7

African Americans, 14, 154, 172, 216 n. 8

Afro-Caribbean women, 14

AIDS, 8, 20, 28, 42, 57, 205

Alameda military base, 4

Alcatraz Island occupation, 164

Alexander, M. Jacqui, 103, 149, 222

Alexie, Sherman, 6–7

Allan, Lewis (pseud.), 212 n. 2

Allende, Salvador, 28

Allison, Dorothy, 15

Alma de Mujer Center for Social Change, 108, 217, 217 n. 1

Alzheimer's disease, 194

Amada (fictional character), 43, 213 n. 12

America, 5–6, 19, 22, 26, 33, 67, 71, 89, 136, 151, 154–55, 157, 159, 162, 178–79, 209 n. 3, 216 n. 7; middle-class, 180; as occupied, 28, 170, 224 n. 7; white, 172, 183

América, 24, 29, 31, 35, 39, 44, 88, 139–45

American ethic, 168–69

American Indian movements, 19, 160, 164–65; writers in, 5

American Indigenism, 8

American principles, 25

Americans, 29, 37, 43, 59, 68–70, 93, 112, 144, 153–54, 158–59, 167–68, 186, 210 n. 2

CHERRÍE L. MORAGA is a playwright, poet, and essayist. Her publications and plays have received national recognition, including the American Studies Association Lifetime Achievement Award, the National Endowment for the Arts Playwrights' Fellowship, and two Fund for New American Plays Awards. In 2007, she received the United States Artist Rockefeller Fellowship for Literature. Moraga is the co-editor of *This Bridge Called My Back: Writings by Radical Women of Color*, which won the Before Columbus American Book Award in 1986. Currently, she is completing a memoir on the subject of Mexican American cultural amnesia titled *Send Them Flying Home: A Geography of Remembrance*. She is an artist in residence in the department of drama and comparative studies in race and ethnicity program at Stanford University.

CELIA HERRERA RODRÍGUEZ (Xicana/O'dami) is a visual performing artist and educator whose work reflects a full generation dialogue with Xicana and Xicano, Indigenous Mexican and North American Native thought, spirituality, and politics. She teaches in the Chicano studies program at the University of California, Berkeley, and in the diversity studies program at California College for the Arts in Oakland. She holds an MFA in painting from University of Illinois, Champaign-Urbana. Herrera's work has been exhibited nationally. Since 2005, Celia Herrera has also collaborated as the conceptual (set and costume) designer for Cherríe Moraga's theater productions, including *The Hungry Woman*, *Digging Up the Dirt*, and *New Fire: 3 Elementos de Consciencia*.

Library of Congress Cataloging-in-Publication Data

Moraga, Cherríe L.
A Xicana codex of changing consciousness : writings, 2000–2010 /
Cherríe L. Moraga ; drawings by Celia Herrera Rodríguez.
p. cm.
Includes bibliographical references and index.
ISBN 978-0-8223-4962-4 (cloth : alk. paper)
ISBN 978-0-8223-4977-8 (pbk. : alk. paper)
1. American literature—Mexican American authors.
2. Mexican American women authors.
3. Mexican American authors.
4. Mexican American lesbians.
5. Hispanic American feminists.
I. Rodríguez, Celia Herrera. II. Title.
PS153.M4M673 2011
810.8′086872—dc22
2010049740